How to Reduce the Cost of Software Testing

Edited by Matthew Heusser and Govind Kulkarni

CRC Press
Taylor & Francis Group
Boca Raton   London   New York

CRC Press is an imprint of the
Taylor & Francis Group, an **informa** business
AN AUERBACH BOOK

CRC Press
Taylor & Francis Group
6000 Broken Sound Parkway NW, Suite 300
Boca Raton, FL 33487-2742

© 2012 by Taylor & Francis Group, LLC
CRC Press is an imprint of Taylor & Francis Group, an Informa business

No claim to original U.S. Government works

Version Date: 20110801

International Standard Book Number: 978-1-4398-6155-4 (Hardback)

Visit the Taylor & Francis Web site at
http://www.taylorandfrancis.com

and the CRC Press Web site at
http://www.crcpress.com

Contents

Foreword ix
Preface xi
Acknowledgments xv
Authors xix

PART 1   What Will This Cost Us?

Chapter 1   Is This the Right Question? 3
Matt Heusser

Chapter 2   The Cost of Quality 19
Selena Delesie

Chapter 3   Testing Economics: What Is Your Testing Net
Worth? 37
Govind Kulkarni

Chapter 4   Opportunity Cost of Testing 49
Catherine Powell

Chapter 5   Trading Money for Time: When Saving Money
Doesn't (and When It Does) 57
Michael Larsen

Chapter 6   An Analysis of Costs in Software Testing 73
Michael Bolton

PART 2   What Should We Do?

Chapter 7 Test Readiness: Be Ready to Test When the
Software Is Ready to Be Tested 103

Ed Barkley

Chapter 8 Session-Based Test Management.................................. 119

Michael Kelly

Chapter 9 Postpone Costs to Next Release 137

Jeroen Rosink

Chapter 10 Cost Reduction through Reusable Test Assets............. 155

Karen Johns

Chapter 11 You Can't Waste Money on a Defect That Isn't
There 169

Petteri Lyytinen

PART 3   How Should We Do It?

Chapter 12 A Nimble Test Plan: Removing the Cost
of Overplanning 179

David Gilbert

Chapter 13 Exploiting the Testing Bottleneck................................ 195

Markus Gärtner

Chapter 14 Science-Based Test Case Design: Better Coverage,
Fewer Tests.. 213

Gary Gack and Justin Hunter

Chapter 15 Clean Test: Suggestions for Reducing Costs by
Increasing Test Craftsmanship 227

Curtis Stuehrenberg

Chapter 16 Rightsizing the Cost of Testing: Tips for Executives... 245

Scott Barber

Afterword.. 261

Appendix A: Immediate Strategies to Reduce Test Cost 263
Matt Heusser

Appendix B: 25 Tips to Reduce Testing Cost Today 275
Catherine Powell

Appendix C: Is It about Cost or Value?.. 287
Jon Bach

Appendix D: Cost of Starting Up a Test Team 297
Anne-Marie Charrett

Index.. 307

Foreword

As I write this, the American economy has just come out of a recession, but in terms of employment, the economy is stagnant. We face a looming risk of a second recession, possibly a much deeper one. Throughout the recession, companies have been driving down costs. And in that context, we have a new book on driving down the costs of software testing.

The authors approach the challenge from several directions. First, we can ask what the *costs* are. In many cases, the costs are overestimated or the return on investment is underestimated. Getting clear on the facts and communicating them persuasively are important skills.

Blended with the discussions of cost are discussions of waste. Many people see testing as waste in and of itself—if we did not have bugs to find, we would not have to spend money finding them. Then again, if we did not have rain, maybe we would not need roofs on our houses. Is that waste? Or weather? Test groups can sometimes recruit or train some staff who have enough programming and glass-box testing skill to help programmers reduce the number of bugs that survive into system-level testing. But this kind of collaboration is something that has to be welcomed by the programming team, not imposed by the testers.

Even if we accept system-level testing as valuable, there is often significant waste. Software testing is an empirical, technical investigation that we conduct to provide stakeholders with information about the quality of a product or service. Testing that is not designed to provide valuable new information is waste. The same standard applies to test-related activities, such as writing test documentation or deciding which bugs to report and to what level of detail. Many practices add value when applied sparingly (such as user-interface-level regression testing) but impose high net costs when applied broadly as "best practices."

We reduce waste by doing less of what we should not do. We increase effectiveness and efficiency by replacing waste with work that yields value. A tester or testing practice that yields more information of greater value is more effective. An effective tester or practice that yields more per unit time (or cost) is more efficient.

One of the key ways to improve effectiveness is to master more of the available test techniques and understand when they are especially useful.

Different techniques are optimized to expose different types of problems under different circumstances. For many types of bugs (think of race conditions, memory corruption, or insufficiency of available resources as software usage increases), we are blind without well-tailored techniques.

One of the key ways to improve efficiency is to improve a tester's skill in applying test techniques. This improvement is primarily fostered by personal coaching or small-group training. However, we need to be cautious about the training investment itself. Too much tester training is superficial and essentially skill free. It does not take much testing skill to pass a multiple-choice certification exam. (I have never seen a hint of evidence that memorizing definitions improves testers' effectiveness or efficiency.) Other training is more focused on skills, but if people cannot apply a new skill to a project they are working on today, they are likely to forget it before they find a use for it. Training can increase value or waste. You have to choose it carefully.

Collections of essays (such as those in this book) are not likely to improve your skills, but they can help you focus your testing more effectively, to identify waste, and to define learning objectives against which you can assess proposals for training. Good luck in applying them. We have a rough ride ahead and this is a collection of topics that we need to make progress against.

—**Cem Kaner**

Preface

It is hard to believe that it was only in January 2010 that Govind Kulkarni posted two simple questions on LinkedIn: *How do we reduce cost of testing? What are the possible ways by which we can reduce cost of testing yet detect defects?* The result of that post was page after page of spirited discussion. We discussed everything from better test planning (big tests up front) to just-in-time test delivery (no test planning), from exploratory methods to model-driven methods, and everything in between. It was a blast; people started blogging about it.

Then Govind had an idea: If these ideas are good, let us share them with the world. So he started to e-mail the most active, strongest, compelling contributors to the group, asking if they would like to contribute to a book on the subject. Bring to a boil, add some salt to season, wait for nine more months, and the result is the book now in your hands.

We like to think of this book itself as an example of the one plus one equals three power possible with collaboration. But we're getting ahead of ourselves.

So Govind had an idea for a book. When he came up with the idea, we were not really sure how it would turn out. Would we have a bunch of overlapping ideas? Would we have a bunch of *conflicting* ideas? Or maybe a bunch of stories that might or might not resonate with the readers? We didn't know. Matt Heusser offered to come on board and help with the project. Eventually, Heusser took on a senior editor role, the book deal came, and we got serious. But we still did not know how the book would turn out.

The good news is that writing a chapter is relatively cheap (compared with writing a book). Writing an outline is cheaper; writing a one-paragraph outline is practically free. So we asked our authors come up with abstracts and outlines, then played the compare-and-contrast game to find out if patterns were emerging.

The entire book was developed on a wiki, a sort of editable Web page—with each contributor's work available to every other contributor. Once we invited colleagues and peer reviewers, the total group of people looking at the work was about fifty. This meant we had continuous and massive peer review of the work *as it was developed*. Authors received feedback on the abstract or the outline; some turned in just a few paragraphs at a time to get feedback before they proceeded. Others turned in a first draft and asked what do you think.

We used this continuous feedback loop to refine the work. As we identified overlap, we advised people to tighten some parts and strengthen others to minimize the overlap. When we identified missing parts, we recruited authors to jump into those areas. Eventually, we had something that was starting to look like a book. So we had to organize it. But where to start? We had a bunch of chapters about specific techniques and others that were more like frameworks for improvement. More important than how we organized it: How should you read it?

If you are a test manager, line manager, or executive looking for ways to cut test costs *right now*, turn to Appendix A, where there are strategies for reducing test costs. Likewise, testers and other doers who feel project pressure and want to get to done faster might want to check out Appendix B, which lists practical, concrete tips to use *today*. If you are under pressure to outsource for cost reductions, you will want to check out Appendix C, where Jonathan Bach discusses the outsource testing value proposition.

We put those chapters as appendixes at the end of the book, and there is a reason for that. The "cut costs now" chapters are prescriptive. They tell you what to do—but as prescriptions, they are sort of like a doctor giving medical advice without first examining the patient. Sure, they might work in many situations, but you will want tools to determine if the advice will work for you. The good news is that the advice and tools for your situation can be found in, well, the entire rest of the book.

First we wanted to cover what value testing brings, what its costs are, how it can be measured, and the opportunities there are for gains. So Part 1 is "What Will This Cost Us?" That is also a bit of play on words, in that doing less testing—the most obvious way to decrease cost—has its own hidden costs. (If you do not have a test team and are considering building one, this part will lay a foundation to help your analysis, but do not forget Appendix D, by Anne-Marie Charrett, on the economics of starting a test team within an existing development group.)

In Part 2, "What Do We Do?", we dive down from theory to practice, giving specific, actionable areas in which to find cost savings in software testing.

Part 3, "How Do We Do It?", moves from strategy to tactics—with concrete examples and suggestions on how to find cost savings without sacrificing outcome.

It has been our pleasure to work with some of the best minds in the software testing world to give you advice on software testing. Some of that advice will conflict. Ultimately, you will have to decide which advice is right for your organization, what to do, and when and how to do it. It is our hope to be a little help in that selection process. And our pleasure.

Choose wisely.

Acknowledgments

Scott Barber thanks Dawn Haynes, Catherine Powell, and Mike Kelly for dropping what they were doing to provide immediate, direct, valuable, and insightful reviews and recommendations. Special thanks to Tyra Twomey, PhD, who I often refer to as my "personal editor," for converting my blathering into something identifiable as English once again. Also a big thanks to my sons, Nicholas and Taylor, for not giving Daddy too much of a hard time for bringing his laptop to their football practice in order to meet deadlines for my chapter.

Ed Barkley acknowledges the discussions held in May 2010 on the Software Testing & Quality Assurance LinkedIn group that started this whole effort. What a testament to the power of the Internet to bring such a diverse bunch of international software techies together to coauthor this book! Thank you Govind Kulkarni, Suresh Nageswaren, Markus Gärtner, and Matt Heusser for being the great catalysts and visionaries you are. Here's a shout-out to those reviewers, especially Matt, who helped me learn about writing in the active voice! I also stand on the shoulders of such giants as Philip Crosby, for my appreciation of how quality can be free, and W. Edwards Deming for championing true process improvement and system thinking. And a final thanks to the folks at Socialtext for providing the stable and user-friendly platform for our work. I'll continue to recommend it to my consulting associates as we interact across the continents.

Anne-Marie Charrett thanks Cem Kaner and Michael Bolton for their reviews and insights while preparing her chapter. Also thanks to Markus Gärtner, Catherine Powell, and Robin for their reviews and comments. A big thanks to Matthew Heusser for his tireless energy and persistence, which are the main reasons this book is here today. Thank you also, Andrei, Alex, and Nikolai, for your warmth and support. You guys are the warmest and friendliest safety net anyone could wish for.

Selena Delesie thanks the editors for the invitation to contribute to this project. Your energy, passion, and drive kept the rest of us hopping. The collective efforts of authors, editors, and reviewers came together to create a book on software testing that provides diverse solutions for managing testing costs. It has been an honor to work with you all. A big shout-out to Matt Heusser for the use of active voice; Fiona Charles for stripping nonessentials; and Paul Carvalho, Josh Assad, and Maik Nogens for feedback on the final touches. Selena also thanks mentors and colleagues for their support over many years; you have been a profound influence. Finally, Selena is thankful to Aaron and Christian for their patience and support through crazy ideas, long hours, and trips away from home—you make it all worthwhile.

Markus Gärtner would like to thank foremost Elisabeth Hendrickson for her vital feedback on early versions of his chapter. Not only did she offer vital ingredients for the content, but she also provided great guidance on including more examples. In the same sense, Michael "GeePaw" Hill provided great copyediting notes to improve the chapter substantially. A big thanks goes out to him for his hints and itches as well. A big thank you also goes to the other contributors of this book project. We challenged ourselves, providing early, vital, and crucial feedback over the course of the past decade, er . . . months. A special big thanks goes to Matt Heusser and Govind Kulkarni, who both pushed us even further to make this book a reality exactly when we needed it. And finally, Markus wants to thank his wife and children for their support. Without their contributions to the few minutes not spent with the book, the pages you hold in your hands wouldn't be the same as they are now.

David Gilbert would like to thank his wife, Sandy, and his daughters, Sarah and Sophie, for putting up with him not only through the writing of this chapter, but through all the software testing stuff he does that so often takes him away from them. Your patience and support are amazing. I would also like to thank Kathryn Stoehr for her countless hours of editing and advising. Finally, I would like to thank Matt Heusser and everyone else involved in driving the project. So many testers have something they want to say but just never take the time or figure out how to get there; this project has given them a voice, and you should be commended for that.

Matt Heusser would like to thank the folks at Linkedin (where the conversation started), along with Socialtext (who offered the wiki). Those two electronic tools made it possible to get this group together. Matt would also like to that Govind Kulkarni, who asked the question on LinkedIn, then noticed all the energy and followed up a month later by creating the book project. Thanks to Sudhindra P, who is the group owner of Software Testing and Quality Assurance LinkedIn group—he created the forum to exchange the ideas and encouragement. During the course of the project, some chapter reviewers and book authors stepped up to offer intensive peer review. Others asked what they could do to help and dived in, in some cases offering dozens, if not hundreds, of hours of help, just to make this the best possible book. I would like to thank Markus Gärtner, Catherine Powell, Pete Walen, and Jon Bach for specific and intense review above anything I expected. And of course, Matt would be nowhere without the family that gave him the support and drive to write this book.

Govind Kulkarni is grateful to John Stevenson and Matt Heusser, who reviewed my chapter; their comments really helped to improve the content. John had family problems, but in spite of that he was able to find time for the review. I sincerely thank my superior, Prem Apte, who also reviewed what I wrote, passed on very good comments, and encouraged me to complete the project. I am thankful to my wife, Sankhya, and my daughter, Rucha, for their patience and encouragement, since this work took a lot of my weekend time and odd hours. I sincerely thank all of the authors who participated in this project and have made this book see the light of the day. Last, but "How can I forget?" John Wyzalek of CRC Press for his support and encouragement. I thank many of my friends at Enjoytesting.com who encourage me to do lot of new things in life.

Michael Larsen would like to thank Glenn Waters for his in-depth review and helping see the "bigger picture" in his chapter. Thanks also to Matt Heusser, Markus Gärtner, and the other "Miagi-Do ka" for their encouragement and invitation to participate in such an amazing project. Thank you, Shannah Miller, for being an early champion of the testing cause, and Charles "Chuck" Hein for showing how much fun "breaking things on purpose" could actually be. Finally, huge gratitude for my wife, Christina, and three children (Nicholas, Karina, and Amber) for their patience while their husband and father went about writing and doing all of this "testing stuff."

Petteri Lyytinen would like to thank Uoma Oy for acknowledging the value of this book project and for allowing me to work on my chapter during working hours. A very special thank you to Nicole Rauch for her careful reviews of the chapter—your feedback was invaluable! I would also like to thank all of the other contributors: I feel honored and privileged to have been invited to contribute to a book project along with such great minds and great personalities. Finally, a big thank you to Matthew Heusser and Markus Gärtner for making all of this possible for me in the first place—I couldn't hope for better mentors on my path through the ranks of Miagi-Do and toward becoming a better tester!

Catherine Powell would like to thank her husband, Dan, for his support and patience through the long days of testing and the long evenings of writing. She would also like to thank Matt Heusser and Govind Kulkarni for taking a discussion and turning it into a book. Last, she'd like to thank all the reviewers and UC Berkeley for teaching her the business of software.

Jeroen Rosink would like to thank Matt Heusser and Govind Kulkarni, who supported me during this project. Also thanks to Markus Gärtner, Catherine Powell, Peter Walen, Kaleb Pederson, and Nicole Rauch for their feedback on my contribution. They helped me with their patience and valuable remarks to translate the chapter as it is now. Last but not least I want to thank my wife, Mirjam, and my kids, Thomas and Anne, for their patience and their mental support. During this project I learned that speaking about testing is one thing, expressing it in written words in a foreign language is more than a challenge; it is a way of learning and growing.

Curtis Stuehrenberg would like to thank all the colleagues and friends who generously provided feedback and guidance during this effort. Your patience and advice were greatly appreciated. I'd like to single out Max Guernsey, Leonard Haasbroek, and James Marcus Bach for their detailed feedback and support. Even if I apparently ignored your advice, rest assured that I did read it at least. I'd further like to thank Jon Bach for encouraging me to start writing, coaching, and generally making a spectacle of myself. Finally I'd like to thank my wife, Julienne, who found a way to constantly and gently remind me of the task at hand even when it moved into the more tedious phase or rewrites and editing. I sincerely hope all my future agents treat me with your kid gloves.

In addition to the authors, the book project had a large collection of peer reviewers, among which John Stevenson, Mike Dwyer, Glenn Waters, Gee Paw Hill, Kaleb Pederson, Ben Kelly, Seth Eliot, and Andreas Leidig all stood out. It was nice to get to know them through the scope of the project, and to them we are grateful.

Carl Walesa offered his time at an incredibly low rate to move the book from wiki form to the official template format of the publisher. To be fair, he basically offered his time as charity. We appreciate it.

Wait—what was that about "wiki form," you ask? The abstracts, outlines, chapters, review, and project management for this book was entirely done on a Web-based tool called a wiki donated by Socialtext.

So what exactly is a wiki? Well, the word *wiki* is native Hawaiian for "quick." So a wiki tool is a quick-to-use, editable-by-anyone Web page. Learn all about wikis at www.socialtext.com.

Authors

Jon **Bach** is manager for Corporate Intellect at Quardev Inc. (www.quardev.com), a testing and technical writing services company in Seattle. He is most famous for his work in exploratory testing, namely, as coinventor of Session-Based Test Management (with his brother James). He has spoken at over 100 testing-related conferences and workshops, and is an award-winning keynote speaker. He is president of the 2011 Conference for the Association of Software Testing as well as  speaker chairman for Pacific Northwest Software Quality Conference 2011. His blog, http://jonbox.wordpress.com, focuses on human aspects of software testing.

Scott Barber is the chief technologist of PerfTestPlus, cofounder of the Workshop on Performance and Reliability, coauthor of Microsoft patterns and practices' *Performance Testing Guidance for Web Applications*, and contributing author of O'Reilly's *Beautiful Testing.* Barber thinks of himself as a tester and trainer of testers who has a passion for software system performance. In addition to performance testing, he is particularly well versed in helping  companies improve the value of their testing programs and departments, testing embedded systems, testing biometric identification and personal security systems, group facilitation, and authoring instructional materials. He is an international keynote speaker and author of over one hundred articles on software testing. He is a member of the Association for Computing Machinery (ACM), IEEE, American Mensa, the Context-Driven School of Software Testing; a signatory to the Manifesto for Agile Software Development; and a life member of the Association for Software Testing. You can find links to Barber's published works, his blog, and his contact information at http://www.PerfTestPlus.com.

Ed Barkley has been in software development in one form or another since 1968. Over those forty-plus years Barkley has contributed in such industries as publishing, manufacturing, service, distribution center technology, finance, telecommunications, advanced digital video imaging technology, call center management, pharmacy claims processing, and work-flow solutions for foreclosures and bankruptcies. In addition to traditional information technology roles such as developer, systems analyst, project manager, and test manager, Barkley has also had business-facing roles including business process improvement consultant, facilitator, change management leader, and trainer. A proponent of ISO, CMMI, and ITIL, and a strong supporter of intelligent approaches to human performance improvement (ISPI/ASTD), he has also worked to translate Lean manufacturing principles into office processes to identify and minimize waste, delay, and rework. After earning a management science degree from the University of Cincinnati, Ohio, he continued his academic collaboration by teaching as an instructor within that discipline. Barkley is currently a business analyst, passionate about requirements definition, IT-to-business communications, modeling, user- and context-driven conversations, test planning, facilitation, change, and issue management. He can be reached at his Web site http://www.edbarkley .com or at his LinkedIn profile http://www.linkedin.com/in/edbarkley/.

Michael Bolton has been working in software development for over twenty years, and in the last ten has been teaching software testing all over the world. He is the coauthor (with senior author James Bach) of "Rapid Software Testing," a course that presents a methodology and mindset for testing software expertly in uncertain conditions and under extreme time pressure. Bolton has been program chair for the Toronto Association of System and Software Quality, and conference chair (in 2008) for the Conference of the Association for Software Testing, and is a cofounder of the Toronto Workshops on Software Testing. He wrote a column in *Better Software* magazine for four years, and sporadically produces his own newsletter. Bolton lives in Toronto, Canada, with his wife and two children. He can be reached at michael@developsense. com or through his Web site http://www.developsense.com.

Anne-Marie Charrett is a professional software tester and runs her own company, Testing Times. An
electronic engineer by trade, software testing chose
her, when in 1990 she started conformance testing
against European protocols. She was hooked and
has been testing since then. She enjoys working with
innovative and creative people, which has led her to
specialize in working for start-ups and small com-
panies. Charrett blogs at http://mavericktester.com
and her business-facing Web site is http://www.testingtimes.ie. She runs
@dailytestingtip, a Twitter account that provides daily tips to software
testers.

Selena Delesie is a consulting software tester and
Agile coach who runs her own company, Delesie
Solutions. She has been managing and coaching on
software, testing, and Agile practices for a range of
leading-edge technologies for about a decade. She
facilitates the evolution of good teams and organizations into great ones using individualized and
team-based coaching and interactive training expe-
riences. She is an active speaker, participant, and
leader in numerous industry-related associations and conferences. Links
to her published works, blog, and contact information can be found at
DelesieSolutions.com.

Gary Gack is the founder and president of Process-
Fusion.net, a provider of e-learning, assessments,
strategy advice, training, and coaching relating to
integration and deployment of software and information technology industry best practices. Gack
holds an MBA from the Wharton School and is
a Lean Six Sigma Black Belt. In addition, he is an
ASQ Certified Software Quality Engineer (CSQE);
a Certified Scrum Master; a visiting scientist with
the Software Engineering Institute (2006), where he coauthored the
"Measuring for Performance Driven Improvement 1" course; and he holds
the ITIL Foundation Certification. He has more than forty years of diverse
experience in the software and information technology industry, including
more than twenty years focused on process improvement. He is the author

of numerous articles and a book titled *Managing the "Black Hole": The Executive's Guide to Software Project Risk*. He can be reached via e-mail at ggack@process-fusion.net, blog http://process-fusion.blogspot.com/, or Web site http://www.process-fusion.net/.

Markus Gärtner has spent four years in software testing, as a tester and a group leader. Since September 2010 he works with it-agile GmbH in Germany as expert on Agile testing. Personally committed to Agile methods, he believes in continuous improvement in software testing through skills and deliberate practice. Gärtner is the cofounder of the European chapter of Weekend Testing, a black belt instructor in the Miagi-Do School of Software Testing, contributes to the ATDD-Patterns writing community as well as the Software Craftsmanship movement. Gärtner regularly presents at Agile and testing conferences, as well as dedicating himself to writing about testing, foremost in an Agile context. Gärtner blogs at http://blog.shino.de.

David Gilbert is the quality improvement advisor for Raymond James, CEO of Sirius Software Quality Associates, and the creator of TestExplorer. He has been a consultant on automated testing for over fifteen years, and for the last ten years has been a passionate advocate of exploratory testing. He is one of a select few testers endorsed by James Bach and Michael Bolton to teach their rapid software testing class. Gilbert is active in local testing groups, has presented at many national conferences, and written editorials for *Better Software* magazine. His testing tool, TestExplorer, was the first software created specifically to support the process of Session-Based Test Management for exploratory testing. He occasionally blogs, and publishes his blog at both www.TestExplorer.com and www.Sirius-SQA.com. He can be found on Twitter at SiriusDG, on LinkedIn at www.linkedin.com/in/davidleegilbert, on Skype as SiriusDG, and via email at dgilbert@sirius-sqa.com.

Matthew Heusser is a software process naturalist and consulting software tester. In the twelve years he has been working in technology, he has worked as a developer, project manager, and test and quality assurance lead. During that time he also managed to serve as lead organizer of the Grand Rapids' Perl User Group. Heusser also served as lead organizer for the Great Lakes Software Excellence Conference and has presented at STAREast, the Better Software Conference, Google's Test Automation Conference, and the Software Test Professionals Conference. In addition to speaking, Heusser is the author of the  influential blog Creative Chaos (http://xndev.blogspot.com) and a contributing editor to *Software Test and Quality Assurance* magazine. He recently completed a contract as an evening instructor in information systems at Calvin College and served as the lead organizer of the workshop on technical debt. His first contributed work was a chapter in the book *Beautiful Testing*, published in 2009 by O'Reilly Media.

Justin Hunter is Founder and CEO of Hexawise, makers of a software test case generating tool. Justin got involved in software testing via a circuitous career path that included stints as a securities lawyer in London, General Manager of Asia's first internet-based stock brokerage firm, and eight years working at Accenture, a global IT and management consulting firm. While at Accenture, Justin introduced testing teams around the world to Design of Experiments- based software testing methods, measured benefits of using these methods in 17 pilot and received a global Innovation Award for improving testing efficiency and productivity. He is passionate about raising awareness of efficiency enhancing software test design strategies that help testers test smarter, not harder. Justin lives in North Carolina with his wife and two boys. He can be reached at http://www.linkedin.com/in/justinhunter or through his company's website http://www.hexawise.com.

Karen Johns, CSTE, is a director with Mosaic Inc., which specializes in helping organizations manage the risk of developing, maintaining, and installing their mission-critical systems. Johns is the product manager and chief developer for Mosaic's methodology products and was instrumental in integrating Mosaic's object-driven test automation process with field-proven testing methodology. With over thirty years of experience, Johns has expertise in information systems quality assurance with emphasis on software testing, test automation, software process improvement, measurement, project management, and training. Johns has planned and implemented structured testing processes for a wide range of industries. In addition, Johns has developed and presented customized testing and project management methodology training across numerous projects and industries. She has also presented at Quality Assurance International (QAI) and Better Software conferences, and at local Chicago Software Process Improvement Network (C-SPIN) and Chicago Quality Assurance Association (CQAA) presentations.

Cem Kaner has pursued a multidisciplinary career centered on the theme of the satisfaction and safety of software customers and software-related workers. With a law degree, a doctorate in experimental psychology, and seventeen years in Silicon Valley, Cem joined Florida Institute of Technology in 2000 as professor of software engineering. His research focuses on the question: *How can we foster the next generation of leaders in software testing?* Kaner is the senior author of *Testing Computer Software* (with Jack Falk and Hung Quoc Nguyen), *Bad Software* (with David Pels), and *Lessons Learned in Software Testing* (with James Bach and Bret Pettichord). The Association for Computing Machinery recently honored him with its Making a Difference Award (http://www.sigcas.org/awards-1).

Michael Kelly is a partner at Developer Town, a venture development firm. His focus is software testing; he is most passionate about exploratory testing, performance testing, and testing in Agile environments. Kelly is a past president and director for the Association for Software Testing, and he has built and managed development teams at both startups and Fortune 500 companies. He regularly writes and speaks about topics in software testing, runs a series of software testing workshops in the Indianapolis community, and is a regular contributor to SearchSoftwareQuality.com. You can find links to Kelly's published works, his software testing blogs, and more information about how venture development works at his Web site http://www.MichaelDKelly.com.

Govind Kulkarni has spent seventeen years in software quality assurance and management. He is a Project Management Professional (PMP), Certified Quality Auditor (CQA), and TicK IT professional. He has worked with Fortune 500 clients, and has provided test strategy and test management solutions. He is one of the reviewers of the test maturity model integrated (TMMi), is actively doing research in model-based testing, and is devising his own test  estimation method called as TPIT. These days he works as a mentor and has trained some two thousand testers all over the world. He manages his own testing Web site http://www.enjoytesting.com and is actively involved in LinkedIn and other forums. He has written more than twenty-five technical papers and is a frequent speaker at testing conferences. He can be reached at govind@enjoytesting.com.

Michael Larsen retired from a career as a rock and roll singer to pursue software testing full time at Cisco Systems in 1992. After a decade at Cisco, he has worked with a broad array of technologies and industries including virtual machine software, capacitance touch devices, video game development, and distributed database and Web applications. He has for the better part of his career found himself in the role of being an army of one or the lone tester more times  than not, and this unique viewpoint is frequent grist for the mill that is TESTHEAD, his professional software testing blog (http://mkl-testhead.blogspot.com/). Larsen is actively involved with the Association for Software Testing (AST), assists as an instructor for AST's series of Black Box Software Testing classes, and is a passionate supporter of AST's vision and approach to software testing education. He is the cofounder of the Americas chapter of Weekend Testing. His LinkedIn profile is http://www.linkedin.com/in/mkltesthead and can be found on Twitter at @mkltesthead.

Petteri Lyytinen is an Agile/Lean and software testing enthusiast with a little over six years of experience in the field. He has participated in testing

in various environments ranging from mobile platforms through Web-based solutions to desktop applications, and has been involved on all levels of testing, including test planning, test management, and, more recently, broader quality management. Lyytinen works as a test manager in a small Finnish information technology-service company where he is responsible for managing the company's quality assurance strategy and competence development, in addition to directing the testing efforts of the company's off-shore test team. Due to his open minded but critical way of thinking combined with technical curiosity and his passion toward software testing, Lyytinen is a strong player in the testing field and rarely runs out of ideas on how to improve the products or processes at hand. His strongest points are his vivid imagination, the "I wonder what would happen if…" approach to just about everything and his excellent ability to make people understand complicated concepts by using real-life examples as analogies. Lyytinen blogs at http://pro-testing.arabuusimiehet.com/, and an easy way to contact him is through his LinkedIn profile at http://www.linkedin.com/in/petterilyytinen.

Catherine Powell is a principal at Abakas, a software consulting company. She has been testing and managing testers for about ten years. She has worked with a broad range of software, including an enterprise storage system, a Web-based healthcare system, data synchronization applications on mobile devices, and Web apps of various flavors. She is an author and a formal mentor to testers and test managers. Powell focuses primarily on the realities of shipping software in small and midsize companies. Her published works, blog, and contact information can be found at www.abakas.com.

Jeroen Rosink has over eleven years of experience as a software tester. Since November 2005 he has worked for Squerist, the Netherlands. In addition to his function as a senior test consultant, he also acts as a coach, teacher and "oracle" for his colleagues. He has fulfilled several roles from test analyst to test consultant in different projects. This brought him experience in branches such as financial services, embedded software, energy market, semi-government, and petro industry. The projects ranged from building a new mortgage system to maintenance of social security systems, and used development methods including RUP, Agile, Waterfall, EVO, and ASAP. Rosink blogs at http://testconsultant.blog-spot.com; his LinkedIn profile is http://nl.linkedin.com/in/jeroenrosink. He also published articles in the second and third edition of *Quality Matters*, *"Be Innovative! Stop Improving Your Test Process"* and *"Skill Based Testing: The Life Cycle of a Tester,"* respectively.

Curtis Stuehrenberg is a classically trained bari-tone and unsuccessful stage actor who stumbled into software testing when a friend pulled him, kicking and screaming, onto a project at Microsoft that would one day become Secure Business Server. The team wisely shunted him into the build and test lab where they assumed he would do the least harm. They were fortunately mistaken. Soon he was stalk-ing the halls, causing fear and anger in developers and architects alike for having the effrontery to break "his" builds. Twelve years later, he has mellowed somewhat and enjoys a challenging, reward-ing, and at times successful career helping companies and teams walk the fine line between craftsmanship and value. In what passes for his free time, he writes a little, leads the odd discussion, and argues passionately about subjects most of the world could care little about until things go wrong.

Part 1

What Will This Cost Us?

1

Is This the Right Question?

Matt Heusser

This book starts with the question "How do we decrease the cost of testing?" In this chapter, I'll push back a little on that question, asking if it is, in fact, the right one—and putting it in its place. After all, one rational answer to the question on how to reduce the cost of testing is the following:

> The easiest way to make testing cheap is to do a quick, slapdash job. Easier than that, don't test at all. Your testing costs would go down, but overall costs would go up. And customers? Those would just go away.
>
> **—Anonymous**

1.1 CONTROLLING COSTS: WHAT DOES IT MEAN?

Say, for a moment, that you are a test director and successfully implementing the ideas in this book. That means you can do the same work with half the test or quality assurance (QA) staff. Assuming the work coming in from development stays constant, what happens, what is the result, the outcome? That's right. "Success" at lowering test costs might just mean having the dubious honor of laying off half your staff.

This sort of thing has happened before. Eli Goldratt saw it happen in the twentieth century in manufacturing. According to Goldratt, one early consequence of his "theory of constraints" was massive increases in throughput for American factories. This actually turned out to be a problem, because the companies now had more supply than demand, so they began shutting down factories due to overcapacity. Goldratt documents these sorts of system effects in the second edition of his book *The Goal: A Process of Ongoing Improvement*.

Laying off half the staff might lead to a bonus or promotion, but it doesn't sit well with me; it doesn't serve the community we work in. No, I want to look at something beyond pure cost. In general business we look at cost and sales (or the "top line" numbers); it may be acceptable to double our costs if sales quadruple. We have nothing like that top line in testing. There is no easy metric for it.

Instead of value, we focus on cost. And again, we know where that ends—success means the unemployment line.

I do agree that brining down testing costs in general is a thing, but is is only part of the equation. In this chapter I will lay some ground rules for evaluating cost, while also including value within the discussion. Without looking at value, we're back to cutting testing completely.

So first, let's look at what *limiting*, *containing*, or *decreasing* cost means, exactly.

1.2 LOOKING DEEPER INTO LIMITING COSTS

Before we discuss value, let's take a moment and look at limiting costs. After all, it's straightforward. It's easy. It's simple. What can be wrong with that? Consider for a moment a typical cost-cutting strategy. We could, for example, cut benefits, bonuses, and salaries for the workers. Over time, this tends to decrease morale, increase turnover, and decrease productivity. When salaries go down, the best and brightest leave for greener pastures—leaving the company with, to paraphrase Ronald Padavan, "the dumbest and the stupidest." I hope you'll agree that's not a useful long-term strategy [1].

The next level of cutting costs is a tad more refined. Instead of cutting benefits or laying off the highly paid staff, we can instead try to break the work down into extremely simple, well-defined component tasks. Then we can hire people for specific, repeatable, well-described jobs [2]. For example, we can separate our front office from the back office, then hire a low-paid "call center" or "help desk" person to manage the queue of incoming work. That allows our more experienced, more well-paid technicians to stay focused on one problem at a time without interruption.

But there's a problem. Psychologist and systems thinker John Seddon labels the problem "failure demand." As Seddon explains it, there are two types of demand in the system: regular demand, where a customer wants something; and failure demand, where a customer comes back a second, third, fourth, and fifth time to ask again for a solution because the initial "solution" did not meet the initial demand.

If you've ever seen a call tracking ticket bounced around a dozen, two dozen, or three dozen times without resolving the issue, you've seen failure demand. And you know that failure demand can be more expensive than the original request in the first place. Seddon goes on to document that this separation of front office from back office and movement of jobs, often to low-cost-of-living, low-wage areas, creates enough failure demand to remove any cost savings. Seddon uses one phrase to describe all this. In his words, "When you try to control costs, costs go up" [3]. We need a better way.

1.3 WAYS TO LOOK AT VALUE

We want to report something to management to get that "exceeds expectations" on the annual review, and we want it to be a number, right? Value in testing defies simple numeric measurement. This is not a new problem. The great W. Edwards Deming, guru of total quality management, used a quote from Lloyd Nelson to explain this: "The most important figures that one needs for management are unknown or unknowable, but successful management must nevertheless take account of them" [4].

The classic example Deming gives is training. If you simply look at numbers on a spreadsheet, training has an immediate cost without clear value. Of course, you could make up numbers in a complex spreadsheet about turnover, or productivity, but those would just be an estimate, a guess, wishful thinking. Likewise, if you only look at a spreadsheet, it makes sense to only hire part-time employees (to save the cost of insurance and other benefits), or to cut benefits and retirement, or to fire the entire staff and rehire cheaper people. Yet we know from the previous section that those strategies fail. So we have a paradox: We have to manage to value, yet value defies numerical measurement.

Managers have been struggling with measuring value for centuries. Even measurements as deceptively simple as cold hard cash in the bank can be manipulated. One sales technique that creates sales right now, without creating real long-term value is known as "channel stuffing." When a manufacturer takes a channel stuffing approach, they convince customers (usually a retail store) to buy many more products than they actually need for a given time period, then allow the other company to return the extra equipment by a certain day. This allows sales executives to "make" monthly or quarterly sales targets without having to do the work of, you know, actually selling more things. This also causes the manufacturer to pay out large bonuses without "real" sales attached. Gil Amelio, former CEO of Apple Computer, claims that channel stuffing was one of the practices that led to the near-destruction of Apple in the 1990s [5].

Another example currently playing out in the courts is Lehman Brothers. According to the U.S. Securities and Exchange Commission, Lehman Brothers manipulated its balance sheet by taking on loans right before its quarterly report, thus creating the appearance of more cash on hand. And then there is Enron, WorldCom, or a host of other frauds.

So much for cold hard cash as an absolute metric. But who said we need metrics, anyway? The most common line used as an argument in favor of metrics is from Tom DeMarco, in his book *Controlling Software Projects* [6]. The actual line from that book was not "without measurement you can not manage," but instead "without measurement you can not control." DeMarco he spent the rest of his career pointing out that control in software projects isn't all that important. Twenty years after that original article, he published an article in *IEEE Spectrum* that formally refuted the importance of controlling software projects [7]. In his words:

> My early metrics book, "Controlling Software Projects: Management, Measurement, and Estimation," played a role in the way many budding software engineers quantified work and planned their projects. In my reflective mood, I'm wondering, was its advice correct at the time, is it still relevant, and do I still believe that metrics are a must for any software development effort? My answers are no, no, and no.

Think about it: You manage to keep your hair looking good without taking a ruler to it every day, right? This can be done by looking at it, understand what is happening, and paying attention. We call this qualitative evaluation. You may not agree with me and I can understand that. I hope you will at least suspend your disbelief long enough to finish this chapter. Let me talk about other tools for your toolbox, to see if they might be helpful. So let's forget about this metrics madness for a bit and instead talk about what actually happens while doing testing, in order to understand.

Once we understand testing a bit better, perhaps then we can generalize some rules for management.

1.4 THE REALITY OF TESTS AND TEST CASES

When I talk to managers and executives I get this vague general impression that there is some correct set of test cases. It seems to be kind of like the holy grail or the North American Big Foot, except that many leaders think they have captured it.

The thinking goes that if the team had this set of correct test cases, we could separate test design from test execution, and pay the test designer more wages as the one "just executing" the tests. Of course that whole idea would send Seddon into convulsions; but, I am sad to say, it doesn't even work.

First, for any given piece of software, there may be an infinite number of possible test cases. If you give the requirement to two test engineers and ask them to create test cases, you'd likely get two entirely different sets of documents. Each would address the risks that the author perceives. Likewise, test cases tend to try to predict errors. Consider the simple web application that converts degrees Fahrenheit to Celsius and back, illustrated in Figure 1.1 [8]. A classic approach to this problem would break the functionality into equivalence classes and boundaries. It might look something like this:

Celsius Value	Expected Fahrenheit Value
0	32
37	100
100	212
One	ERROR
(blank)	(blank)

We could make quite a list, and it might be a good one.

Framed this way, the tests have a flaw. They assume the software will be used by something like a computer, with a specific input and output. This frames the problem like a function in computer programming. But applications are not consumed by software, they are used by humans. And the

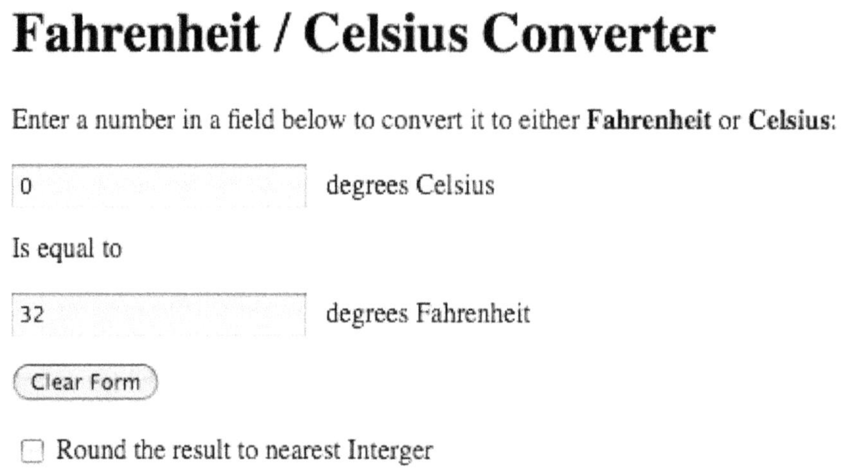

Fahrenheit / Celsius Converter

Enter a number in a field below to convert it to either **Fahrenheit** or **Celsius**:

| 0 | degrees Celsius

Is equal to

| 32 | degrees Fahrenheit

(Clear Form)

☐ Round the result to nearest Interger

FIGURE 1.1
Matthew Heusser's host of Martin Carlsson's F to C conversion code. Used with permission.

human has many more ways to interact with the software than simplistic input–output.

With this particular software, the problem is that the page does a conversion immediately when you type anything into the textbox. So when I want to test 100 Celsius, I need to type in a one, a zero, and a second zero. The software does an interpretation at every step—converting 1 to 33.8, 10 to 50, and 100 to 212. Watching these numbers change is an odd experience. As a customer or user of the software, the interaction makes me feel uncomfortable. Out of control. Something is wrong; I would prefer to use conversion software where I press a button for the conversion, not where it happens automatically with the onkeypress event.

In my experience consumer Web applications are full of these little usability issues that can be found and fixed easily once a user can actually explore the application, but might not be found in hours, days, or weeks of reviews, inspections, and walk-throughs. It is also unlikely to be found by testing up front.

So this is our first insight: We need to understand the type of defects that can be found by those up-front processes, and the type that can be found by exploring the software. Then we need to get really good at exploratory testing and effectively planning the tests that *can* be done up front.

1.5 WHERE IS THE VALUE?

So far I see value in several different places in the spectrum: First while the software is being conceived, using tests as examples to help clarify the requirements, and then again toward the end of the process, finding the most important problems quickly. In addition to finding problems, we can create value by providing information to management to help them make ship–no-ship decisions and in writing "good" bug reports that help developers identify and find specific problems quickly. For the next section I will cover each of these four areas and how to do them more effectively.

1.6 TESTS AS AIDS TO REQUIREMENTS

Consider the deceptively simple requirement "User can apply multiple discount codes to an order." It sounds trivial. Consider that the user applies three 50 percent discount codes. What happens to the order? Do we stop at 100 percent or keep going, discounting the item 150 percent and giving the customer money back? Or we could apply the first discount to 50 percent, the second takes off half of what is left, down to 25 percent, and the third again discounts by half, taking the price to 12.5 percent of the original. While I would expect the third discount takes things down to 12.5 percent, it is also possible the company has a business rule to never discount below 25 percent. We could make requirements that express these discounts as business rules, and we probably should. But think about it another way: Isn't a concrete, defined-expectation test also an example [9]? These examples have a fair amount of value to business users who now understand in specific terms how the software will behave, and they can also serve as guideposts to developers.

When I think of tests as examples, two kinds spring to mind: both the confirmatory "press the button and get the answer," but also the out of bounds, the incorrect, and the exception case. These can be extremely important, not only because they define what the software should do when something goes wrong, but because they remind the programmers to program for cases when something goes wrong.

It is becoming more common that product owners and developers come up with those confirmatory tests. Oh, it might take a little effort, but if a product owner and developer cannot articulate the "happy path" of the software and come up with an example or two, your team probably has bigger problems than shaving a little bit of testing cost off the process. In some cases, we can automate them and turn them into checks, things that simply must pass for the real inspection to occur. The negative tests, the exceptional ones, could probably benefit from a professional critical thinker. That is where testers can step in and add a lot of value quickly.

Having a tester involved to define the product might appear to make the cost of testing go up, but think about it: Better examples and better thinking early means the product will be of higher quality before it gets into a tester's hands. Which means there will be less defects, less back-and-forth between developers and the testers.

To be brutally frank, it seems to me that every five years or so a new expert comes along and "discovers" this idea of being involved up front. Actually, there are several chapters like that in this book, and some of the ideas are good. My advice here is a little different though: Don't be involved up front in order to come up with test cases in parallel with requirements gathering. I do not want a drawn-out twelve-month period where people are having meetings and writing things on paper. No, I want to move from concept to prototype to code quickly, so things do not have a chance to become stale.

Instead of hampering the process, running around complaining that we need better specifications or we need a certain type of plan or we can not proceed without this or that box checked, I see the testers actively contributing to figure out what we are going to build and how it ought to work. That is what I mean by involved up front.

When I see a tester ask "What happens if the software can't connect to the database?" (and I do), I immediately see him also making a suggestion: "We should try again in five minutes, and, after three failures, send e-mail and pager notices to the database administration team." The idea here is to keep the process light, fast, and moving. (If you noticed that the example is just a test turned sideways, well, you are catching on.) That means faster time to market, fewer defects, and happier customers. If you would rather have cheaper testing but greater overall time to market, I do not know. Maybe you need a different chapter. If what you really care about is delivered value to customers, read on.

1.7 FINDING THE MOST IMPORTANT DEFECTS QUICKLY

Years ago, when I was a young programmer at "The Title Office," we had a gentleman on our staff named Mohammed. Mohammed was a programmer too, but as a service to the team he also did testing. That guy could break an application in seconds. He would mouse around the screen, tap-tap-tap, crash your application, and say something like "You need to handle rapid resizing" or "This calendar app crashes when I try to schedule a meeting with five people a year from now that's a week long." Mohammed would make you cry. One time, I'm pretty sure I heard him cackle with glee.

What Mohammed was doing was a technique called *quick attacks*. He didn't need any long set-up time nor did he need to document a great deal. Instead, Mohammed would look at every input and overwhelm it with data. Yes, he would also occasionally walk the happy path to get further into the application, but mostly Mohammed was checking to see how the software handled exceptions. His theory being that if the application handled exceptions well, the programmer had thought of most of the cases well; and if it didn't, the programmer likely had to go rethink all of the possible combinations of inputs in the program.

Beyond quick attacks, we can do something called domain modeling, where we actually look at the problem the software is designed to solve or the capability it is designed to enable. This gives the tester a sort of vision, or model, of how the software should work. Good testers can exploit this to find the difference between the software as envisioned by the customer and what was actually built.

Other jumping-off points to test ideas include the historical failures of the software (unless this is a brand new application), the historic failures of our mode of software environment [10], what the key business functions are, and what our key risks are. This is classic risk management, and there are several ways to do it, the simplest being to multiply the risk percentage of occurrence by impact and sort, and test for the riskiest problems first. During that process itself the tester will learn more about the software, the problem, and how the programmer implemented his solution.

I find it surprising that in all the test literature, so little effort is spent on quick attacks and domain modeling. Think about it: We just sort of assume that anyone can come up with "good" test cases, and then we are surprised when we spend a lot of money on testing but bugs slip through. To borrow a quote from John Ruskin:

It's unwise to pay too much, but it's worse to pay too little. When you pay too much, you lose a little money—that is all. When you pay too little, you sometimes lose everything, because the thing you bought was incapable of doing the thing it was bought to do. The common law of business balance prohibits paying a little and getting a lot—it can't be done. If you deal with the lowest bidder, it is well to add something for the risk you run, and if you do that you will have enough to pay for something better.

This kind of investment in test excellence doesn't have to cost much actual money. A few dollars, perhaps a training course, and a few hours of committed time. One good resource on this is *Lessons Learned in Software Testing,* by Cem Kaner, James Bach, and Bret Pettichord. Two more, slightly dated texts are the pair of books *How to Break Software* and *How to Break Web Software,* by James Whittaker, and a fourth is Lee Copeland's book *A Practitioner's Guide to Software Test Design.* Beyond that, there are numerous test challenges and exercises [11] that any test team can go over, sharpening its skills in the process.

I would rather have one tester that can find the bugs quickly than a dozen untrained people writing testing scripts that essentially run one test per page. A good quick tester can test a dozen items in a minute. (Or more. It depends on the type of the problem.)

1.8 PROVIDING MEANINGFUL INFORMATION TO DECISION MAKERS

For the sake of simplicity, let's define the role of executive as "to execute," or get things done. Chiefly that is done by making key decisions. To make those decisions business leaders need information. That's where the tester comes in. We can probably predict the kind of questions the executive will ask: How long will testing take? When will the software be done? Perhaps, just perhaps, the executive may ask what is the state of the project, and what is the difference between the official story and what is actually going on in the field.

That is a critical moment. If the testing group says something like "We have run eighty-five out of one hundred test cases with a 75 percent pass rate." Or "A test cycle takes three days and we are on test cycle number two," we've lost our moment. To our executives (and lets face it, to anyone outside our small team), this kind of statement sounds a little like the adults in the world of Charlie Brown: "wah wah wah wah wah." What we've just done is ceded the field and made testing simply another step in the process, another thing to do in order to ship the project. Pretty soon management will be claiming unreasonable things like "the role of testing is to validate that the software works," [12] something impossible to do if the software doesn't actually work in some way, which it is a whole lot of the time.

What we can do is provide meaningful information. We can perform actual evaluation into the state of the software (a big part of which is testing), then condense and summarize that generally in three ways: Systems thinking, anecdotes, and statistics.

Sometimes all the king's horses and all the king's men are saying that yes, the project will be done by November 1. They may be under extreme pressure from multiple layers of management to support this date. The ironic thing is that if the team cannot make it, and the executives know this early, executives can often make better financial decisions for the company.

As the only folks touching and watching all parts of the system, often the testers are in a place to know more about what is really going on than any individual programmer, project manager, or "architect." (On one project, I overheard two developers talking in the restroom, saying things directly contradictory to the happy-happy sunshine meeting they had two hours earlier.) Lesson: Don't underestimate informal communication channels. And consider the value of providing critical information on the project.

1.9 ASSISTING OTHER TECHNICAL STAFF: BUG INVESTIGATION AND COMMUNICATION

Next consider the run-of-the-mill, mediocre test group at a large company. For any given project the team is assigned as available, and the team members pull out scripts from a document repository to run. One particular test is to add accounts to a given "group"—a group is a collection of users.

It's a simple test: Go into the control panel, select a group, go to the "add accounts" textbox and type in the name of the account you would like to add. As you type, the possible list of accounts should appear, as in Figure 1.2. The tester creates an account called Test1, a group in account Test2 goes to the control panel, types in "T," then "Te," then "Tes," then "Test" . . . and nothing shows up at all. The tester could file the bug now,

Accounts (1)

Add Group to Account: Sq|

| SquareCalc |
| SquareRootMathematicians |

0 rows selected: Sh ... ion (Remove from account)

Showing 1 - 1 of 1

	Name	Workspaces	Users	Primary
☐	BudgetCorp	0	1	⊙

FIGURE 1.2
Searching for accounts in the software control panel.

with a clear error and a reproduction strategy. Or the tester could experiment trying other accounts. For example, most "older" accounts on the system worked just fine.

It turned out the software was limiting the list to the accounts that the business administrator themselves "belonged to," yet the specification called for the control panel to show all accounts in the system. If the tester had done the same unthinking test with an account the logged-in user belonged to, he would have seen no error at all [13]. Likewise, if the bug's reproduction steps were documented incorrectly, it's possible the programmer would not have seen the error.

This is a clear-cut case where expertise and investigation could make the difference between completely missing a bug, or filing it with the wrong cause, or bouncing the bug back and forth between developers and testers for several days—versus finding it and fixing it in minutes.

For the record, this is a bug I found last week, and yes, we fixed it before it went out to customers.

1.10 DRIVING OUT WASTE

One thing I like about the business term *Lean* is the appeal to eliminate waste. In manufacturing, you can physically see waste in terms of leftover scrap or thrown-away inventory. So, for example, the burgers your fast food place throws away uneaten are waste. Waste for software is harder to define. When I interviewed Mary Poppendieck, author of *Lean Software Development,* she defined *waste* as "anything the team itself feels is not helpful in accomplishing the mission" [14].

About the same time, I started interviewing testers about how they spend their day. I wanted to know how much time was spent in meetings, how much in e-mail, documentation, writing status reports, working on compliance activities—things that are not testing. In many cases the testers that I was interviewing were spending up to 80 percent of their time on activities they themselves agreed did not add value.

If you use just one suggestion from this chapter, consider this: For two weeks, write down exactly how you spend your time, in fifteen-minute increments. That will transform your anecdotes and stories about time wasted into hard data.

When someone asks how you can improve performance on projects, trot out the pie chart: Look at how many things the testing group is asked to do that are not testing. If we are only testing 20 percent of the time, then by only shaving a few percentage points off here, here, and here, we can get that number to forty. This will double productivity.

Occasionally I have the chance to interview testers who are wildly productive compared with their peers or the industry at large. These are people who may cost one and a half times as much but find two, three, four, or five times as many defects, often more important and serious defects, often defects other testers will not find no matter how much time they are given.

These supertesters have a number of things in common. Two key things I notice are that they rarely get blocked [15] and they are always testing. If that means shifting work hours to when no one is in the office, they'll do it. If it means sneaking off to work in the cafeteria, they'll do that too. When it comes to avoiding nontesting work, good testers can be surprisingly effective.

If the result of that is that the 80/20 becomes 20/80—that means we can reduce the cost of testing not by hourly rate, but by simply eliminating waste and obstacles [16].

1.11 PUTTING IT ALL TOGETHER

Any group of humans doing work is going to have a bottleneck, the process that slows things down. In many organizations, this is claimed to be the software testers. Let's take that to its logical extreme: Consider a project scheduled for release in ninety days where the code is sent to the testers on day eighty-nine. Is testing actually the bottleneck? As soon as the testers find the first showstopper bug, the true bottleneck becomes the development group, so the statement isn't supportable. But more than that, it is not a helpful statement; it is a wrong-headed way of looking at the problem.

Testers could have helped the project in lots of ways, the first of which was likely to identify the schedule risk in the first place and to suggest alternate ways to build the software to avoid that risk. Testers could have been involved in the beginning to clarify requirements, or, more likely on this project, to remind folks that the shared understanding of what was meant to be built was missing and the documentation vacuous.

If management were to break that ninety-day project into smaller chunks, or if the technical staff were to create stubs, scaffolding, and drivers for the code earlier, then the testers could begin exploring the software earlier. That means they would be finding defects earlier, giving the test team time to fix the defects more quickly. (Also, when the new code is fresh in the mind of the developers.) This kind of exploring would mean earlier fixes and quicker time to market.

Good testers can provide more information to the technical staff about what went wrong, with everything from the environment, to what has changed since the code used to work, to insights about a family of related defects. These insights can further reduce developer time and time to market.

Finally, testers are faced with the impossible goal of evaluating an infinite number of possible tests in order to create a quick summary for management. If done poorly, this leads to extra time spent testing and debugging when the software could have gone to customers. Or worse, the tester could miss some important tests, which means early delivery of buggy software. All of these, combined with the desire to eliminate waste in our test processes, tell me that a truly expert tester is not only much faster and efficient than a new tester, but that the active, engaged tester can find defects the dilettante cannot.

The entire world has a constant complaint about bottom-barrel quality software. Instead of trying to shave a few pennies from the software testing process, we might be better served to develop and grow software testers who are technically adept, personally flexible, and experts in the domain of the business. In other words, maybe we can decrease the overall cost of testing—I've listed a half-dozen ways to get there. Notice that to do it we focus not on shaving a nickel, but on delivering real value by driving out waste, redundancy, or eliminating work-in-progress inventory. To do that, we'll have to change the perception of testing. Instead of thinking of testers as those "other people" who "verify" the software is correct, we communicate and explain our value for what it is—strategic partners and contributors.

Who's with me?

NOTES

1. Laying off the highest paid staff and rehiring at a low wage happened to be the exact strategy pursued by Circuit City. See "Why Circuit City Busted, Why Best Buy Boomed," *New York Times,* http://www.time.com/time/business/article/0,8599,1858079,00.html, or Google "Circuit City bankruptcy layoff."
2. Frederick W. Taylor suggested separating the worker from the work in his book *Scientific Management,* published in 1903. I used to argue that Taylor was (literally) a hundred years out of date, but recent textual criticism and investigation indicate that most of Taylor's published results were bogus and simply never occurred. For a detailed explanation of this, I recommend "The Management Myth: Why the Experts Keep Getting It Wrong," by Matthew Stewart. In practice, I do not recommend separating the worker from the work. Instead, I recommend engaging the worker in the work.
3. John Seddon, *Freedom from Command and Control: Rethinking Lean Service* (Productivity Press, 2005).
4. Edward W. Deming, *Out of the Crisis* (MIT Press, 2000).
5. Gil Amelio, *On the Firing Line: My 500 Days at Apple Computer* (Harper Paperbacks, 1990).
6. Tom Demarco, *Controlling Software Projects: Management, Measurement, and Estimates* (Prentice Hall, 1986).
7. Tom Demarco, "Software Engineering: An Idea Whose Time Has Come and Gone," *IEEE Spectrum,* available at http://www2.computer.org/cms/Computer.org/ComputingNow/homepage/2009/0709/rW_SO_Viewpoints.pdf.
8. You can find a copy of the app and play with it at http://www.xndev.com/downloads/convert.html—no charge!
9. My colleague Brian Marick has said "An example would come in handy about now" so often that I want to attribute the phrase to him. Certainly he deserves credit for popularizing the idea that concrete, defined tests can be thought of as examples. Here is an example from his Web log: http://www.exampler.com/blog/2007/06/11/my-first-marketing-event-in-sixteen-years-of-business/.
10. For any Web-based system where I am about to create a permanent transaction of some type, I want to know how fast the Submit button works. I also want to know if I see no result immediately can I click it again, and does that create a second, additional transaction? I've never seen a requirements document that says, "Limit number of orders to one at a time," yet we still have that as a reasonable expectation, and it seems to still fail a relatively large percentage of the time.

11. A few good challenges to get you started are the GRR Airport Test: http://adam.goucher
.ca/parkcalc/ (Requirements: http://www.grr.org/ParkingRates.php—scroll down)

> The activities widget test: http://www.softwaretestpro.com/Item/4621/How-would-
> you-test-this/User

> And, of course, the triangle problem: http://www.testinggeek.com/index.php/
> testometer/154-triangle-test-in-software-testing

Making these up isn't hard. Mostly any brainteaser will do, but if you can add a
graphical user interface it gets even better. Currently I like to carry around these tap-
activated LED dice at conferences and ask people to test them.

12. The actual quote I am thinking of is this: "Software quality testing is the systematic
series of evaluation activities performed to validate that the software fulfills technical
and performance requirements." Yes, it is from Donald J. Reifer's *State of the Art in
Software Quality Management,* from 1985, but worse, that specific line was quoted in
the *Handbook of the Software Quality Engineer* on page 16 as part of the definition of
test and evaluation.

13. This kind of hidden "equivalence class," by the way, is something you rarely see
referred to in textbooks. When Cem Kaner talks about "problem of local optima," he
is referring to a similar problem where the programmers create equivalence classes
by optimizing common maneuvers. In this case, it was the good idea of code reuse
overapplied to a situation where it didn't help.

14. "The Poppendiecks Speak: Two-Pizza Teams and the Software Development Experience,"
InformIT.com, http://www.informit.com/articles/article.aspx?p=1380369.

15. My favorite quote along these lines is "Three strikes and you are not out! There is
always one more thing you can to do influence the outcome!" from the American
war movie *We Were Soldiers,* starring Mel Gibson. In a software context I first heard
it from Robert C. Martin at a Great Lakes Software Excellence Conference (GLSEC),
where he stood onstage and said, "Never be blocked." In other words, if you need a
decision made, and everyone's hedging, just make it for them. Odds are they will go
with the precedent you've set, and, if not, you'll at least be able to reuse some of the
stuff you built along the way. In a testing context, that means declaring what is and
is not a bug, and possibly working with programmers to get some way to access the
code that is written but not yet under test.

16. The tester who can avoid being blocked and spends 80 percent of his or her time
actually testing is four times more effective than the one who spends 80 percent of
his or her time being blocked or otherwise in meetings. Four times. Think about
that the next time a tester tells you he or she is blocked, or some guru offers a whiz-
bang piece of automagical software offering hundreds of percents of performance
improvements.

2

The Cost of Quality

Selena Delesie

If you are anything like me, you may find it challenging to develop quality products that exceed customer expectations. Making high-quality products does not come cheaply. Some costs may be obvious, like sales, marketing, and employee salaries. Other costs, like employee training, testing, fixing errors, retesting, and reporting on information, may be less obvious and are often neglected by organizations. Of those indirect costs, testing is most bemoaned by executives as an expense with little value. But pictured as a way to prevent market loss or as information to make decisions with, testing stops being a problem and becomes part of the solution. The real problem is the cost of developing and supporting software that is valued by the customer, and testing can help reduce that cost. This is the cost of quality. This chapter explores approaches an organization can take to improve product quality. Consider approaches you have tried. Did they work, and if so, at what cost?

2.1 WHAT IS QUALITY?

Even though quality cannot be defined, you know what quality is.

—**Anonymous**

How do you define *quality*? Does quality software meet requirements, is it user-friendly, or does it have no reported problems? These are different and valid perspectives. Quality can mean different things. David A. Garmin suggested that product quality is multidimensional and definable using five approaches (*Sloan Management Review,* 1984). People still use these approaches today to assess product quality.

1. The product-based approach views quality as a precise measurement. Measures are calculated for products against different software quality attributes.
2. Under the manufacturing-based approach, quality products conform to requirements. Products are measured against defined requirements to discover inconsistencies. Improvements to product quality are managed using process control methods.
3. In the user-based approach, quality products satisfy user needs, as determined by a fitness-for-use assessment. Clear decisions about the most important customer needs are required to complete the assessment.
4. The transcendent approach views quality as "innate excellence"—quality cannot be precisely defined but can be recognized through product use. Quality decisions are based on experiences with a product.
5. In the value-based approach, quality is related to product costs. Product quality is good when a product is profitable and its value outweighs the time and money spent to create it.

Companies often use product or manufacturing-based approaches to assess software quality, even though software is composed of too many elements for an effective whole-picture measurement. The same software will not be used the same way by all users, or even by two people. Even if people use software the same way, they may have different opinions of the defects they find. If each user's experience is different, how can we turn that into a single meaningful number? It turns out software quality is more complex than a simple one-number scale.

Let's look at one last definition—a humanist definition:

Quality is some value to some person.

—**Gerald M. Weinberg**

This definition is compatible with Garmin's, is simpler, and allows additional perspectives when deciding the quality of a product. Weinberg suggests quality is a subjective and context-specific idea that it is different for a particular product, person, and point in time. Using this definition, think about what quality means for your product. Who does your product solve a problem for? What value do customers place on your product? What do they expect of it? How will they use it? What ways could they use it that you would not expect?

Creating high-quality products requires understanding your target user and what quality (value) they expect from it. This requires sleuthing, but results in sales and happy customers when done well.

But wait! Creating a high-quality product also requires high-quality work. As William A. Foster said, "Quality is never an accident; it is always the result of high intention, sincere effort, intelligent direction and skillful execution; it represents the wise choice of many alternatives."

With this combined understanding of quality, let's look at different approaches a fictitious company may take to develop high-quality software, the challenges it experiences, and the associated costs.

2.2 WE DON'T NEED TESTERS

NewStuff Corporation is a software company seeing increases in revenue and customer complaints. The CEO, David, believes improving operations will reduce complaints and help NewStuff become a success story. Our journey at NewStuff begins with Tim, the development manager. Tim is proud of his team. They work hard to develop quality software, and have released two new software products in the last year. *Who needs testers when the developers are so good?* Tim thinks.

Tim looks up when his boss knocks on his door. "Come in," Tim says. "What's up?"

"We need to hire a tester," David says. "I want you to own the interview process. Are you up for it?"

"Why? My department is doing great! The last two releases were on time, on budget, and satisfied requirements. Why ruin a good thing?" asks Tim.

"I'm concerned. Recent reports from Customer Support consistently identify serious problems. We are missing things. I want everything tested, but it doesn't make sense for your team to do it all," says David.

Tim frowns. "Testers won't add much value to what we do. My team does code reviews, unit tests, and has 90 percent line and branch coverage. We can add edge-cases and integration tests if that helps. Frankly, we're better off hiring more developers so we can release new features faster."

David leans back to consider this. *I'm sure we can improve product quality with process changes and additional people. Maybe Tim feels threatened or thinks I don't value their work. How do I get him on board?*

David responds, "your department is doing great work. A tester will allow Development to do more new feature development and less testing. I want you on board with who we hire. Talk to Tina about the quality costs she tracks to put this in perspective for you."

"All right, I'll talk to Tina," Tim replies. After David leaves, Tim reflects on the situation, *I don't think Tina's information will change my mind, but David seems confident about this.*

Later that week Tim meets with Tina, the project manager, to review a cost summary.

Tina fills Tim in: "I collect employee data for time spent on customer reported issues. It's summarized by average time per week, per employee, across each department. Using an hourly rate of fifty dollars, NewStuff has a yearly cost of more than eight hundred thousand dollars for customer issues."

While reviewing the data (see Table 2.1), Tim realizes it includes some hidden costs for developing quality products. *I remember reading about quality costs—these costs belong to the external failure costs category. Every company has them, so I'm not surprised. But why is it more than eight hundred thousand? Should Development spend 30 percent of the week on external quality issues? I wonder what we should aim for.*

"That seems high, Tina. What should costs be in this area?" asks Tim.

TABLE 2.1

External Failure Costs at NewStuff Corporation

Department	Average Time (Hrs/Week)/ Person on External Quality Issues	# of People	Yearly Cost for External Quality Issues	% Time on External Quality Issues
Executive/Mgmt	9	5	$117,000	20%
Customer Support	35	3	$273,000	78%
Sales	6	3	$46,800	13%
Marketing	3	3	$23,400	7%
Project Mgmt	16	1	$41,600	36%
Development	14	8	$291,200	31%
Manufacturing	7	2	$36,400	16%
Total	**12.8**	**25**	**$829,400**	**28%**

Loaded average employee cost/hour = $50
Average work week = 45 hours
External quality issues = Customer reported issues, returned product, maintaining/improving customer relationship, maintenance releases

"The fewer issues reported by customers, the better. Development spends 30 percent of their time on these issues. Though impossible, aim as near to 0 percent as feasible," Tina replies.

Tim considers the situation as he returns to his office. *If the testing Development does now is given to testers, then we'll spend less time on customer issues. Then we have more time to develop new features! Testers may help reduce the number of bugs released to customers, but if not, we'll know hiring them was a waste of time.*

Recap

While Tim agrees that reducing external failure costs will help NewStuff, he mistakenly believes that shifting work to test without improving development work quality will reduce those costs. Let's fast-forward a couple years to find out what happens at NewStuff Corporation after hiring a tester.

2.3 TEST QUALITY IN

It's Friday at 3 p.m., and Michelle, NewStuff's newest tester, sighs as her manager explains that they must work this weekend.

"The project is three weeks behind schedule, so a decision was made to release next week no matter what. Development will promote a new build tonight containing fixes for critical bugs. This weekend is the last chance to improve quality, so clear your schedules," Mark says.

"This is the fourth weekend in a row!" John exclaims. "I'm exhausted from all the overtime, and my wife will not be happy." Other team members echo his sentiments.

Mark replies, "I understand guys. I'm not happy about it either, but it's our job to find bugs and show that the software works."

The testers have been working around the clock testing new builds and reporting many bugs. Every time they take a step forward, it feels like they take two steps back.

"Mark, I'm concerned about the pattern we're in," Michelle says. "It seems Development is trying to fix the bugs we report, but is unable to keep up. I suspect they are taking shortcuts with fixes, which is introducing even more bugs."

"That's possible..." says Mark.

"So what are we trying to accomplish? What is our role on this project?" asks Michelle.

"What do you mean?" Mark asks.

"Well, Development is writing code, but are they writing *good* code? Do they confirm that they code what the customer wants?"

John interjects: "From my conversations with developers, they work independently based on the requirements. When something is unclear, they make their own interpretation. The developers all say they're glad we're here to find bugs, because they don't have time to test."

Mark replies, "I think you're right. With the frantic pace, I haven't looked at things objectively. I'll talk to Tim about how we can change. Pushing bug detection to Test just before release isn't saving time or money. Unfortunately, I still need you this weekend, at least for a smoke test. I'll talk to stakeholders about the expectation of 24/7 test coverage, especially on weekends."

"That's a start Mark, thank you," Michelle says. The other team members echo her sentiment.

Mark then visits Tim to talk about his team's discussion.

After quietly listening to Mark, Tim responds, "Why blame the issues with this project on my team? Maybe the problem is that your testers are bad at finding bugs."

Mark changes his approach: "I'm sorry Tim, I'm not trying to blame the developers. I'm concerned that we're all losing valuable time fixing and retesting bugs. I want to reduce extra work, and hopefully, the overtime people are doing. Can we work together to improve things?"

Tim replies, "Sure. What are you thinking?"

"We need to know how much time is spent on these issues. Then we translate that into money lost," Mark says. "Senior management is more receptive to suggestions when we identify the financial impact."

"OK, let's try that. Tina was collecting data like this for external quality issues a couple years ago. Maybe she can help us," Tim replies.

"Excellent! Knowing how much time we spend on internally found issues will help us identify the problems we need to address. This might even reduce people's workloads."

It turns out Tina had already been collecting this data in the time-tracking software for both internal and external quality issues. Tim, Mark, and Tina meet the following week to review the information.

Tina begins, "These are the comparative quality costs based on the collected data. While external failure costs have reduced in the last two years, our internal failure costs are high." (See Table 2.2.)

TABLE 2.2

Internal Versus External Failure Costs at NewStuff Corporation

Department	Average Time (Hrs/Week)/Person		# of People	Yearly Cost		% Time	
	Internal Quality Issues	External Quality Issues		Internal Quality Issues	External Quality Issues	Internal Quality Issues	External Quality Issues
Executive/Mgmt	10	5	6	$156,000	$78,000	22%	11%
Customer Support	4	30	3	$31,200	$234,000	9%	67%
Sales	1	3	3	$7,800	$23,400	2%	7%
Marketing	1	1	3	$7,800	$7,800	2%	2%
Project Mgmt	15	5	2	$78,000	$26,000	33%	11%
Development	17	5	10	$442,000	$130,000	38%	11%
QA/Test	20	7	3	$156,000	$54,600	44%	16%
Manufacturing	7	3	3	$54,600	$23,400	16%	7%
Total	**10.9**	**6.7**	**33**	**$933,400**	**$577,200**	**24%**	**15%**

Loaded average employee cost/hour = $50

Average work week = 45 hours

Internal quality issues = Design changes, redesign rework, defect analysis, defect measurement and reporting, defect fixing, retesting

External quality issues = Customer reported issues, returned product, maintaining/improving customer relationships, maintenance releases

"This is higher than I expected," Mark says. "Sixty percent of testers' time is spent on rework activities relating to retesting, defect measurement and reporting, analysis, customer reported issues, and maintenance releases; while nearly 50 percent of developers' time is spent on rework. We need to improve work quality earlier in the project lifecycle, because these defects are costing too much between Development and Test alone."

Tim agrees.

Mark and Tim jointly discuss their concerns with the CEO. David agrees that better quality processes are needed, particularly to improve defect detection earlier in project life cycles. David decides to hire an Operations vice president to take ownership of the needed quality processes. Tim and Mark also agree to immediate changes, like having requirements and design reviews for all new features and changes. It is a step forward in getting quality costs under control.

Management recognizes that quality needs to improve earlier in the product life cycle after reviewing the cost summary. But why is the data needed to recognize this? Some testers at NewStuff saw a problem that others missed: Repeatedly handing off software between Test and Development isn't improving product quality but masking underlying issues. High product quality results from high-quality work. Read on to find out how NewStuff Corporation fares after introducing process controls to reduce internal failure costs.

2.4 METRICS TELL ALL

"We have a quality problem," David says at the senior management meeting. "Why can't we deliver quality products to our customers? Though we tripled in size the last two years, we can barely deliver two new releases this year, and those are providing little new value. What are we doing to fix this?" he asks his executive team.

Michael, the Operations VP, speaks up: "Our teams follow a stringent quality process, as we invested a lot into process control for product development, including software. We are ISO 9001 certified and have achieved CMMI Level 3. Given these processes, I don't understand why the software organization can't deliver what we need."

Christine is annoyed. As the Software VP, she has shared her concerns about the effectiveness of these processes with both Michael and David.

Although cross-departmental discussions have improved, it takes a lot of time to complete each process step. It seems little time is spent on value-adding tasks that will improve release delivery.

"Let's take a step back. As I understand, ISO 9001 and CMMI Level 3 certification were obtained to reduce internal and external failure costs. Is that correct?" asks Christine.

"Yes," David begins. "We didn't spend enough time defining requirements, or get sign off on requirements or design decisions. So, most quality issues were only found close to release dates."

Michael chimes in: "We also didn't have good measures to indicate whether to proceed with later project phases, release products, or track customer feedback. These quality processes helped solve those problems. We now have many measures to tell us we aren't meeting targets."

"Does everyone feel these add value? My department, the test teams in particular, spend a lot of time producing and tracking measures. I think we lose valuable time on process tasks that could be better used for development and test tasks," Christine suggests.

"I like that data, because it helps make decisions," Michael replies.

"I don't agree," says Joe, another VP. "We review charts every week and talk about how numbers have increased or decreased, but I don't really know what's going on. For example, tracking the number of defects customers report tells me that customers are finding problems, but nothing about the defects themselves. I think we should review the metrics to confirm they provide the value we think they do."

David makes a decision: "Michael and Christine, at our next management meeting I want you to summarize our internal quality costs, external quality costs, appraisal costs, and prevention costs. I need concrete data to base our discussion on, before making any big decisions."

Two weeks later, Michael and Christine share a cost summary (Table 2.3) that surprises everyone.

"As you see," Christine begins, "Development and Test each spend about 30 percent of their time on their primary responsibility, quality detection in the case of Test, and design and coding in the case of Development. They both spend more than 60 percent of their time on prevention, internal, and external quality issues. Development spends a little time on detection—testing their software before it goes to Test—but not enough."

Disbelieving, Joe exclaims, "These numbers seem too crazy to be real!"

TABLE 2.3

Quality Costs at NewStuff Corporation

Department	Average Time (Hrs/Week)/Person				# of People	Yearly Costs				% Time			
	Prevention	Detection	Internal Quality Issues	External Quality Issues		Prevention	Detection	Internal Quality Issues	External Quality Issues	Prevention	Detection	Internal Quality Issues	External Quality Issues
Executive/Mgmt	3	0	8	5	15	$117,000	$0	$312,000	$195,000	7%	0%	18%	11%
Customer Support	5	0	2	26	6	$78,000	$0	$31,200	$405,600	11%	0%	4%	58%
Sales	1	0	1	1	7	$18,200	$0	$18,200	$18,200	2%	0%	2%	2%
Marketing	1	0	1	2	5	$13,000	$0	$13,000	$26,000	2%	0%	2%	4%
Product Development	6	0	6	8	6	$93,600	$0	$93,600	$124,800	13%	0%	13%	18%
Project Mgmt	12	0	9	5	3	$93,600	$0	$70,200	$39,000	27%	0%	20%	11%
Development	13	3	9	4	28	$946,400	$218,400	$655,200	$291,200	29%	7%	20%	9%
QA/Test	17	13	7	4	15	$663,000	$507,000	$273,000	$156,000	38%	29%	16%	9%
Manufacturing	5	6	7	3	5	$65,000	$78,000	$91,000	$39,000	11%	13%	16%	7%
Total	**8.9**	**3.4**	**6.7**	**5.5**	**90**	**$2,087,800**	**$803,400**	**$1,557,000**	**$1,294,800**	**20%**	**8%**	**15%**	**12%**

Loaded average employee cost/hour = $50

Average work week = 45 hours

Prevention costs = Project quality planning, metrics data collection, quality assessments, configuration management, change management, inspection and reviews, process improvement, data analysis and reporting, SQA program planning, compliance audits

Detection costs = All verification and validation activities, test planning, test execution and reporting, etc.

Internal quality issues = Design changes, redesign rework, defect analysis, defect measurement and reporting, defect fixing, retesting

External quality issues = Customer-reported issues, returned product, maintaining/improving customer relationships, maintenance releases

Michael shakes his head: "I'm the last to admit it, but we need to make some changes. The data isn't perfect, but it helps us understand some problems we have in delivering regular quality releases.

"We need Development and Test to focus even 50 percent of their time on their primary responsibilities. Detection costs are good quality costs, which is what Test is here for. Prevention costs are also good if we're not blindly doing process work.

"Internal and external failure costs need to be eliminated; we have too much rework, which means no bandwidth for new work. Reducing these 'bad' costs in Software will have a domino effect and reduce these costs in other departments, too."

Christine offers: "I've heard that a lot of companies are using Agile approaches. I'm told they help deliver highest value functionality first, new releases more often, and improve release quality. I'd like to investigate and create a proposal if Agile seems a viable change for NewStuff."

David sees several executives nodding their heads: "OK, Christine, create a proposal and we'll decide whether this Agile stuff is worth doing. In the meantime, everyone work together to reduce some of the bigger costs. Perhaps the time spent on data collection, analysis, and reporting is costing us more than benefiting. I want you all to report back at the next meeting on how we'll free up needed time in Software."

Recap

While introducing quality process controls helped achieve consistency in how NewStuff Corporation developed products, the management team discovers that some controls are more hindrance than help. Processes should guide how work is done, not dictate blind allegiance to forms and methods that add little to the development of a product. Let's find out if Agile helps NewStuff Corporation reduce the overhead of unwanted quality costs.

2.5 AGILE WILL SAVE US

"This Agile stuff doesn't work," Don says at a sprint retrospective. "We're supposed to discuss requirements, pair with testers, and talk about solutions with team members. This is wasting our time. How are we supposed to write code when we spend so much time talking to people?"

Tina isn't surprised to hear Don say this. He has complained about Agile since training began six months ago. So far Agile has provided small gains for NewStuff Corporation. Their Agile coach says this is normal and that bigger gains will result in upcoming months.

Don continues: "Things were better when we worked the way we wanted—we could deliver several releases a year. Now management says when to deliver what, but not how things should be developed. . . . And how are we supposed to estimate work using a user story on an index card?"

As the team's ScrumMaster, Tina wants the team, project, and Agile to succeed at NewStuff: "Don, I understand you're frustrated, but I don't think you understand why we transitioned to Agile. We are trying to reduce time to delivery, improve quality, and reduce unnecessary costs. This requires communication and collaboration, that everyone be responsible for their actions, and everyone be a team player. This isn't about you, but the entire team and our ability to provide value to our customers."

"So when can testers actually talk to developers?" Michelle asks.

John adds, "When I talk to developers, I'm usually told they're too busy."

"We are!" Don responds. "We're trying to develop an entire feature in a few days. You should be able to figure out what to test on your own."

Softly, Maria voices her thoughts: "I always feel rushed. I don't think we estimate story size well, not because requirements are bad, but because we don't do it as a team. We also don't include time to do our work well. When we estimate based on minimal coding and testing, we'll constantly feel pressured. We need to include time to write unit tests or do test-driven development, and time for discussions to understand requirements and make design and testing decisions."

"But everything will take longer," says Don.

"Yes, at first," Maria begins, "but with practice we will get faster. Were you fast at coding when you started to learn? I suspect not. Over time you got faster with practice though, right? It's the same principle for all these new things. It won't take long before we're faster at delivering higher quality software."

"I would also like time to improve skills at work, instead of doing it at home all the time," Michelle pipes in.

"And get training in new technical areas, or testing and programming techniques!" exclaims John.

"OK, folks," Tina interjects, "the retrospective got hijacked, but we do have things to work on. Each of you, write down one thing you want improved this week. We'll then vote to pick one, then define success criteria for it so we know when we're done."

After everyone writes down a suggestion, the team votes. The winning entry is "write unit tests."

"That's a broad improvement. Can you make it more specific?" Tina says.

"We can break it down into smaller tasks to be completed different weeks," suggests John.

"Good idea. I think the first task is learning why unit tests are important. If we understand how cutting corners affects other work, then everyone may agree to write unit tests," says Maria.

"Sure. If you can convince me it will save time, I will try it," Don concedes.

"I will take that as an action," Tina offers. "When we meet, I will share data on current company costs so we can later see how writing unit tests changes them."

The team accepts Tina's offer. Later that week the team has a lunch-and-learn on the costs of unit testing (Table 2.4).

Tina begins, "The first chart shows the cost of a unit test, and the cost of a bug that a unit test could have found. These are estimates based on data in our bug tracking system and discussions with team members. Actual costs may be higher or lower."

Tina continues, "Using this data, I estimate the average cost to write a unit test is ten dollars, based on a salary of fifty dollars an hour. This assumes twelve minutes to write a unit test, though actual time may be higher or lower depending on complexity, person, and so on.

TABLE 2.4

Cost of Unit Testing vs. Customer Reported Bugs

Average time to write unit test (min)	12
Billable rate /hr	$50.00
Avg cost to write a unit test	**$10.00**
Average combined time to fix a bug (hours)	4
Includes time spent by customer support, project managers, testers, managers, developers	
Billable rate /hr	$50.00
Avg cost of a bug	**$200.00**
# Customer-reported bugs last release	368
Total cost of bugs	**$73,600.00**
Total cost of unit tests (if written, assume 2 unit tests find each bug)	**$7,360.00**

"If a bug isn't found by a unit test, it might be found by code review, acceptance test, system test, or even customers. If a customer reports a bug, there are a lot of people, time and costs associated with it: customer support to talk to the customer and log the bug, testers to review and reproduce it, project managers to watch its progress, executives to ask about it, developers to discover a root cause and fix and test it, testers to retest to ensure it's gone, customer support to report back to the customer, as well as do a maintenance release.

"This time adds up! It gets higher if the bug isn't fixed properly the first time. Based on this data, a bug takes an average combined four hours of employee time from start to end of this cycle in a best case situation. So, a bug costs the company two hundred dollars.

"The last release had 368 bugs reported by customers, which cost NewStuff $73,600. If two unit tests could catch each bug, it costs $7,360 to write them all. Which cost do you think management would rather invest in to improve software quality?

"Developers, consider how long it takes to identify a root cause and fix a bug. Is it less than the time to write a unit test, about twelve minutes? Here alone writing a unit test will save you time. Writing unit tests saves time in other areas too: code is less likely to regress so less time is needed finding, fixing, and talking about bugs. You can also refactor code without fear of breaking it."

"That makes sense," Maria says. "This supports the idea of paired developer–tester coding too. If a tester pairs with me when I write unit tests, then writing unit tests for those bugs would be $7,360 × 2 = $14,720. Still a big difference."

"Wow," Don says, "I had no idea. I don't buy into the numbers, but this actually makes sense. I agree that writing a unit test will take less time than investigating and fixing a bug. I spend a lot of time on bugs, and I'd rather spend my time writing new software."

Tina adds, "The same principle applies to why collaboration early in a project helps find user story problems, discover what the customer wants, and decide on designs and tests. Collaboration costs are cheaper than bug costs resulting from collaboration that didn't happen.

"Here is a chart summarizing company quality costs. While our prevention costs have reduced since our days under heavy quality processes, our other costs have slightly increased. Imagine how they'll change if we invest time in unit tests and more collaboration. We can review this data in six months to see how we improve." (See Table 2.5.)

TABLE 2.5

Quality Costs of Using Agile at NewStuff Corporation

Department	Average Time (Hrs/Week)/Person				# of People	Yearly Cost				% Time			
	Prevention	Detection	Internal Quality Issues	External Quality Issues		Prevention	Detection	Internal Quality Issues	External Quality Issues	Prevention	Detection	Internal Quality Issues	External Quality Issues
Executive/Mgmt	4	0	7	4	15	$156,000	$0	$273,000	$156,000	9%	0%	16%	9%
Customer Support	2	0	2	26	6	$31,200	$0	$31,200	$405,600	5%	0%	5%	60%
Sales	1	0	1	4	7	$18,200	$0	$18,200	$72,800	2%	0%	2%	9%
Marketing	1	0	1	2	5	$13,000	$0	$13,000	$26,000	2%	0%	2%	5%
Product Development	5	0	5	7	6	$78,000	$0	$78,000	$109,200	12%	0%	12%	16%
Project Mgmt	5	0	6	7	3	$39,000	$0	$46,800	$54,600	12%	0%	14%	16%
Development	2	3	12	4	29	$145,600	$218,000	$873,600	$291,200	5%	7%	29%	9%
QA/Test	2	20	11	5	15	$78,000	$780,000	$429,000	$195,000	5%	47%	26%	12%
Manufacturing	3	5	6	3	5	$39,000	$65,000	$78,000	$39,000	7%	12%	14%	7%
Total	**26**	**4.5**	**7.9**	**5.8**	**90**	**$598,000**	**$1,063,400**	**$1,840,800**	**$1,349,000**	**6%**	**11%**	**18%**	**13%**

Loaded average employee cost/hour = $50

Average Work Week = 43 hours

Prevention costs = Project quality planning, metrics data collection, quality assessments, configuration management change management, inspections and reviews, process improvement, data analysis and reporting, SQA program planning, compliance audits

Detection costs = All verification and validation activities, test planning, testing execution and reporting, etc.

Internal quality issues = Design changes, redesign rework, defect analysis measurement and reporting, defect fixing, retesting

External quality issues = Customer reported issues, returned products, maintaining/improving customer relationships, maintenance releases

The team agrees to focus on improving quality earlier in the project, starting with unit tests for all new and changed code, and by embracing frequent collaboration to eliminate problems early and often.

Recap

Although the team follows an Agile process, they aren't embracing the concept of consistent feedback, a key principle for success with Agile. Agile is more than this concept but is more likely to fail without frequent feedback loops. Some helpful feedback loops include unit tests, early communication about user stories with the customer and management, demos, retrospectives, and daily communication and collaboration within the team. Let's jump ahead eight months to see if the agreed-upon changes help NewStuff Corporation further reduce undesired quality costs, and improve product quality and delivery.

2.6 IT'S ABOUT PEOPLE

Eight months after the first lunch-and-learn on the costs of unit testing, Tina smiles as she shares the latest quality cost summary at a company meeting (see Table 2.6). It's a big turnout as nearly all employees are in attendance.

"This chart summarizes the time everyone spends on the quality cost categories of prevention, detection, internal, and external issues," Tina begins. "I calculate yearly costs using a base rate of $50 per hour, then determine the percentage of time spent per category.

"Eight months ago one team improved dramatically by incorporating consistent feedback loops, writing unit tests, and embracing frequent collaboration to eliminate problems early. The other project teams adopted these changes soon after. I think they saw how little time the first team spent on bugs, and how much time they worked on fun work like new features."

Many employees laugh and nod their heads in agreement.

Tina continues: "I'm pleased to share that overall quality costs have reduced, most dramatically being our internal failure costs. Both Test and Development now spend more than 70 percent of their time on work we want them to do—find bugs, and design and code software. As a result, we've had two successful releases in the last two quarters that customers are raving about. We're on a roll!"

TABLE 2.6

Quality Costs Six Months Later

Department	Average Time (Hrs/Week)/Person				# of People	Yearly Costs				% Time			
	Prevention	Detection	Internal Quality Issues	External Quality Issues		Prevention	Detection	Internal Quality Issues	External Quality Issues	Prevention	Detection	Internal Quality Issues	External Quality Issues
Executive/Mgmt	2	0	1	1	15	$78,000	$0	$39,000	$39,000	5%	0%	3%	3%
Customer Support	2	0	2	25	6	$31,200	$0	$31,200	$390,000	5%	0%	5%	63%
Sales	1	0	1	1	7	$18,200	$0	$18,200	$18,200	3%	0%	3%	3%
Marketing	1	0	1	1	5	$13,000	$0	$13,000	$13,000	3%	0%	3%	3%
Product Development	2	0	1	1	6	$31,200	$0	$15,600	$15,600	5%	0%	13%	5%
Project Mgmt	3	0	5	2	3	$23,400	$0	$39,000	$15,600	8%	0%	8%	5%
Development	2	10	3	2	28	$145,600	$145,600	$218,400	$145,600	5%	25%	8%	5%
QA/Test	2	28	3	2	15	$78,000	$78,000	$117,000	$78,000	5%	70%	10%	5%
Manufacturing	3	5	4	2	5	$39,000	$65,000	$52,000	$26,000	8%	13%	10%	5%
Total	**2.0**	**8.1**	**2.3**	**3.2**	**90**	**$457,600**	**$1,885,000**	**$543,400**	**$741,000**	**5%**	**20%**	**6%**	**8%**

Loaded average employee cost/hour = $50

Average work week = 45 hours

Prevention costs = Project quality planning, metrics data collection, quality assessments, configuration management, change management, inspection and reviews, process improvement, data analysis and reporting, SQA program planning, compliance audits

Detection costs = All verification and validation activities, test planning, testing execution and reporting, etc.

Internal quality issues = Design changes, redesign rework, defect analysis, defect measurement and reporting, defect fixing, retesting

External quality issues = Customer reported issues, returned product, maintaining/improving customer relationships, maintenance releases

Recap

Active communication, collaboration, and a high-quality work ethic are now the standard at NewStuff. While employees are happy spending time on fun and value-adding activities, management is happy about reduced costs, higher quality releases, and improved time to market. Although it took longer then the CEO had hoped for, NewStuff Corporation is finally poised to become a success story.

2.7 MANAGE THE COST OF QUALITY

NewStuff's story allows us to see different processes and approaches you can try to reduce costs, improve quality, and accelerate time to market. Though fictional, NewStuff Corporation's journey to improve product quality and reduce costs has happened in many companies, perhaps your own. Did any approaches NewStuff use sound familiar? How about the challenges they experienced?

By choosing activities worth investing in—like communication, collaboration, feedback loops, detection activities, and some prevention activities—you are making a conscious decision to improve product quality, accelerate time to market, and reduce product costs. Not investing in these activities results in spending many times more in internal and external failure costs—the costs you most want to avoid.

Regardless of the process or approach experts tout as the solution to solve your software development problems, or reduce your testing costs, there is no way to guarantee it is the right solution for your company. Your organization is unique in its projects, organizational structures, people, ideas, interaction models, processes, strengths, and even shortcomings.

Though I can't give you the right answer without becoming familiar with your company, I do know you need a solution that is custom tailored for your company and the quality costs you are willing to pay for. It is hoped this chapter provided some ideas to help you in that journey.

Remember, creating high-quality products is a choice. You can choose to invest in the activities needed to create high-quality products, while reducing the cost of testing or not. You get to decide if improved customer satisfaction, increased revenue, higher product quality, and reduced costs are worth the effort.

3

Testing Economics:
What Is Your Testing Net Worth?

Govind Kulkarni

Compact fluorescent lamps were discovered as an alternative to normal bulbs and tubes to reduce electricity consumption and cut bills. After fifty years of shared experiences in testing we in the software testing community have a few ideas, techniques, and tricks to reduce waste during testing and pass those savings on to customers.

3.1 BOARD ROOM DISCUSSIONS

Imagine you are a software test manager, invited to your first big meeting with the chief operating officer (COO), along with a few of your peer test managers. You prepare your charts on test cases, defect counts, and organizational improvement; all combined into a twenty-five slide PowerPoint deck. You move to plug in your laptop and the COO laughs. He points you to a seat and says:

"I just want to ask you one question: Is your testing resulting in profit?"

That's not the question you were expecting. And you sort of know what the COO is getting at: If it would be cheaper to not test, why do it? Gulp. If you never expected to get a question like that as a test manager, you're not alone. After all, profit and loss is a corporate concept, not a team-level one, right? How does it even matter for testing projects?

So you want more detail. You ask a counter question to the COO: Could you please elaborate and enlighten us what you are talking about?

The COO responds with financial terms. "Well, can you tell me the net worth of the testing? You don't know, do you?"

Then the COO starts explaining testing in the context of corporate balance sheet. "Imagine that I placed a hundred thousand dollars in your pocket. What can you do with that? Spend the money for testing, you say. Hire another tester or two cheap ones; maybe bring in five contractors for a month. I know, you say it's a necessity. But we could also put the money in the bank and earn interest on it, right?"

Joe, the senior test manager at the company, stands up, saying, "We have to spend money in testing, because it is a need, in much the same way as food is for living. It is very important to know our mistakes—we have legally binding contract with the customer! If software quality is really poor then we must correct it before we ship it, otherwise they could return the software. That means refunds. So I consider spending money in testing as an investment."

For the first time since you tried to plug in your laptop, the COO actually smiles. He replies, "Well, Joe, I happen to agree with you, that is the reason I asked what is the net worth of testing?"

As a client or senior manager, if you spent money on software testing and felt happy with your costs or pleased with the reports, graphs, dashboards, and software value, well, this chapter is not for you. If you wondered whether it result in profit, then read further.

3.2 INTRODUCTION

Whether you are in the United States, Europe, South Africa, or India, you have probably felt the effects of the current global recession. Yes, I said global; among my coauthors on three continents, we've all felt it. That global reality keeps, saving money on the forefront of our minds. Software projects, like any other initiative, are compelled to look for opportunities to decrease the overall cost. Looking at testing as a *nonessential, nonbuilding* cost (after all, if it all "just worked," or everybody did great job we wouldn't need to test at all, right?) makes it a highly likely target for cost cutting. Two different ways to do this are hard measures or soft measures. Some hard measures include retrenchment; lay off, stopping the contract, using a cheaper vendor, deferring testing to future or not doing it at all. Soft ones are those where projects are forced to increase efficiency by reducing waste that otherwise would add up to cost.

In this chapter, we look at a concept called net worth, primarily taken from the world of finance and accounting. We are extending this concept to software testing projects with an objective to know whether the money spent on a testing project was a sound investment. Finally we look at certain metrics that could be collected as a part of test deliveries in order to increase net worth, release after release.

I am of the opinion that test managers today need to be trained in financial analysis and ratios. I think these subjects should become mandatory in the learning curve. By doing so, test managers should be in a position not just to create test strategy but also provide cost savings by way of eliminating waste over the life of the test project.

Let's assume a test project that contains the following traditional phases:

1. Test planning
2. Test case design and construction
3. Test data creation
4. Test execution
5. Test closure

I'm using a traditional model here for ease of demonstration; of course you could use an Agile or rapid model that implements a series of all of these test activities in thin slices and the idea of net worth would still hold. I'll choose to focus on test execution because this phase is vital—it's the one where we find the defects and retest the fixes.

3.3 NET WORTH

Net worth is the difference that exists between the assets and what is owed. Calculating net worth involves totaling the amount of all debt obligations and subtracting that figure from the total worth of all assets. Net worth is a part of any balance sheet and shows where a company's money came from, where it went, and where it is now.

When the cumulative value of all the assets exceed the total of all liabilities it can be said that a positive net worth exists. In other words, if you have more money than you owe, you are in the black. A negative net worth means an individual or a business is in debt. Unless the company has an ace up its sleeve—a new product, a change in the value of its assets, or something—a negative net worth is likely the path of failure and bankruptcy.

If better net worth means more money for the business, then what really matters is not sales but sales minus liabilities. For example, if you estimate a project and sign a contract for $2 million and the project ends up costing you $4 million you are, as Americans say, up the creek without a paddle. Also note that net worth is not a constant factor but changes year after year depending on business performance

As a sample let us look at the net worth of four companies. Note the company names given are not real they are used just as an example and data presented is imaginary; if these companies really exist then it is just a coincidence.

Number	Company Name	Current Assets [A]	Current Liabilities [B]	Net Worth [A]–[B]	Net Worth% ([A]–[B])/ [A]
1	Abbara Inc.	$100 million	$43 million	$57 million	57%
2	BetaMax Records	$80 million	$27 million	$53 million	66%
3	Chipmunk LLC	$119 million	$121 million	–$2 million	–1.68%
4	Delta's Designs	$216 million	$215 million	$1 million	0.46%

Note: There may be very specific formulae for calculating net worth but this table suffices for our discussion.

We say that company BetaMax Records is better off compared to other companies. It is because even with fewer assets, compared to other companies, its net worth is high.

Let me give you one analogy: Imagine you have fixed a meeting with your friend and when you meet her for coffee, she asks, "Can you take care of me, do you have enough money?" You reply, "I came by BMW car but I have taken an 80 percent loan, I just filled the gas tank, and paid it by credit card. I have a duplex apartment and I have mortgaged it." After hearing all this, the girl starts thinking. Your net worth is too low and perhaps may reject because you owe a lot more than what you possess.

So if you ask a question to yourself—Why do the net worth's differ? It is simple; if a business takes a loan from a bank and does not use that money then the liability keeps increasing by way of interest. Some other reasons that affect a company's net worth are decreasing sales, mismanagement of cash flows, and not having control over expenses.

3.3.1 Implementing Net Worth in Testing

So what happens if we take the net worth financial model and apply it to software testing? In the following example, we have considered a sample project, which has completed four releases in a year, and there is a road map for subsequent releases. Please note that a project release cycles could be shorter or longer depending on how the release management has decided the release to go to production.

Now we are wondering what is the net worth of our testing. We are asking this question because for each release the client spent different amounts of money based on scope and timeline of testing. Testers did a great job by testing and ensuring fixes are working; releases have gone successfully. There are a few production issues here and there that are taken care by support staff.

So with this information how can we measure net worth of testing? Let me show you.

One of the main elements of testing is to find defects and retest the fixes. Since this defect information is readily available during the life cycle of a software project, we propose classifying project defects in two categories like *assets* and *liabilities* so we could use this information to calculate net worth.

- System testing defects—We treat defects logged by the testing team as the only asset. Everything else is a liability. The more defects testers find during system testing better it is. So count all defects found by testers during system testing for our calculation. It does not matter how you found that defect, it may be by running automated scripts or manual.

- User acceptance testing (UAT) defects—We consider genuine UAT defects, those after leaving the duplicates, confirmed as not a defect, as liabilities. These are found by business analysts or users by spending their efforts and energy. Testers should have ideally caught these. Since testers missed them, it is a liability on testers part. Bluntly put, the tester says to a business analyst, "Sorry, I should have found it, but thank you for finding it." However, in some projects UAT is done even before the testing team completed its system testing. In that case, count only those defects found by analysts in the already tested functionality.

- Open defects—One pest control advertisement has a slogan: "We find and kill all pests." That is fine with pest control. These people spray pesticide and in the end they find and kill the cockroaches, bed bugs, rats, lizards, and so forth. In contrast, when the testers test, they only detect and tell the defect and its severity. In addition, UAT may find some more defects and when the system is deployed to production, end users will likely find a few more. Management may decide a certain defect is too expensive to fix or would not occur often for users, and may conclude that it is costlier to fix and leaving it open is more economical.

We must note that the quality of application will not automatically improve by just finding defects. The defects found have to be fixed, retested, and confirmed to be working. Then only we can say that quality of application has improved. Believe me, the sponsors will not thank testers for finding defects, but they do appreciate the bugs that are fixed and also the working functionality. In reality, not all defects that are found are fixed. Even if defects are fixed, some new ones may pop up or the same one may pop up. What I wish to say is that the project team tries its best to fix as many defects as possible, but in the end there is some percentage of defects open in a deployed system. Having a workaround for a defect is fine, but a defect is a defect unless it is fixed. It is like finding a cockroach but not killing it.

So all open defects of any severity or priority that are not fixed for any kind of testing that is performed and left in the system are considered liabilities. We do not care why they are open, it may be a business decision; we only worry that the longer they stay open they can do harm in some way to someone at some point of time. The testing community can only try to get a maximum number of defects fixed, retested, and closed.

- Production defects—Many projects collect data on production defects soon after the application goes live. These are the defects detected just after the deployment is done and go live was successful. These are the defects either tester could not find or user acceptance testers (if you had them) did not encounter and in the end the user found it. It may be a deployment issue, it may be data issue, or it could be open defects causing the problem.

Many releases do contain open defects but for our calculations we need to collect only the legitimate defects reported by end users after the release went live. If end users complained about a defect but it was kept open or it worked in the system-testing environment but not in production, then do not count such defects for calculation.

We treat production defects as a liability. But note, we attach weight to production defects based on the seriousness of the defect. Simply put, it does not matter how many thousand defects testers find, if they left one defect to production that crashed the entire database, harmed the company's reputation, or someone is trying to sue the product maker, then no good is done.

3.3.2 What Does Production Weighting Mean?

Production weighting is the figure given in column E in the following chart for how much a defect would cost the customer or users. It is based upon a range from 1 to 10, where 1 means cosmetic or little cost to business and the defect can be best left as is and 10 indicates a serious problem and additional cost. They are then added up for each defect and divided by the total number of defects found in production to give an average weighting score.

So if we have compiled the above information on system testing defects, UAT defects, production defects, and number of open defects then this is how we can arrive at let us say defects net worth (Defects Net Worth = Assets – Liabilities).

Number	Release	Number of Defects Caught by Testing Team during System Testing (A)	Number of Defects Caught by Analysts during UAT (B)	Number of Open Defects (C)	Number of Production Defects/Issues Found Post Go Live (D)	Production Weighting (E)	Net Worth [A] – [B + C + (D × E)] (F)	Net Worth% F/A × 100 (G)
1	June 08	1000	55	53	2	20	852	85%
2	Sep 08	1200	40	29	7	1	1124	93%
3	Dec 08	800	25	55	5	3	705	88%
4	Mar 09	1500	120	100	11	1	1269	84%

Did you wonder what this table is about? Wait a minute. This tells a story. It tells how much the release is worth in terms of assets and liabilities. In the table, we may say that the Sep 08 release yielded more returns than other releases in terms of handling of defects though testers found more defects in the March 09 release. The March 09 yielded lesser return; it does not matter how many defects testers found but when it is compared to liabilities the March 09 release definitely did fewer compared to other releases.

Let us attach money to our discussion. Say the client spent $100,000 for a June 08 release on the testing project. Then each defect detection costs $100. In addition there are other costs for UAT defects, production defects, and leaving the defects open.

Imagine a happy day scenario: no UAT defects, no production defects, and all defects found were fixed—that is, only assets and no liabilities, a situation all testers dream of. Then the net worth would have been 100 percent. But that is not the case here. There were liabilities in each of the releases. That is the reason net worth dropped to 93 percent for the Sep 08 release, which means the release carried 7 percent of liabilities. Conversely, the more the liability the lesser the return on testing spending. We could also conclude that the client possibly had only 93 percent of the return on $100,000 spent.

We also need to note that net worth cannot be 100 percent at any point of time and in any release and in any project, simply because exhaustive testing is out of question. Testers cannot find all defects, analysts and end users continue to find defects, and no project fixes 100 percent of defects. But can this be an excuse; we must worry when net worth falls considerably below the figure that is fixed by us (I mean the client). For example, you as a client can set up a contractual clause or demand from your suppliers a minimum of 85 percent net worth. If you did this clause and got a net worth figure as 80 percent for a release, then this means testing is not resulting in a profit.

You and I might get into a debate for hours on the aforementioned points, because we all talked about functional testing. But, what about other tests? Say, performance testing was not conducted or if conducted, it was done poorly and when the system went live, functionally everything was all right but performance-wise it faltered. So should we say with 90 percent above net worth resulted in profit? But the system, as a whole, did not meet expectations. So, unless the testing team has logged all types of testing defects in the defect management system and included in this net worth calculation, this calculation may be meaningless or true for functional tests.

3.3.3 Some Steps to Increase Net worth

We noted from the previous discussion that the net worth can be increased by having more assets and fewer liabilities. But in testing it is not an easy task to increase assets (defect discovery). We can only improve the chances of finding defects by learning lessons from past releases, correcting mistakes, and instituting a process to study why UAT and production defects surface. In general, there can be three possibilities when a genuine defect, which was left out by testers, is reported at UAT or in production:

1. A test case exists, but was not executed during system testing.
2. A test case does not exist so no execution happened.
3. Tests did happen but not for the reported data combination, product, or user types used during UAT or production.
4. Certain tests (performance, security, usability) are not conducted at all due to short timelines, budget, or constraints, or even if done, not done properly or functional testing took precedence to other tests.

Here is a sample table. By doing a retrospective study of each of the UAT and production defects and taking preventive actions, we can only increase the possibility of defect detection in future releases (provided the product continues to have releases).

Defect ID Reported	Reported At What Stage?	Did Testing Team Test This Functionality?	Do We Have A Test Case?	Why Did We Miss This Defect?	Preventive Action
23461	UAT	Yes	Yes	The specific data combination used at UAT was not used by the testing team.	1. Add the data used during UAT in test suite. 2. In next release give priority to test the UAT data combination missed by testing team.
Issue 10	Production	No	No	Quality assurance ran out of time and this functionality was done using ad hoc testing.	1. Create a test case. 2. Execute in the next release.

It is not that by doing the above postmortem UAT or production will reduce defects, but this analysis only helps the testing team to improve the regression suite and give due importance and attention to UAT and production issues in the forthcoming releases. To increase the chance of finding defects, the testing team can also take note of the following points.

Goal	Question	Metrics	How It Helps
Have test cases for all listed requirements.	Do we have test cases for all requirements? *One or many test cases must be traced to listed requirements.*	Number of requirements not having test cases divided by total number of requirements	Ensures that 100 percent of listed requirements have one or many test cases attached to them. This helps to ensure that all requirements are met for testing.
Test all previous hot fixes, patch releases in main release.	How many test cases were created for hot fixes? Patch releases? How many of them are tested?	Number of test cases created for hot fix, patch divided by total test cases suite size Number of test cases executed as a part of hot fix, patch deployment divided by total number of test cases created	Improve the regression test suite by executing the previous patch/hot fixes helps to ensure that code merge issues are taken care of during testing.
Execute all planned tests in the release	How many test cases we planned to test but did not test in the release?	Number of test cases executed divided by total test cases planned for execution	If all planned test case were executed, then it decreases the chance of testers missing defects.
Test execution coverage to cover 100 percent of the requirements.	Did we cover 100 percent of the requirements?	Number of test cases not executed but attached to requirements	Leaving some requirements untested will increase risk of defects seepage.
Test with different data sets to increase chance of finding data related defects. *For example, a laptop with different configurations can be called as each set.*	Did we use the same data sets to test two consecutive releases? Or different data sets? If D1, D2...Dn are different data sets, then do we use only D1 all the time or different sets at different executions?	Number of test cases executed with same data sets in last two releases	If a test case passed with D1 data set, then it is not a guarantee that it would still pass with other data sets. Testing with different data sets increases chance of finding data discrepancies.

3.4 OPEN DEFECTS

If we have set an objective to reduce the count of open defects then the testing team needs to address the following:

1. Why did the defects remain open even on the last day of go live? How many defects have workarounds and how many do not? Why were they left open, are the defects deferred to future releases or just ignored? Usually the less priority or severity ones became scapegoat.
2. How many past releases open defects are still in the defect tracking system? If they are too many, then is the project management or sponsors aware of it (they should be anyway)? If yes, did any debate happen with stakeholders?
3. Was a cost–benefit analysis done? What is the cost of fixing, retesting, and deploying a fix against the business loss or legal bindings.
4. Did quality assurance spend reasonable effort to work closely with business analysts and convince project management and development as to why the defects are important to fix and why they should not be kept open, or is the team just busy retesting the ones given by the development team.

By doing so, we cannot say the open defects count will come down. The testing team can only make an honest effort to improve quality of application, and many times not fixing a defect is a political and economic decision on cost verses benefits.

3.5 CONCLUSION

The COO said, "I hope all of you must have got the message now as to how important it is to compare defects with a balance sheet!" What money is to a balance sheet, defects are to a product or application. In corporate you manage money and in software testing you manage defects. You spend so much money to detect them, and once you have detected them if they are not fixed then what is the use? Alternatively, if the testing process was so messy that defects were passed to end users, what is the use?

The COO then said, "I think we need to compare testing with sweeping a floor: the more the dirt, the more you sweep, the lesser the dirt the lesser you sweep. If you did more sweeping when there was little dirt, you spent more time, energy, and money, and if you did less sweeping when there was more dirt then you made the floor look dirty even after you finished sweeping because you did not match the sweep with the amount of dirt." Similarly, in testing too, if the application contained lot of defects and less testing was done, then you have undetected defects still residing in the application and thus cost because sooner the users are going to find them. If you did lot of testing and fewer defects were found, then you spent money unnecessarily. If you are cost conscious, keep one thing in mind: Testing is done for defect discovery only because testers themselves fix the problems they find, so you spend a lot of money for defect discovery. If the defects found are not fixed and are stinking in the defect management system or end users start finding more serious problems than the testers, then testing should be called just a farce and is not worth it.

4

Opportunity Cost of Testing

Catherine Powell

4.1 GIVING AND GETTING: OPPORTUNITY COSTS AND TEST MANAGEMENT

For every ten tests that we perform, we don't perform a thousand other tests. For everything we know, there is a lot more we don't know. Every choice we make to do something means choosing not to do others. These opportunity costs, the roads not taken, are everywhere in software. It's time to make those costs explicit.

4.2 WHAT IS OPPORTUNITY COST?

If a teenager decides to go to summer camp, and the camp costs a hundred dollars, that means the explicit cost is a hundred dollars. However, if he had the option of staying home and earning two hundred more, there is a hidden cost—an opportunity cost—of two hundred more dollars to attend the camp. In other words, the opportunity cost of something is the benefit we would have gotten if we'd chosen to do something else.

A testing example: We have a release in one day and a number of tests we'd like to run. We can choose only one of the following:

A. Run a small throughput test to confirm that performance hasn't degraded
B. Run a quick load test to see how many users we can handle before our system falls over

If we do A, then we do not get the benefit of doing B and vice versa. Put another way, the opportunity cost of doing A is the benefit we would have gotten if we had done B. Because we ran a throughput test (option A), we learned how fast one user could use the system. Because we ran a throughput test (option A), we did not learn how many people could log in—and this is opportunity cost.

4.3 WHY MEASURE OPPORTUNITY COST?

We measure opportunity cost because resources are not infinite. There is never enough time, machines, or people to do every test we would like. Measuring opportunity cost helps us make the best choices given the limits that exist in the real world.

4.4 OPPORTUNITY COST APPLIED

Let's take an example application. It's a Web application that lets us log in, order pizza, see what pizza our friends ordered, and upload pictures of pizza we've eaten. We expect it to be very popular. Of course, if it's going to be popular, our pizza application should work. We had also better ship it at some point—seven weeks from now sounds good. Our testers came up with a set of tests they want to perform:

Test	Estimated Duration
Image upload tests with various file types and sizes	3 days
Login/logout tests	1 day
Signup tests—including automation	5 days
Security tests for cross-session exploits	5 days
Order payment (integration with third-party system)	8 days
Friends features—find, make, reject	7 days
Profiles—create, view, edit	4 days
Upgrade tests	3 days
Load tests up to 10,000 users	10 days
Load tests up to 1000 users	8 days
Cross-browser testing—5 browsers	5 days
Cross-browser testing—2 browsers	3 days

Let's assume these are all realistic estimates. We've got sixty-one days worth of tests and only thirty-five days until we ship; we're not going to get it all done. We have to decide what to do—and what the opportunity costs are of doing the things we choose.

4.5 IDENTIFYING OPPORTUNITY COST

The opportunity cost of doing one test is the benefit we would have gotten from the other test we would have done. In other words, the opportunity cost of image upload tests is the information we would have gotten from upgrade tests (since we don't do upgrade tests because we're busy with image upload tests). The opportunity cost of upgrade tests is the information we would have gotten from cross-browser testing (but we skipped cross-browser testing and chose to do upgrade tests instead).

Taken at a more macro level, the opportunity cost of doing a set of tests is all the tests we don't do, and all the information we don't get from them. Let's look at that list again, sorted according to priority:

Priority	Test	Estimated Duration	Reason Behind Priority
1	Upgrade tests	3 days	Failing here would cause total system unavailability
2	Login/logout tests	1 day	No access, no pizza
3	Signup tests—including automation	5 days	User's first experience should be near perfect
4	Cross browser testing—2 browsers	3 days	JavaScript-heavy site is prone to error
5	Order payment (integration with third-party system)	8 days	Money makes the world go round
6	Profiles—create, view, edit	4 days	Prerequisite to sharing
7	Image upload tests with various file types and sizes	3 days	We're using a third-party library we don't quite trust here—integration might be tricky
8	Friends features—find, make, reject	7 days	This is a differentiator but not strictly necessary for the first release; if we have to pull it we can
9	Load tests up to 1000 users	8 days	Will be good to have but we can tweak it after release if needed

(continued)

Priority	Test	Estimated Duration	Reason Behind Priority
10	Security tests for cross-session exploits	5 days	We're using libraries for html rendering that help us prevent this
11	Cross-browser testing—5 browsers	5 days	60 percent of our users are on two browsers, the others are mostly corporate (e.g., IE6)
12	Load tests up to 10,000 users	10 days	Maybe we won't be that popular quite yet

We have thirty-five days, so we're going to get through the first eight items on our list, and have a little time to spare. We're not going to do items 9 through 12. These items, therefore, are the opportunity cost of doing items 1 through 8. Because we choose to do the first eight items, we are also choosing not to do the remaining items, and that's opportunity cost. There are also tests that we didn't even consider doing. These tests are also opportunity cost, although they are unseen. Any decisions we make to change the opportunity cost will leave the tests we did not think of just as they are, as opportunity cost.

In some places, opportunity cost is measured in dollars as a company policy. If this policy is in place, find a senior business stakeholder to assist the test team in assigning those values, as the translation to a dollar figure is highly specific to each individual organization.

4.6 THE DECISION TABLE

Twice now we've seen a table of test options and some information about those options—their cost, their priority, and their perceived benefit. This table is known as a decision table. Using a decision table makes the priorities, tests, and trade-offs explicit—for all audiences. Decision tables can be used for many different decisions, like what features to build, what tests to run, which tool to purchase, and so forth. Please note that the decision table used in this chapter is an unofficial format, simplified from the official standard [1] for ease of use.

To create a decision table, we need the following information:

- Our options
- Benefits of each option

- Cost estimates
- An understanding of our priorities

Defining our options is the most important part of creating a decision table. We need to understand the universe of possibilities before we can make informed decisions. No option list is ever comprehensive—there are often near-infinite ideas and variations—but we should cover everything we reasonably might do.

Along with the options we have, understand what we'll get from that option. What is the benefit of doing this? For example, performing cross-browser tests confirms that our application looks good and behaves in the various ways people are likely to view it (or allows us to identify a problem and fix it before our customers find it). Some benefits are subtler than others, but if we can't identify any benefit at all to doing something, then we probably shouldn't be doing it. When we identify benefits explicitly, a lot of the things we do simply because we've always done them are likely to fall off—or at least to get lower priorities.

Once we understand each option, it's time to estimate it. How the estimate is expressed doesn't matter much as long as it's consistent. We can use person days, ideal engineering days, estimated duration, or some other method of our choosing. After we've estimated each option, look back at the options and their estimates. Each estimate should be roughly comparable—all in days, or all in weeks, or all in hours. If an option has a significantly longer estimate than any of the others, break it up into smaller pieces. The goal is to compare apples to apples, not apples to planes; keep choices of similar size.

Last, we need to prioritize our options. This is not something for the tester to do alone. These priorities will define what we, the testers, do and more important the information that we gather. Go to the consumers of the information provided by the tests (often called stakeholders) to see what they need to make an informed decision. We as testers provide information to someone or some group; that someone or some group should be the ones deciding what information is necessary and what is not. From this will come the priorities. Note here that it is essential for this to be a force ranked list (a list in which every element is in a strict sequential order, and no two items have the same rank). There can't be more than one top priority. For the purposes of calculating opportunity cost and planning this test cycle, something is either more or less important, not equal. This way we don't end up with sixty-one days of top priority tasks and thirty-five days left until release—an impossible situation.

4.7 CHANGING THE OPPORTUNITY COST

Once we understand the opportunity cost of an effort, then the trade-offs become more visible. There are two things to trade off here: time and tests. The more days there are before release, the lower the opportunity cost of that release—because we can do more tests. The fewer days there are, the higher the opportunity cost of that release.

Thus, to reduce the opportunity cost of a release, there are a number of things that can be changed:

- Extend the release and make the release date later
- Add more people to the project
- Reprioritize tests

Extending the release effectively increases the number of things that we can do, and that decreases the number of things we're explicitly choosing to not do. Opportunity cost declines. Whether extending a release is a feasible option depends on whether your releases are date based (must release on some date regardless of what's in it) or feature-based (must release with some feature set, regardless of when that occurs). It's worth asking whether the release date is a target or a deadline.

Adding more people works similarly to extending the release: the number of things that we can do between now and the release date increases, resulting in a decline in opportunity cost. This is a dangerous path, however: adding more people to a release doesn't always allow the team to do more. This is an option that is much more likely to be effective early in a release, but the later it gets, the less likely this is to work. This is also only possible to the extent that the work can be broken up and done in parallel.

Reprioritizing tests changes the nature of the opportunity cost, although it doesn't necessarily decrease that cost. We can, as in our pizza application, reduce our opportunity cost in the area of security in exchange for increasing the opportunity cost in the area of browser compatibility. This changes the nature of the cost, but the total opportunity cost does not change. And in the end, this is a business decision: drop a feature or add some risk to a feature; it's all still tests that we do or do not do.

4.8 LIMITS TO CHANGE

There are limits to the opportunity cost we can change. Think of changing opportunity costs as moving pieces around on a puzzle board—the fewer spaces we have, the fewer things we can move around. As time passes, the chance to change opportunity costs declines. For example:

- If it takes two months for a new engineer to be a contributing team member, then adding engineers a month before release is no longer an effective option; it won't reduce our opportunity cost. If anything, Brooks's law may apply [2]: adding manpower to late projects makes them later.
- If all the opportunity costs are five days or more and it's two days before release, then changing the priority of tests won't help—nothing that's isn't already done will fit in.
- As we move through the release, product management is talking about it with customers, potential customers, and even the public. At first, they say it's coming next year, and we have a lot of ability to move the release date, thus changing the opportunity cost. As time passes, those dates get more and more precise: second half of 2011, third quarter of 2011, October 2011. Each increase in precision gives the team less room in which to change the release date and therefore less chance to change the opportunity cost.

The earlier you are in a given release cycle, the more options exist for changing the opportunity cost. Make a decision table as soon as you start thinking about a release. Exposing opportunity cost early gives you freedom to change. Make a decision table, see the opportunity cost, change it. Make a decision table, see the opportunity cost, change it. Repeat.

4.9 CONCLUSION

Every opportunity has a cost. For every test we perform, there exists a test that we could have done but didn't. For every scenario we try, we skip something we could have tried but didn't. Opportunities meet release dates, and opportunity cost is what we would have done tomorrow, if there were a tomorrow.

Testing is a battle against time. There is an infinite number of things that could be tested in a given system. Because there is infinite variety but not infinite time, there is opportunity cost. Bring the opportunity cost into the open, where we can understand it and affect it.

NOTES

1. Decision Tables, CSA Standard Z243.1-1970.
2. Frederick P. Brooks, *The Mythical Man-Month* (Reading MA: Addison Wesley, 1975). Note that Brooks's law also famously applies to nine women attempting to have a child within a month—it's not going to happen.

5

Trading Money for Time: When Saving Money Doesn't (and When It Does)

Michael Larsen

> How you spend your time is more important than how you spend your money. Money mistakes can be corrected, but time is gone forever.
>
> **—David Norris**

In any endeavor I participate in, I have choices. In many of life's transactions, I can spend money to have something done, or I can spend the time to do that same thing. For some things, it's worth it to invest the time to make up or offset the amount of money to be spent. At other times, there is a level of involvement and a required expertise that makes not spending the money a barrier to achieving my goals. There is a trade-off: money for time, or time for money. The problems arise when we don't give each of these areas proper consideration. In the world of software development, containing costs is important, but so is delivering a good quality product at the right time. Containing costs when a project is on time is a good thing, but losing time and not delivering a product when scheduled can cost both time and money, often in the lost revenue from dissatisfied customers. At the furthest extreme, the resulting loss of time could result in legal action for not being able to deliver on commitments. This chapter examines the trade-offs between money and time, and demonstrates examples where time investment has meant financial gain, and where lack of understanding of time has negated or even negatively affected a company's finances.

5.1 A NEW PROJECT GETS UNDER WAY

It's time for another software project to begin. Each time I go through this process, I have a similar set of experiences. Each time I need to:

- Address physical infrastructure needs
- Determine where to set up machines
- Gather and install software applications to support the testing needs
- Consider the scope and types of testing that will be required

Physical infrastructure needs include buying and setting up the server and client system and networking equipment. It may also involve internal or external hosting considerations plus the adequate securing of these resources. When we consider physical machines, potential lab space for the devices and the need for adequate cooling must be considered. Our software application under development also has infrastructure requirements. Software development kits (SDKs) and integrated development environments (IDEs) are needed for software development. We must configure and maintain file services, database services, Web services, and so forth. We also have to consider deployment of the application(s) for testing and for general use. The specific testing areas (and the software testing tools that we utilize) must also be considered. Unit testing. Functional testing. Load testing. Performance testing. Parafunctional and human factors/user experience testing. The number of areas to manage and maintain is dizzying.

I have witnessed various companies and their management teams wrestle with the goal to improve the testing and development process. These goals may be to speed delivery or add testing coverage for initiatives that haven't adequately been tested. Many management teams also provided fanfare and cheering about the time savings due to some new enhancement. It might be a new tool to automate all of the regression testing. It could be a new server to run a battery of virtual environments. A robust versioning and backup system to keep all versions of files updated, tagged, secure, and available would streamline the application life cycle. These are admirable goals, and when implemented, the net result can be more productive testing. Work can be completed more quickly.

All of these initiatives cost us something. To set up any of these enhancements, our teams have to spend something to bring them to fruition. With organizations squeezing budgets and economizing where possible, some businesses are reluctant to spend. During economically challenging times, many organizations opt to soldier on using tools already in place (if any exist) and machines that are already at work in their current state. Money is not spent, so our costs are lower. What this "cost saving" doesn't address is the time trade-off made to perform these tasks. The cost of testing is not exclusively about money; very often we must include time in that cost analysis as well.

5.2 WHERE ARE WE SPENDING OUR MONEY?

As our development project ramps up, the resources available will dictate the total time needed to complete it. The number of people on a project certainly adds to the total price tag of a project as well as the total amount of time a project may take. With a testing team, two testers working together will very likely complete more testing than one tester will. The combined test coverage is often much greater than the sum of individual tester's standalone efforts. Having more powerful computers will certainly shave the time it takes to build applications. Likewise, having more machines makes it possible to deploy more test environments.

Support for multiple operating systems provides additional challenges. Microsoft Windows, Mac OS, and HP-UX are examples of operating systems that have an up-front licensing cost for each installation. Linux and FreeBSD are examples of open source operating systems that are available for free. Beyond just the cost of the operating system is the time needed to give each system thorough testing. Each supported platform adds a time multiplier as to how long it will take. There are also variations in database software, Web server software, office productivity applications, and other components that may be required to evaluate the functionality of the application under test. In addition there are variations in the way the software is written and deployed (precompiled code such as C++ vs. dynamic application code like Java). Each variation requires another environment be set up and tested.

Testing these multiple operating systems requires choices be made. We can purchase and maintain individual hardware machines. We can also utilize virtualization technology to reduce the need for multiple physical computers. The host server will require many orders of magnitude more capacity and performance than the individual computers we would have virtualization replace. If a project requires six systems of equal capability, virtualizing those machines will require sufficient resources on a single server to be able to house and run those six environments. That host server will require enough disk space, RAM, and system resources for the six virtualized environments to operate and respond as though they were standalone machines.

Testing tools range from free, open source options all the way to very expensive proprietary commercial systems. The application under test often determines which tools, if any, will need to be used. There are many free and open source test tools for testing Web applications. By contrast, most of the tools that test a compiled application from a "black box" perspective are commercial products (though there are also a number of open source options available that allow us to create tests and automate many tasks).

As I have seen over the years, not spending for these items or areas can provide a short-term cost savings. We made do with the servers and machines we had on hand. We also managed to get by with a limit on software licenses (within reason and within the bounds of what is legal; I do not advocate piracy to cut costs at any time). I have set up test beds and test labs using free operating system software using a variety of Linux variations. I have also used both commercial and free virtualization software, where the host was running Linux, and the guest machines likewise represented a variety of free operating system options. These test environments also have been set up to use as many free or inexpensive variations of open source tools for testing purposes. There is no question that using these techniques has saved money.

5.3 WHAT'S THE TRADE-OFF? THE TRADE-OFF IS TIME

There is an adage that says, "You can have a system that is cheap, fast, or of good quality. Pick two." Price, time, and quality rarely move up and down together. If one area gets incremented, others are decremented. When we spend less to perform a task, the time to accomplish the task often increases. The quality of the resulting output may also decrease. In my experience, companies want to bring costs down, while keeping the quality level as high as possible. To make both goals succeed (lowering costs and improving quality), in most cases we will have to allow time to increase.

Let's use a build server as an example. If we chain a number of computers together to perform builds, the overall time to complete the build process will diminish. What could shaving 25 percent of the time off completing a build do for your development and testing teams? Think of the amount of time that could be applied to testing and fixing issues discovered rather than waiting for the build to finish. The quicker the turnaround from development to testing, the quicker issues can be discovered, addressed, and fixed. Quicker builds allows for better integration of new code. Quicker builds allows for a system that is up and running and more frequently available. With the effort to set up the scripts and tests needed, the quality of the build process can be improved. The productivity gains were produced by spending money to add server horsepower. Paying for the human brainpower to create scripts and processes makes for fewer errors in the build process.

To contrast, let's consider what would happen if a new initiative of ours requires a server, but our budget doesn't allow for it. We could share the workload on the existing build servers. We could pull one of the machines out of the build process and make it a standalone server. What happens? Cost savings are immediate; we didn't have to purchase a new server. The quality of the builds may be unaffected, but the time to complete the builds has increased. If the system performs daily builds, the time we have lost because of the server change will be multiplied by the number of days for as long as the projects are active. The benefits of quicker turnaround for development and testing will not be achieved.

I have used test environments with open source operating system software and open source testing tools. On the surface, the environments appear to be totally free or have a very low physical cost to implement. In my experience, deploying, maintaining, and administering these operating systems and applications requires a significant time commitment on the part of the development, test, and information technology (IT) teams. Open source software (and the communities that help with bug fixes, documentation, and implementation of new features) is on par with the development of many commercial applications. The ease of installation and maintenance of the installed software has likewise improved dramatically. Still, a high level of knowledge and skill is required to keep multiple open source applications and tools running smoothly. That knowledge development and maintenance requires time.

Several groups I have been a part of, especially at the beginning, had no formal tools in place. Most of the testing steps are performed manually.

Many tasks are best suited to active manual testing, but when all our testing is manual, the time required to complete it can be significant. Multiply our manual testing efforts by the number of projects and the time commitment to do all of the needed testing rises exponentially. Few organizations have the luxury of long periods of time to make sure all testing is performed. What tends to happen is that testing time gets cut (or at best held to the required scheduled time). The total amount of tests gets cut, which can lead to a lower quality product. When we apply a risk-based test approach, we aim to maximize the potential of covering areas we consider most critical. Even with this method, consider how long it would take to cover all areas in the time limit. Where will the cuts be made? Should we eliminate human factors testing? Will considerations for user experience go untested or receive a lower priority? Will features that are desired but can't be fit into the timeline be moved to later releases? If so, how long will it be until we will be subject to the hands of Kronos once again?

5.4 WHAT IS TIME REALLY WORTH?

Let's say an average developer earns $50 per hour. That includes all benefits. Fifty dollars per hour is not unreasonable given wages, vacations, holidays, benefits, and sick days. What other aspects of the workday need to be considered? We do not have the ability to simply wake up, teleport ourselves to work, meet our objectives, and then immediately zip away to do other things. We commute and we spend money to make those commutes. When we work at home, we pay for infrastructure to allow that ability. We purchase clothing and food to support us while we are in the mode of working.

Some commentators have said that our full twenty-four-hour day should be viewed in light of what we earn. To really determine the value of our time, we would need to take the total amount of time in a week, and divide it into an hourly figure. If we were to divide those hours in comparison to our average developer earning $50 per hour, that individual is really earning $11.90 per hour.

This is the concept of the "real wage," and it was popularized in the book *Your Money or Your Life*, by Vicki Robin, Joe Dominguez, and Monique Tilford [1]. By using this approach, the real wage is almost 80 percent less than what our midlevel developer earns while working. We can also look at a less extreme example. When all activities and expenses that immediately impact our work are considered, the difference in the real wage can be anywhere from 30 to 50 percent lower than our earned hourly rate. When we realize just how much our real wages are, we feel prompted to do significantly different things with our spending and behavior.

The value of time becomes more critical as additional people come into the picture. Time is multiplied, and each nonoptimized hour affects all of the individuals involved in a project. Going back to my previous build server example, imagine a daily build currently takes three hours. Adding another server could bring the time of the build process down to two hours. Put into monetary terms, if a team of ten developers was able to save just two hours each per week, the team would then have twenty hours more per week to add value to the product. That is a saving of one thousand dollars per week or close to fifty thousand dollars per year.

The real wage for an organization can be greatly increased by its ability to save time. It can also be greatly decreased by the time it loses.

5.5 IS TIME ALWAYS THE ENEMY?

It is possible to lose money when time is not taken into account. Time can also be used to an organization's advantage as well. Using the build server example again, we will need to spend money to get the hardware and to achieve the time savings. What if we could get the same hardware for half the cost? Could we get double the hardware for the same cost? For the past thirty years, computer and networking equipment has roughly doubled its performance every eighteen months. This doubling capability has also been closely tied to improvements in RAM, disk space, peripherals, networking devices, and the cost of internal components of motherboards and expansion cards. We can see a general trend that machines effectively double in power every eighteen months to two years, while staying relatively even costwise.

With this in mind, does the time not saved, and the subsequent lowering of the real wage of the organization, offset the potential of gaining double the power in machine performance in eighteen months? If the answer is no, then waiting could potentially lower costs while still getting a better return on time. Consider what the cost–benefit analysis of buying a piece of hardware now versus later would be (specifically with the idea of the gained time for our example team providing a fifty thousand dollar cost savings each year).

What other steps could be put off until later? Consider what happens when automating tests. I have a natural tendency to want to get in early and start working with the system as soon as the user interface (UI) or other elements are coded. By automating tests early, the ability to test the system early and often should yield a good return on the time spent to automate the steps. What happens if the UI changes? Additional fields are added (or removed) or just relocated to a different part of the screen. My automation efforts will have to be modified (best case) or completely redone (worst case). In this instance, is it better to wait until the UI is finished? The odds (and risk) of the UI being changed are now greatly lessened, and my automation efforts are less likely to require reworking or redoing.

5.6 BALANCING SHORT-TERM AND LONG-TERM GAINS AND LOSSES

When I look to balance and consider the costs associated with money and time, it's important to look at both short-term and long-term views. There is always a return on investment when it comes to the time put into any process versus the value of the output. Whether the return is positive or negative, and by how much, is up to the team and the organization. This may also be dictated by issues that we have little control over. Using automation as an example, there is a formula that Deon Johnson refers to as the automation return on investment (ROI) [2]. The automation ROI is determined by comparing cost savings, increased efficiency, and reduced risk. The equation we use for this is:

$$ROI = (Gains - Investment\ Costs)/Investment\ Costs$$

The larger challenge is for us to convince management that there is likely to be a positive return for our investment. It may cost our organization one hundred thousand dollars to automate a series of tests. If the net result of that automation is quicker time to market and an increase in sales, that's a strong incentive to make the changes. If the hundred thousand dollars spent for automation does not generate additional revenue to equal or surpass the initial investment, it can be argued that the return on investment is negative. In this situation, a manager would be unlikely to recommend continued automation efforts.

What I think needs to be considered is the window of time being used. One financial quarter may be far too short a time period to determine the value of a testing effort. Sadly, quarterly numbers are what drive many organizations. In this instance, a one hundred thousand dollar deficit may doom a project. However, if a longer view is taken, that initial deficit will be erased. As seen in Figure 5.1, if an investment is made up front and that investment can get a modest performance increase over an extended period of time, the return on that investment can be considerably higher than not making the investment. Compared to a longer time period (say, three or four years) the benefits and cost savings will become more apparent [4].

As an example of balancing short-term expense with long-term benefit, Cisco Systems offers an interesting example. It invested time and resources between 1992 and 1995 to create a robust automation framework around the Tcl language. This framework was then used to create extensive automation libraries and script suites to test the Cisco Internetwork Operating System (IOS). Scores of testers were responsible for developing these scripts. These scripts would then communicate on the routers' console ports and send commands that would set up the routers' internal configuration parameters. These Tcl commands, using the Expect extension, were capable of initiating numerous test sequences. The scripts allowed the testers to confirm results, determine the pass–fail criteria, and then tear down the tests.

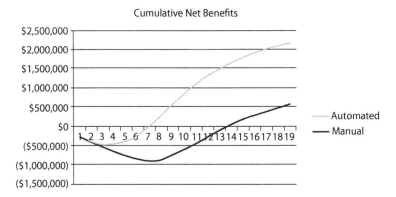

FIGURE 5.1
The cumulative benefits over time comparing a range of tests performed manually versus with some level of automation (numbers are in months). (From J. Scumniotales, "Why Incremental Development is Better: An ROI Perspective," http://agile.scumniotales. com/2009/02/why-incremental-development-is-better-an-roi-perspective.html.)

Decades of cumulative man-hours were put into creating the libraries needed to allow the test framework to be completed and enhanced over the initial three years. Large lab facilities were created to house all of the equipment required to run the tests. This required a large up-front expense, but it proved to be an excellent way to run regression tests and to capture information for reports and for issue tracking. Today, Cisco's investment in Tcl goes beyond testing. Cisco IOS has an extension that allows administrators to use Tcl directly. They can use it on the console port to configure routers and switches in production environments, as well as to create queries for SMTP (Simple Mail Transfer Protocol) messages and also for accessing SNMP MIBs (Simple Network Management Protocol Management Information Bases) [5].

I have also had many experiences when the short-term benefits of saving money outweighed the long-term issues. One of the favorite war story examples used by many testers (and yes, I've experienced my share, too) come from experiences with outsourcing. It's considered a boon when outsourcing efforts help you and your team get more done and increase profits. It's seen as a bane when that outsourced team ends up taking over your job. I've been in both situations and can speak to exactly how both situations feel. The business case I've heard most often used to justify outsourcing testing efforts is that the organization can save money. To be fair, when it is done correctly, with a high level of communication and collaboration, and with a motivated and well-synced team, outsourcing can be beneficial and can be a cost saver.

For outsourcing to save money, the entire business case must be considered. For example, I was part of an outsourcing process when I worked with a Japanese video game company. For our group of testers, we were the outsourcing group working on the video game company's behalf helping to ready titles for release and distribution into the U.S. market. We reaped the benefits of that relationship and provided a good service with a high degree of quality and satisfaction to our client.

By contrast, a number of years ago when I was working with a technology company, there was a large initiative where management decided to have an outsourced group assist in the development and the testing. The reasoning was that there was more than enough work for our group to do and this would allow us to quickly get a large number of tests completed and have the reporting turned around to management quickly. That was the goal, a way to get a lot of testing done quickly and at minimal cost. At first, it looked like the organization would save a lot of money. Over time it became clear that what management had hoped would be tested and in the timeframe it wanted wasn't. Several meetings were required to clarify the situation. Each meeting needed to be conducted with the management team in one location and the development and testing team half a world away. This made the effective time between each daily build and receiving results to be two days. Days turned into weeks and weeks into months. It became clear that any short-term cost savings was consumed when the product was not ready to be shipped on time. As the team continued to try and get the product ready, more issues appeared. Some issues were related to usability, some with performance, and quite a few issues affected the overall user experience. Ultimately it was determined that the project would not meet the needs of the customers, and both development and testing were halted. Subsequent work was brought back in house. The cost benefits originally envisioned never materialized. In this case, the cost in both money and time was significant, with a negative return on investment.

So, if outsourcing is an option to consider, here are a few questions we should be asking:

1. What is the cost of trying to collaborate across greatly differing time zones?
2. What are ways that the collaboration can be improved?
3. Would tools aid the process of collaboration? If so, how much would they cost?
4. How much travel will be required to keep the two groups in sync?
5. How long will it take to fully ramp up an outsourced team?
6. How will these changes affect the designers of the system?
7. How much does the design team have to document for the out-sourced team to be effective in its testing?
8. How much will it cost to produce that documentation?
9. Will there be any long-term value in the documentation produced?

Asking these questions up front, and many more, plus considering all costs associated with them, will give a truer picture of the expense in terms of both money and time.

5.7 HOW CAN WE OPTIMIZE COSTS (MONEY AND TIME)?

Finding the magic point where we can save money and keep to a good amount of time while ensuring high quality is a delicate balance. Many might say it can't be done. I say with an eye toward having all three perfectly balanced, it's unlikely. I do believe, however, that there is a way to get to where the monetary cost is "low enough," the overall time is "long enough or short enough" and the quality is "good enough" to be effective and release a good product to stakeholders who want it in a timely manner. There is no magical incantation or special formula to let the organization know exactly where that good enough is, but there are a number of areas that I think can be examined and, when taken into context, useful to gauge whether a project or application will fulfill the needs of the customer in a way that is timely and provides for good cost savings to implement [6].

1. Determine the most critical areas to the stakeholders.
2. Focus on the highest risk areas first.
3. Make sure to ask the right questions.
4. Fix the showstoppers, and understand what constitutes a showstopper.
5. The perfect is the enemy of the good.

5.7.1 Determine the Most Critical Areas to the Stakeholders

Who is the product for? What is their expectation? Does our solution meet it? If the answer is yes, then it is safe to say we are on the right path. If it does not, no amount of cost cutting or optimization will matter. When I was sitting in a development and testing meeting, discussing a particularly time-sensitive software project, our development manager asked the assembled group: "Do we make software here?" When the developers and testers said yes, he shot back "No, we do not! We make a solution that solves a problem for our customers. At the end of the day, if we don't get that part right, it doesn't matter what else we did get right!"

5.7.2 Focus on the Highest Risk Areas First

The areas that matter most to our stakeholders are ultimately the highest risk areas. It doesn't matter if we agree or not, they are the ones who want the application, and their wish list is what's driving the purchase of the application. An example might be to make sure that any UI screens can be viewed in an 800 × 600 window. It may seem like a trivial issue, but it isn't when the target application is going to run on a kiosk where that is the maximum resolution. Screens that do not look good or require scrolling, especially in an application that uses a touch screen or does not have a method for scrolling, will be a major problem. If this is a key consideration, testing with an 800×600 screen better be one of the first priorities in the test plan.

5.7.3 Make Sure to Ask the Right Questions

Who are the intended users? Does a product already exist that meets this need? If we are first to market, does the application do what our customers want it to do? If we are not first to market, what differentiates us from the competition? Is that difference significant enough to make for an appealing alternative with the established players? What kind of environment will the application be deployed in? Does the product live up to the expectations set for it? Are there any legal requirements we need to be aware of? Each of these questions provides valuable information to help testers set their priorities on the right areas. This information helps make sure that, again, the areas that matter the most get the most coverage. Areas that are less important, or not important at all, get prioritized appropriately.

5.7.4 Fix the Showstoppers, and Understand What Constitutes a Showstopper

Many testers are trained to look at crashes as showstoppers, but they may not understand that a key business rule is being violated, or that a poorly worded paragraph or stray punctuation could prove embarrassing should it get out. If we press a combination of keys, and the application crashes, that looks bad. Many testers will rightfully state that this is a big issue and a showstopper. But is it? Is the combination of keys a regular occurrence, such as a combination of regularly used shortcut keys, or is it an unusual combination that is very unlikely to come into everyday use? By comparison, look at the main text that spells out what the users of the software will do as a service for a customer. Imagine that the text is misspelled and the punctuation is wrong. Many testers would consider text issues to be a low-level cosmetic bug. That may be true, but in this case, it may be an issue that really sets off an alarm in the customer buying the product. The random key presses that caused the crash was a way lower priority compared to the text on the page that spelled out the agreement between the service provider and its client.

5.7.5 The Perfect Is the Enemy of the Good

There may be many small issues that have been found, and there may be many low traffic areas that may not have received thorough testing. The ship window is two weeks away, and we determine that we can cover all of the remaining areas, and many of these little niggling issues can be resolved and retested, but only if we get six weeks of additional testing time. What do we do? When faced with this option, I tend to look at the areas that have not been tested and evaluate the risk if any of those areas were to house a monster bug. What are the odds that area will be hit? What are the chances that the issues I have discovered will be seen as catastrophic? In this case, I rate on a scale of 1 to 5, 1 being really critical and 5 being virtually unlikely to happen. I then rank them in order of that gut feeling, then I see what I can hit and what I cannot. I may have to leave several 5s on the table, but I better make really sure that I have covered all the 1's in question. After doing that, the project manager, development team, and test team, along with any other key stakeholders, will have to make a judgment call. Do we keep digging and testing to see what else we can uncover and risk not making the release date? Do we roll with it and decide it's time to let the product go, because we have all decided that, based on the criteria we have received, the risk areas we have covered, the questions we have asked, the answers we have received, the feedback we have received from end users, and the showstoppers we have fixed, have given us the gut feeling that we are ready to go live? Different situations will inform either of those decisions, but there are times when good enough really is, and waiting for perfection will prove more costly than beneficial.

5.8 CONCLUSION

The cost of testing is real. There is always a price we have to pay if we want to improve the quality of the software. Sometimes that cost is in dollars, sometimes that cost is in hours, days, weeks, or months. Many times, we have to make trade-offs to deal with the costs of money and time. When we look to save money due to not taking additional time into the equation, it's entirely possible that the money saved will be outweighed by the opportunity costs of the time we have lost. Take the time to determine what is your real wage as a tester, as a manager, or as an organization.

Consider the value of your time actually, and make sure to include that when trying to determine how to reduce the cost of testing. With an eye toward looking at both money and time, it's possible to strike a balance where both can provide a positive return on investment.

NOTES

1. Vicki Robin, Joe Dominguez, and Monique Tilford, *Your Money or Your Life: 9 Steps to Transforming Your Relationship with Money and Achieving Financial Independence; Revised and Updated for the 21st Century* (New York: Penguin, 2008).
2. Automated Testing Institute, "How Is Automation Return-On-Investment (ROI) Calculated?" http://www.automatedtestinginstitute.com/home/index.php?option= com_content&view=article&id=1097:faq-roi&catid=54:faqs&Itemid=84> (accessed August 18, 2010).
3. J. Scumniotales, "Why Incremental Development is Better: An ROI Perspective," http://agile.scumniotales.com/2009/02/why-incremental-development-is-better-an-roi-perspective.html (accessed November 15, 2010).
4. Dion Johnson, "Test Automation ROI," Automated Testing Institute, http://www.auto-matedtestinginstitute.com/home/articleFiles/articleAndPapers/Test_Automation_ ROI.pdf (accessed August 18, 2010).
5. Cisco, "Cisco IOS Scripting with Tcl," http://www.cisco.com/en/US/docs/ios/12_3t/ 12_3t2/feature/guide/gt_tcl.html (accessed August 18, 2010).
6. Jon Bach, "Do We Really Need All This Testing?" http://www.quardev.com/content/ whitepapers/do_we_really_need_all_this_testing.pdf (accessed August 18, 2010).

6

An Analysis of Costs in Software Testing

Michael Bolton

Before we get started, I have some questions for you:

> Why are you reading a book on reducing the cost of testing?
>
> Are you a development manager? Are you concerned that you're not getting good value for the money you're spending on testing?
>
> Are you a tester, trying to figure out a way to help management cut costs just enough so that your company's management decides not to outsource the work that you do?
>
> Are you a test manager, hoping to increase the efficacy of your test group without increasing headcount or equipment cost?

If the answer to any of these questions is yes, I might be able to offer some useful suggestions. If you'll indulge me, I'd like to tell you a made-up story. It's based on a number of real experiences that I've had in several years of hands-on testing work, consulting, and teaching. As you read parts of the story, I'd encourage you to identify *factors* of cost.

What is a factor? A factor is an element, attribute, or dimension of an object or event that might be useful in evaluating it and making decisions about it. Factors are recursive; factors themselves have factors. The braking system on a car is a factor in evaluating the car, but there are factors to the braking system, too. I'll be identifying cost factors here as the story progresses. Most of them will be testing costs, but I'll also point to some other development costs. These are not intended to be formal definitions; that is, the descriptions and definitions that I provide are intended to highlight elements of the story, not to add to the program management or testing lexicon.

In addition, I've included some questions—puzzles that I encountered in the real-life situations that informed the story. I'll answer them along the way and provide some additional observations at the end of the story.

* * *

Several years ago, I was hired to do testing on a ten-week contract at a big bank (which, for this story, I'll call VaultBank). The project involved testing the front end of a teller workstation application (I'll call it TellerPlus) for which the underlying service layer was being changed. Some minor changes that had been requested by the bank were being made to TellerPlus as well. Although the bank had in-house programmers, most of the programming had been contracted to MegaDev, a very large and expensive consultancy that also provided testing services.

MegaDev had hired a team of contract testers to do most of the testing for TellerPlus's initial release. For this update, a year later, MegaDev had recruited an all-new team of contractors—none of whom had had any previous experience with TellerPlus—to test the existing application against the new service layer. I was one of those contractors. A few weeks into the contract, I discovered the extent to which MegaDev was marking up the cost of testing services: it was collecting an additional 30 to 50 percent of each tester's hourly wage.

If most of what banks do involves using—and therefore developing and testing—software, why would they contract it out at great expense rather than treating it as an essential part of business? Both programming and testing are complex cognitive activities that are aided by extensive domain knowledge. Why keep firing the programming and testing groups?

To answer these questions, let's look at some factors of the cost of testing.

Recruitment cost—The cost of finding, qualifying, selecting, and contracting testers.

Training cost—The cost of getting and keeping people up to speed on skills, tools, techniques, and domain knowledge.

Staffing cost—The cost of employing people in a particular role, including salary, benefits, equipment, tools, administrative overhead, and office space.

Hiring, training, and retaining a development group is expensive. As in many large corporations, VaultBank used an accounting model that treated software development as a set of discrete projects with clearly defined start and end dates. This allowed VaultBank to hire contractors—keeping full-time employees off the books—and treat development work like one-time charges rather than ongoing efforts.

MegaDev offered the service of providing a qualified test team, deemed ready to work from the day it arrived. When viewed through a particular accounting model, hiring contractors does *lower the cost of testing.*

In this division, VaultBank had two testers, Ron and Rick, and a test manager, Maurice, all of whom were providing support for several other large applications. I reported to Maurice, and also to Dennis, MegaDev's project manager. As I was working, none of these people observed me directly. Rick acted as a test lead for TellerPlus, but was too busy to offer anything but minimal training and supervision to me and the other contractors. Ron was around a good deal of the time but didn't work on TellerPlus. Since all of the other testers were hired guns brought in for this assignment only, there was no clearly established team culture.

I wasn't aware of a specific person holding the customer role (in the Agile sense) for the project, but there was a subject matter expert named Jeremy. Maurice recommended that I direct questions about the business functions of TellerPlus to Jeremy—but also warned me not to take too much of his time, since he was busy with other matters.

My mission, Maurice told me, was to perform as many test cases as I could each day, to note bugs in the tracking system, and to fill in a personal daily progress report. The report was in the form of a table, identifying a test case number, the pass-or-fail status of the test case, a bug report number where applicable, and notes. The VaultBank people seemed to pay careful attention to the daily progress reports. Other than that, no one seemed to be watching very carefully.

The first round of testing, a year earlier, had produced two kinds of documents explicitly for testers. One was a large binder of painfully detailed test scripts. Each one described a numbered, ordered series of specific actions and observations, some of which were illustrated by screenshots. The instructions and the screenshots often disagreed with each other. Mercifully, I was not assigned to test using these scripts, but four other testers were. They plodded mechanically through the scripts and recorded the problems they found. Since there were no functional changes intended to the service layer, and the scripts hadn't been updated to address the minor changes in TellerPlus, most of the problems the testers found were problems with the scripts.

Why wouldn't MegaDev or VaultBank make sure that each tester was carefully trained and that each tester had ready access to important business information? When testers aren't supervised, there's a risk that they'll end up wasting time and money. Why weren't the testers watched more closely? Scripted tests are expensive to develop and to maintain, so why use them?

Managers, supervisors, and subject matter experts are highly paid, so their time is precious. Training and supervising testers is a costly and time-consuming business. Scripting is an approach to testing that separates the processes of test design, test execution, result interpretation, and learning in person or in time, and that emphasizes process, planning, and control of testing by focusing on documents to mediate management, supervision, and direction of the individual tester. This approach increases some of the costs of testing but reduces others.

> Test design cost—The cost of identifying a potential risk and developing a test idea to address that risk.
>
> Test programming cost—The cost of turning a test idea into a script or sequence of instructions to be executed either by a human tester or by a machine.
>
> Data generation cost—The cost associated with developing, acquiring, processing, filtering, selecting, or (where necessary, for privacy reasons) obfuscating test data.
>
> Execution cost—The cost of actually performing a specific test.
>
> Repetition cost—The cost of repeating a test that has been run before.
>
> Recording cost—The cost associated with creating an ongoing account of the tester's activities.
>
> Supervisory cost—The cost of guiding, observing, and providing feedback to an employee.

Managers for both MegaDev and VaultBank reasoned that test execution is the most important aspect of testing and that testing productivity corresponds to the pace at which testers can run through test scripts. By that measure, testers can indeed be productive from the moment they're handed a test script. Designing tests, programming them, and generating data for them takes a good deal of effort and must be done by skilled people whose time is relatively expensive. However, the managers reckoned that this phase of testing needed to be done only once. After that, performing, recording,

*and repeating the test is relatively cheap, since test execution can be per-
formed by relatively unskilled people who need not know anything about the
business domain. The script tells the testers what to do and what to observe;
recording cost is virtually nil; and managers can believe that they have a
clear picture of what the testers have done, even when the managers are not
directly supervising the work. The daily progress report helps to focus testers
on individual productivity, where productivity is measured by the number
of test cases performed per day.*

My reputation as an exploratory tester had preceded me, so I was given
a different testing assignment (foreign exchange) and a different kind of
test artifact (an Excel spreadsheet). The first column contained a list of
two hundred test ideas for foreign exchange transactions. Other columns
noted the customer's instrument (cash, bank account, bank draft, personal
check, money order, traveler's check, and the like), the currency on hand,
the currency desired, service fees, the exchange rate, and VaultBank's
profit on each exchange. The sheet specified the expected profit margin for
each transaction, along with scanty information indicating which of the
bank's general ledger accounts should be credited or debited. There were a
few references to use cases that I hadn't seen. After a few days, Rick found
a copy of them for me.

The sheet was poorly structured, disorganized, out of date, and inflexible (which is why I'll call it the Messy Worksheet in this story). Comments
were sparse. Many cells had been merged by column; others by row. There
were occasional notes randomly interspersed in the cells. Sometimes a
note linked the test idea to a particular risk or to a specific use case; sometimes there wasn't any particular motivation listed. For the application in
production, exchange rates changed daily, but in the Messy Worksheet,
the exchange rates had been hard coded and were therefore out of date.
Over the year that had passed since TellerPlus had been released, some of
the listed currencies were no longer being bought or sold by the bank at a
retail level, and other currencies had been adopted.

**Leaving a document or a testing tool to be interpreted by a new tester
is risky. Why would a tester produce such a poorly structured and hard-
to-maintain document? Why had management allowed it? Why hadn't
the sheet been maintained?**

*Testing always involves trade-offs, and some parts of any business domain
are complicated. One of my colleagues had been around for the first round
of testing. From him I learned that work on foreign exchange had started
late, and that my predecessor had been under enormous pressure to learn*

the domain and to execute tests. To the managers at the time, test execution was more important than other costly activities, so they decided to reduce other costs.

> *Transfer cost—The cost associated with making the test understandable to others for the purposes of analysis, maintenance, adaptation, execution, or interpretation.*
>
> *Documentation cost—The cost of transcribing transferable information into a time-bound form—writing, illustrations, program code, video recordings.*

In management's view, the people who were on the project a year earlier had sufficient working knowledge to proceed with test execution, and they could communicate with one another face to face. Since TellerPlus had been subject to schedule pressure for its first release, there was no particular incentive at the time to polish the sheet, either during development work or after the system had been deployed.

There was another Excel artifact, too: a very elegant workbook (which I will call the Elegant Workbook) designed to track money flows through the batch reconciliation process, using one worksheet for each test. Each sheet identified a test idea, details about one or more steps in the transaction, and tables that showed where the money was expected to go, and where it had actually gone over the course of each day. (In a batch processing environment, some transactions take several days to work their way through all of the different systems and accounts.) Summary sheets at the beginning and the end of the workbook rolled up the results for daily and weekly analysis. This was a wonderful artifact, but there were a couple of problems with it. First, the version that I saw seemed only to incorporate domestic transactions, with no foreign exchange activity. Second, the workbook could have calculated the movement of funds automatically, but it didn't; the sheets had to be filled out manually. Nonetheless, the Elegant Workbook was a very powerful tool. I was surprised to see that it wasn't being used at all in the current round of testing.

Why hadn't the Messy Worksheet been developed to the standard of the Elegant Workbook? Faced with a pile of unhelpful test scripts, why wouldn't the testing group use an available, useful, powerful artifact to help structure and support its work?

Again through my colleague who had worked on the first round of the project, I learned that the managers had intentionally decided to keep areas of the test effort separated from one another. Managers perceived that testers working on the domestic, foreign exchange, and general ledger elements of the mission were too busy learning about their own areas of specialty to be able to integrate aspects of other areas. The decision not to automate the spreadsheet had also been conscious. The managers hadn't believed that the there was sufficient time for development (and testing) of testing tools. To the managers, putting a lot of automation into the spreadsheet would have reduced the time available for important tests that needed to get done.

> *Domain learning cost—The cost associated with providing experience or knowledge of a particular business area.*
> *Tooling cost—The cost of developing or adapting tools specialized for a particular testing task.*

In the current round of testing, the focus was on the scripted tests, since the development of those tests was seen as a sunk cost. The tests were presumed to fulfill a specific purpose: to provide guidance to people like the current set of testers, who had been selected and mandated to run scripted tests. The managers reckoned that these testers had neither the time nor the skills to comprehend the business domain, the risks, and the spreadsheets all at once, so the managers perceived domain learning cost and transfer cost to be high. In addition, the mission of the project was primarily to make sure that existing functionality hadn't changed. In that kind of situation, the managers perceived that checking [1] (repeating tests with the primary goal of confirming that what we knew about a product is still true) was more important than testing (performing new tests, or performing old tests in a new way; investigating the product with the primary goal of revealing new information).

The final significant piece of documentation—the one that Rick found for me after a few days—was a small binder of around fifty use cases, with some description of what TellerPlus and its back-end system were supposed to accomplish. Each use case was a description and a single example of a transaction supported by the system. Each started with a customer's desire to move some round-number amount of money from one form to another. Some transaction included a foreign exchange component in terms of a desire to buy and/or sell a particular currency. Each case ended with a desirable set of outputs, specifying the amount of money to be credited to or debited from each of the relevant general ledger accounts. There were no separate cases of extreme or exceptional conditions that would have required error handling, although there was a list of error codes and descriptions as an appendix in the binder. The use cases had evidently informed the contents of the Excel sheet, but the links between the two were identified inconsistently. Some tests included a reference to a particular use case; others didn't.

Why didn't the use cases include extreme or exceptional conditions? Why wasn't there documented traceability between each requirement and each test?

Use cases have many purposes. One goal of a use case is to guide programmers toward creation of a set of functions that will fulfill the business need that the use case represents. It's common for subject matter experts and programmers alike, especially in early stages of development, to focus on creating something that fulfills the central idea of some business task rather than on addressing problems that may arise during the performance of that task. In early days of the project, the aim is to produce something that can work; dealing with how it might not work is often a task left for later. In the middle and later stages of the product, new requirements are being added, implicit requirements are being recognized, old requirements are changing, and problems are being discovered, reported, and fixed. From the way VaultBank and MegaDev looked at it, keeping up with changes in the formal requirements documents tended to be seen as expensive and not worthwhile when compared to the development work needed to complete the project.

> *Traceability cost—The cost associated with developing mechanisms or narratives that link requirements and tests.*
> *Product development cost—The cost of developing, testing, and maintaining the product (as distinct from the cost of testing it after the fact).*
> *Maintenance cost—The cost associated with keeping a document, test, or product current, accurate, and relevant.*

Some of the use cases described behavior that was covered by several tests. Some of the tests (albeit only a handful) explicitly covered implicit requirements that had not been specifically laid out in the use cases. Some of the tests were clearly variations on their predecessors as listed in the spreadsheet. Requiring an explicit link between every requirement and every test would have taken extra time, and would have inhibited probing into new risk ideas as they came up. At crunch time—at least in the earlier round of testing—the testers and managers sensibly preferred investigation of risks and problems over compliance with standards for written documentation.

For me, the situation clearly required a lot of rapid learning and that pointed to a heavily exploratory approach. Maurice, VaultBank's test manager, seemed to be very nervous about that. He seemed concerned that the test cases listed in the Excel sheet should be covered and was adamant that I finish with them before I took on anything of an exploratory nature. I pointed out that exploratory testing didn't mean rejecting previous test ideas, but that it did mean learning about the product, the testing mission, and the test ideas in parallel with one another. I also noted that when we're testing in an exploratory way, learning, test design, and test execution are all happening in tight loops. Although the goal is for those loops to be as tight as possible (sometimes so tight as to be invisible), sometimes we're in a high-learning mode whereas at other times we're in high-search mode. Sometimes our discoveries, our investigation, and our learning lead us off one anticipated path and down another one for a time.

I assured him that I recognized covering the existing test ideas in the time available was central to my mission. I also warned that from time to time, I'd discover problems and follow up on them; that at the beginning of the test cycle I'd be focused on modeling and learning about the product; that progress would sometimes be intermittent and lumpy. Maurice acknowledged this, but he appeared to remain nervous. In particular, he seemed nervous about how to explain exploratory testing to his senior managers and to the bank's auditors.

Exploratory testing affords rapid learning about the product or system under test. Why don't more people use the approach?

Many managers around the world equate exploratory testing with "fooling around with the computer." They see exploratory testing as unstructured, when in fact it can be highly structured; undocumented, when it can be very carefully documented. Nonetheless, the managers perceived exploratory testing to have a much higher recording and supervisory cost than scripted testing. There are other costs, too.

> *Reporting cost—The cost of reporting the testing's status to other members of the project community.*
> *Compliance cost—The cost of demonstrating adherence to corporate policies, audit requirements, regulatory standards, and the like.*

Maurice in particular was wary of exploratory testing, at least in part because he had difficulty envisioning how to observe and report test progress to his senior managers and the rest of the project team. With a scripted testing approach, Maurice could simply report the number of scripted tests performed so far, the number performed today, and the number of tests left to go. From that, he could extrapolate the date when testing could be completed. Lumpy progress made Maurice nervous because it made productivity trends less linear and the completion date for testing less certain.

With Maurice's very tentative consent, I began testing using an exploratory, investigative approach. I diagrammed the structure of the front-end and back-end systems, and reviewed the diagram with the project manager, the architect, the local test manager, and several of the programmers. After each interview, I did a session of interactive testing with the application to challenge my understanding of what I had learned. Sometimes I found a bug. Just as often, I found that I was confused, which prompted a return trip to the interviewee or to Jeremy. I annotated my copy of the binder of use cases with observations, questions, and test ideas. I began loops of reading the sheet, performing some tests, and fixing the sheet.

The first real issue I encountered was that the sheet, as designed, was locked into using a set of exchange rate data that was a year old and therefore out of date. One of VaultBank's programmers had already been assigned to the task of querying another system for tables of real, up-to-date exchange rates. He was completing that work just as I came on to the project. I developed a bit of Excel VBA (Visual Basics for Applications) code to obtain and import the table at the push of a button, and routines to look up those rates to avoid the problem of hard coding. Maurice seemed pleased with that.

Automating the download from the database clearly saved a lot of time and effort, and made the spreadsheet much more flexible and powerful. Why hadn't automatic updating been implemented before?

Although automating the sheet might have reduced the cost of testing, the task took programmer time, and the managers considered programmers' time to be more important than testers' time. Moreover, working on the spreadsheet meant that the programmer had less time available for other tasks.

> Opportunity cost—*The cost of engaging in an activity such that it prevents you from engaging in other activities.*
>
> Support cost—*Costs associated with supporting the work of test group.*

I started into cycles of designing a test, executing it, interpreting it, and learning about the system. I started with some very standard and simple transactions to demonstrate reasonable behavior. Soon I tried submitting some extreme amounts of money. These tests, interestingly, often produced crashes or unexpected error messages. Along the way, I found many problems and inconsistencies in the product. Very few of them seemed to have been anticipated by any of the test ideas I had been given from the previous round of testing.

One problem was fairly mundane. I created a receive-cash transaction in which I entered the maximum accepted data for every field—9,999 five-dollar bills, 9,999 tens, 9,999 twenties, 9,999 fifties, and 9,999 hundreds, plus $9,999.99 in coins. The application immediately crashed, displaying a Java exception error on the screen—surprising, considering the application was written in Visual Basic. According to Rick, the local test lead, this was a corner case—"no user would ever do that"—but it led me to wonder where "normal" cases ended and "corner" cases began in VaultBank's usage models. I also wondered why this problem had not been noticed before. Maybe it had, but it hadn't been logged. Or if it had been logged, no one could find it in the bug database.

The crash was trigged by a very basic example of a boundary test. Why hadn't the problem been noticed before? Why wasn't the bug in the bug tracking database? Why did Rick give such a dismissive answer?

Before busy people undertake any activity, there typically needs to be some justification for that activity. The busier people are, and the more productive they appear to be, the harder it will be to justify spending time to pause and reflect. Rick's response was quite reasonable, on the face of it: there was clearly no business case in which a teller would ever accept a couple million dollars in cash. It would have cost him time and effort to take the problem seriously, to report it, and to explain why the problem hadn't been found earlier. (Eventually, he did report it to the programmers, and it did get fixed.)

A scripted testing approach—and a culture that rewards executing scripts over investigation—tends to drive testers away from finding problems. Testers who are under pressure to get test cases completed have a disincentive for exploring risks outside the test cases. After the initial round of test design, the mandate to execute tests may be far more powerful than the mandate to review the extents and limitations of the existing test suite. So the simplest and most likely explanation for the bug not being noticed was that there was no test case for it.

Perhaps the bug had been noticed but lost in the database somehow. As a project progresses, it generates more artifacts. Storing artifacts requires a library, organizing things in a library such that they can be found requires curatorship, and curatorship comes with a cost. A bug database needs attention and maintenance, and the larger it becomes, the harder it is to maintain.

> *Analysis cost—The cost of revisiting and reviewing existing models, test plans, and test ideas.*
>
> *Curatorship cost—The cost of creating, saving, maintaining, updating, sorting, and searching for artifacts and historical information about the product.*

Anything that we do in testing—including analysis and review—takes time and effort. Review of the test strategy is testing, but it isn't test execution. In the previous year's project, getting all of the prescribed tests performed by the project deadline had been the clear management priority for both MegaDev and VaultBank. Any activity other than test execution would have had an impact on management's perception of productivity. MegaDev teams tended to be dissolved at the end of the project. What would have been the point of retaining costly contractors for a retrospective when the managers and team members wouldn't be working together again anyway?

With respect to curatorship, the managers kept the cost of testing lower by deciding that important information would be retained by the people who needed it, in their own heads, and on their own hard drives, and that not-so-important information wasn't worth retaining. All the information that testers would need in the future was in the test scripts.

Another problem was marginally more interesting; I occasionally observed what seemed to be miscalculations, but I wasn't able to reproduce the problem. I reported it as a "Flying Dutchman" problem—intermittent sightings followed by lengthy disappearances. Several days passed, and I found myself at my own bank, observing tellers just like the people who would use TellerPlus. They were all using their keyboards for data entry, whereas the testers, including me, mostly used the mouse. When I returned to the test lab, I put my mouse aside and used the tab key to navigate the application. The miscalculations came back immediately. I noticed that because of an incorrect tab order, TellerPlus was resetting a particular field near the bottom of the screen without my noticing it. Interestingly, tab order problems had been reported before, but were marked "cosmetic, low priority" in the bug-tracking system.

Tab order is an easy problem to fix. Why not fix it?

> *Gold-plating cost—A form of development cost in which the application is decorated or polished for cosmetic purposes.*
>
> *Advocacy cost—The cost associated with investigating a problem and constructing a story that shows the problem in its most meaningful and significant light.*
>
> *Mitigation cost—The cost of addressing problems that manifest themselves either in development or in the field.*

Most people assume that addressing a problem will cost some amount of development time and effort, even if the fix is cheap. But there's an even cheaper way to fix a problem: you can ignore it. That is, you can decide that either the person observing the problem or the problem itself doesn't matter.

In large corporations, most development groups don't care about cosmetics for internal applications. As Joel Spolsky has pointed out, there's no money in it [2]. To the corporation, the program is just a tool and doesn't have to look pretty for the internal users. Until I reported the consequences of the problem, the bank's testers and the contract testers alike had thought of tab order as being a trivial cosmetic detail. The contract between MegaDev and VaultBank didn't mention anything specific about tab order. MegaDev would have cheerfully declared the fix to be an enhancement request (and implemented it for a fee), and the bank was understandably reluctant to reopen negotiations. Ignoring the problem was an easy way to lower the cost of development. VaultBank's managers reasoned that any problem in a transaction would be spotted quickly at a minor inconvenience for the bank and the customer. The tab order business was an annoyance, perhaps, but tellers are well-trained people who would notice that the field has been reset and would mitigate the problem at no cost.

The trouble with this argument, of course, is that people use software at various levels of training, skill, and awareness. Indeed, one job of software is to reduce cognitive load on the user. We'd like to believe that software users are always capable of spotting a problem and always paying attention to what they're doing, but they're not. It's unrealistic to expect tellers to spot a problem in their data when so much of it goes flying by them [3]. Similarly, scripted testers were under pressure to execute test cases and didn't have time for investigation and bug advocacy [4]. In my bug report, I provided a scenario that showed how easy it was to overlook the problem, such that it incurred a financial risk to the bank. At that point the development team finally took the "cosmetic" bug seriously.

As I explored, I found more problems, many of which didn't appear in the bug tracking system. In one of our occasional chats, Maurice expressed surprise that I was consistently finding problems that had not been revealed by previous tests or by the help desk. He asked, "How is it that you can do that?" I explained that part of the exploratory approach involved continually asking new questions and performing new tests rather than repeating tests that had been run before. I also noted that users of software often find their own workarounds to problems; maybe TellerPlus's users had experienced problems but hadn't bothered calling the help desk. Meanwhile, support staff members often put priority on addressing problems for their clients rather than on recording or reporting those problems to the development team. I couldn't confirm this; I never met nor conversed with a member of the support staff.

The cost of testing can be greatly reduced by providing access to information. Why weren't there close connections between the testers and the support staff?

It's common for managers to measure the productivity of support staff by measuring the number of problems that have been fielded and closed. It's less common for support staff to be rewarded for bringing a problem to the attention of the development team.

> Interruption cost—*The cost associated with diversions from the principal business task, including the cost of breaking and restoring flow.*

When support staff escalates a problem, they interrupt themselves from the measured task of handling support calls. Not only that, but a problem report represents an interruption for the development team as well. VaultBank maintained support productivity and reduced development cost by severely restricting the flow of information between groups.

About halfway through the ten-week test cycle, a new tester, Sandy, was added to VaultBank's internal test team. She was an ex-teller with considerable experience who had been reassigned to a testing job. She hadn't been trained at all in testing. She knew how to spot problems that would affect a teller's effectiveness, and she was good at that. Yet she often had a hard time investigating those problems on a technical level. Moreover, because the problems she found were related neither to the test scripts nor to specific requirements in the use cases or other supporting documents, she also had difficulty deciding what problems she should report and how she should report them.

Dealing with her questions cost time and effort for everyone on the project. Why had she not received training in testing?

For the bank, testing was a clerical activity that didn't require much training at all. Better still, Sandy had domain knowledge and experience with the product being tested, and so (the thinking went) she could be more productive even more quickly than a contractor. It might have been a better idea to pair her with an experienced tester for a while, but pairing made the measurement of individual progress more difficult. Besides, in the managers' view, there wasn't much learning required to run through test scripts.

A few weeks into the project, I was summoned for a meeting with Dennis and Maurice. Maurice was concerned: although I had been reporting many interesting bugs, it seemed as though I hadn't been as productive as the other testers. My test case completion rate to that point, as detailed in the day sheets, was something like two or three test cases per day. The other testers, working from the test scripts, had got started into test execution straight away and were making progress, finishing between fifteen and twenty-five scripted tests per day.

Or rather it appeared that they were making progress. By and large they were running through actions specified in the scripts, but I saw no evidence that they were understanding or testing TellerPlus on anything other than a shallow level. Indeed, the scripts—and the pressure from management to complete them—seemed to have relieved the testers of any desire to comprehend the application. Yet as they walked through the scripts they maintained an illusion of progress that reflected unfavorably on me, which left me with some explaining to do.

In a forty-five-minute meeting, I noted the problems that I had needed to resolve in the spreadsheet—and that I had resolved many of them. I pointed out that piecework-style measurement didn't work with an exploratory approach (although I resisted the impulse to say that it doesn't really work with a scripted approach either). I emphasized the fact that I was learning about the product in a way that would make later test execution go more quickly. I also remarked that the previous day I had managed a breakthrough that would allow me to work through thirty of the test ideas in a single day. If I were able to accomplish thirty new tests today, would that help to relieve the concern? The project manager and the test manager agreed that it would, so that's what I did. The breakthrough had been real, but there was another factor that let me work at top speed: those thirty test ideas were all variations on what was essentially the same transaction. The only thing that varied was the amount of money involved in the transaction, which ranged from zero (intended to force an error) through a wide range of valid amounts (intended to show that the foreign exchange rate was calculated correctly) and over the maximum boundary to the minimum invalid amount. For extra points, that day I was able to perform another set of forced-error tests that were highly similar to each other. Each test involved a sale or purchase of a currency whose exchange rate was so low or so high that transactions generated errors and exceptions due to overflows of some intermediate calculation. All of these tests produced the anticipated error messages.

Why repeat tests (or minor variations on them) that don't reveal new information? And why weren't the managers measuring progress in a more discerning way?

If you reduce variation in the structure of tests themselves, they can be easily adapted into new tests. In this way, the test designers were able to produce more tests at a lower cost.

> *Adaptation cost—The cost of changing some factor(s) of a test to create a different test.*

Moreover, tests that are similar to one another can, in general, be performed more quickly and easily than tests that require a lot of variation. When tests are more similar to one another, designers and managers don't have to do as much work to demonstrate that two tests represent the same amount of effort.

> *Measurement cost—The cost of gathering observations of attributes of events or objects, and applying them according to a quantitative model or theory with the intention of describing them [5].*

For testers who wish to introduce a more exploratory approach, there's a challenge: explaining exploratory testing costs time. Managers are often told that you can't manage what you can't measure, and they're often under pressure to make and justify decisions. Consequently, managers generally find it much easier to account for progress on a piecework basis, and test cases have a straightforward, intuitive appeal that fits the bill admirably. Other forms of measurement require more complex models and are harder to explain to the project community and senior managers. When a tester discovers a problem through an exploratory test, managers who use a simplified model of testing are likely to ask difficult questions: Why wasn't this problem found earlier? Why didn't the tester simply do what he was told? How do we change our scripted tests to find a problem like this? Answering such questions requires the skill of test framing—the ability to draw a set of coherent logical connections between the mission of testing and the interpretation of the test result [6]. Framing a test might include ideas on the oracles used, the coverage obtained, the risks addressed, the cost–value trade-offs considered, and justifications for each. In my experience, many testers are not well versed in this skill. If they were, managers might be more inclined to extend trust and relax control.

All in all, it took me the better part of seven weeks to untangle the sheet, to learn how to use the application, to learn about the business domain, and to test the ideas expressed in the first column of the sheet, such that I could call the testing "complete" with respect to those test ideas. The scripted testers finished their work at about the same time. I had reported more problems (and more severe problems) in the product than the five scripted testers had reported.

Why would VaultBank or MegaDev continue to use an approach that requires more people, finds fewer problems, and takes more time?

As I've already noted, there are significant costs associated with introducing—or even explaining—exploratory testing. But let's answer that question a little later.

With three weeks left in my contract and no more prescribed test cases to complete, Maurice approached me and—apparently—having gained confidence in my approaches, asked me if I would continue with exploratory testing. At the time, I didn't believe that I could discover many more problems in the product, and I was concerned that pending changes to the code might invalidate the results of further tests.

However, I had an idea that I thought might be more useful. While testing, I had spent a lot of time trying to identify and calculate exchange rates and money flows using formulas crafted as special cases for each test. I had wanted a fast, generalized oracle—something that, given any transaction or a scenario, would help determine whether the rates and flows were correct. Such an oracle would have been able to aggregate the results of many transactions over several days. This would have taken my testing into batch processing flows that represented different (and riskier) areas.

I had a ready-made starting point: the transaction sheets from the unused Elegant Workbook. However, Dennis (MegaDev's project manager) assured me that an Excel-based oracle couldn't be built; he had tried to create one and had abandoned the effort. I pointed out that developing the oracle—even if I were unsuccessful—would afford me the opportunity to do more exploration of TellerPlus and its problem space, just as Maurice had asked. Since there appeared to be nothing else for me to do for the following three weeks, Dennis and Maurice gave me the mandate to develop the oracle.

I had some experience with Excel and with VBA programming but had not used it to the extent that I would need for this project. I started with the Elegant Workbook, since it already incorporated many factors of transactions. Each worksheet listed general ledger accounts to be credited and debited. The workbook already had several sample customers and bank accounts, and the data associated with them could be plugged into pick lists. Using the live foreign exchange table and routines that I had programmed earlier, I could automatically calculate appropriate exchange rates by concatenating currency and transaction codes, and then using lookups and a bit of math to select the appropriate rate from the table.

The tricky part was figuring out how to apply the business rules to credit and debit the right accounts. I soon discovered Excel's array formulas, a phenomenally powerful way to aggregate calculations. At first, I started with some basic Boolean logic statements to determine when and where to apply the appropriate rules, but I soon found out that this didn't work. After a day and a half of trying to figure it out, I still couldn't understand why.

I went to the local bookstore and perused a few books on Excel. One noted that due to a bug in the version of Excel that the bank provided, Boolean functions (AND, OR, NOT, XOR) simply didn't work in array formulas. I'd have to figure this out without the help of the built-in functions. I bought the book [7] and took it with me when I went to work.

Why had I spent a day and a half on trying to understand the problem before I reached for other resources? When you have staff working on a multimillion-dollar development project, why not give them authority to spend forty dollars on a book that would help them do their jobs more efficiently?

When I discovered that I was unable to do what I wanted with Excel, I assumed that the problem was with my code. I was happy to experiment for a while in order to understand the problem, since investigation and experimentation can help to fix a problem or refine a solution, and I had ample disposable time. Disposable time is the time you can afford to invest while being self-managed without being noticed or getting into trouble—and disposable time is rarely wasted unless you reject any learning from the experience. I had obtained some credibility with Maurice, and the pressure was off the testers to execute test cases, and so I was able to allocate time to try to figure out the problem. When I got stuck, I wrote off the investment in time and money, sought other resources, and ended up buying the book. (I still have it, and I still refer to it.)

> *Investigation cost—The time and effort associated with researching and understanding an observed problem.*
>
> *Experimentation cost—The time and effort required to design, set up, perform, and analyze tests such that you might learn something.*
>
> *Resourcing cost—The cost of seeking and obtaining resources that allow you to perform your job more quickly and efficiently.*
>
> *Education cost—Costs associated with training or reference materials.*
>
> *Justification cost—The cost of explaining actions or expenditures.*

VaultBank may have had a training budget or even a petty cash fund for employee purchases, but money spent on contractors would have been wasted from the bank's perspective. To VaultBank, learning resources for contractors were MegaDev's responsibility. To MegaDev, learning resources were clearly the contractors' responsibility. These policies kept costs down for both organizations. It's common for managers to have to explain their expenditures to their superiors or to the auditors. It's much less common for them to have to explain why they didn't *spend money.*

Figuring out how to apply the business rules was quite challenging. Some were simple, and others involved several intricate conditional calculations. Starting with the simple ones, I implemented each rule one by one. Because of the Excel bug, I had to learn to express Boolean operators in terms of arithmetical operations, which was interesting. Often when I programmed a new rule, there were side effects that broke previous rules, so retesting was very important. After a couple weeks of development, some things about the business domain were puzzling, even to Jeremy the business analyst. Rules that were difficult to understand pointed to risks in TellerPlus, so I did extra testing around those risks.

Late in my development effort, I found one bug to be particularly interesting. I devised a test scenario that involved multiple transactions and multiple foreign currencies, which required a conversion into an intermediate domestic currency. Depending upon the sequence in which the transaction was performed, there was a difference of up to 10 percent in VaultBank's profit. Done in one sequence, the customer got a bargain and the bank didn't make as much money as it could have; in another, the bank made a more reasonable profit; and in a third, the customer paid extra to the bank's benefit. In the field, TellerPlus would allow the teller to work through the scenario in any order he chose, but the use cases and tests prescribed only one path. I raised this issue with Maurice. He responded that this was a training issue. I was surprised; here was a multimillion-dollar piece of software that could have easily calculated an optimal sequence, whether "optimal" meant a solution that favored VaultBank, that favored the customer, or that was balanced between the two. A teller, no matter what level of training, would not likely be able to determine the optimal order, and never as quickly and as accurately as TellerPlus could have done. However, the scenario hadn't been specified, and MegaDev considered the problem to be outside the scope of the development project. VaultBank agreed.

> *Epiphany cost—The cost of dealing with new information that has been revealed or recognized during development and testing.*

Testing is a process of discovery, and some discoveries lead to new problems. As someone once said, once you've opened a can of worms, putting them back requires a bigger can. It would have been interesting to see what more senior managers might have thought of the discrepancies. From the managers' point of view, further inquiry might have exposed issues in VaultBank's requirements development, in MegaDev's architecture for the product, and in the process of test planning and design. It was easier for everyone who knew about the problem to put it aside and depend on the variable behavior of tellers to even things out.

After three weeks I had produced a tool that was very close to what I had envisioned. I had combined the original Excel spreadsheet with the Elegant Workbook to produce a reasonable oracle for the money flows for all the use cases. Testers could update exchange rates at a keystroke, duplicate the master sheet, enter one or more transactions representing a scenario, and observe the results for individual scenarios, or a rolled up daily or weekly balance sheet. I carefully documented the application. I included a glossary, a description of how to use the tool, and notes on some of its limitations. I also included a detailed description of some of the concepts that a tester might need in order to understand rapidly how transactions at the bank worked. Most important, I included my contact information so that anyone who wanted to use the tool would be able to get support on it. My testing of the tool had shown that there were a few minor problems (most of which cropped up when one tried to feed the oracle an invalid transaction), but nothing that I wouldn't be able to resolve remotely.

No one ever called or wrote. I can't imagine that there were no problems with the oracle.

So was the oracle simply a make-work project? Had Maurice simply been placating me? I had learned a remarkable amount; why didn't the bank take advantage of it and use what I had written?

> *Bench cost—The cost of allowing potentially productive paid employees to be seen as doing nothing. (This automatically incurs additional justification cost.)*
>
> *Dithering cost—The personal and organizational cost of being perceived as an individual or organization that is unable to make a decision.*

Note that there's a difference between doing nothing and being seen to do nothing. Even if Maurice hadn't been willing to put the oracle to work, letting me work on the oracle was easier for him. The alternatives—given that I might be seen to do nothing, or given that I might do something actively and find no important bugs—were risky. For Dennis, there was potential embarrassment in having hired testers for too long. Meanwhile, the story that I might be working on a testing tool—even if it were never used—could be easy to justify.

In addition, transfer cost (mentioned earlier) affects a number of people; not just the transferer and the transferee, but also the managers who are responsible for allocating time for the transfer.

By way of an epilogue, a couple of years later I was chatting with a long-time friend who worked for a test outsourcing firm. We realized that we had been doing work for the same bank, he a year later than I. We then realized that we had been working on the same application, too. His assignment? To take that stack of confirmatory test cases (or as I've noted before, checks) that the other testers had been using for TellerPlus and translate them into automated checks at the graphical user interface (GUI) level, using a standard and very expensive GUI automation tool that happened to have serious functional problems of its own. He had found his task quite difficult in that that TellerPlus had not been designed to be automation-friendly. He had had to implement various hacks to automate the manual scripted checks. He remarked that to him the checks as specified weren't terribly useful. By now they were even more out of date, and even more inconsistent with the application as it had evolved. Worse, he found them to be safe, confirmatory, trivial, happy-path tests that didn't exercise the application to its extremes, and thus were very unlikely to reveal a problem, especially since the programmers had become increasingly diligent about unit test coverage. He was reasonably certain that test automation could be applied more effectively and inexpensively below the GUI level, and could thereby exercise business rules with more precision. He had repeatedly remarked on all this to his own managers, to MegaDev's managers, and to VaultBank's managers, but to no avail: they wanted these test cases automated.

He also reported that he had had to figure out how to translate the business logic from the use cases into program code. I asked him if he had seen the oracle that I had developed, which would have provided him with a leg up. No, he said; no one had ever told him a thing about it.

Why would the managers have been so enthusiastic about automating all these checks? Why the expensive GUI tool? Why had no one given him access to the oracle? Had everyone forgotten about it? Did they not understand how valuable it would be for him?

After two or three cycles of development and testing, a new set of managers had arrived. To this group, test execution was still paramount, and testing was still checking. Since the product was in maintenance phase, they perceived that the biggest risk was not in new functionality (there wasn't any) but in breaking existing functionality for which tests already existed. They reckoned that since the activities described by the test scripts were trivial, human testers could be replaced by automation, and that automated scripted tests could be run more quickly and less expensively than manual scripted tests. They compared the cost of the tool and the programmer to the cost of several testers but apparently didn't recognize the extent to which GUI test automation is a software development project of its own. Having spent the money on the expensive tool, they were reluctant to stop using it and kill the project.

And my answer is almost certainly yes: everyone had forgotten about the oracle.

* * *

Through the course of this story, I've identified several cost factors for testing and for other aspects of development. Many of the decisions that people made in this story might seem costly to you based on the factors that I've identified and your own experience. Yet for the managers, the decisions were perfectly rational and justifiable in terms of their vision of a high-quality development project.

If you disagree, that's natural, based on Jerry Weinberg's definition of quality: *Quality is value to some person(s)* [8].

Weinberg's definition of quality is a special case of a pattern that I call the relative rule: For any abstract X, X is X to some person, at some time [9].

People like to think of cost as something that is absolutely and clearly measurable in terms of money, time, or effort, or some combination of the three. These measures seem convenient, because they're relatively easy to quantify, and they might even come with a patina of objectivity. Yet it's important to note that neither time, nor money, nor effort stand alone; they're always related to one another, and they're always relative to some person at some point in history. Anything can appear cheap when you plot cost or value over time, and then look at a small enough section of the curve. Moreover, quantitative measurements of time, effort, and money are always relative to some model or construct. Numbers might be applied to a model "objectively," but the models and the functions that apply numbers to objects or events are always designed or chosen by some person(s) for some purpose(s). As such, the "objective" numbers are anything but objective. Like all quantitative measures, costs can be subject to enormous problems of construct validity [10].

In my travels, I've observed that people often discount, dismiss, or ignore things that they do not measure quantitatively. For example, throughout the story, I didn't mention anything at all about something that is quite hard to quantify: the *value* of testing. My omission was deliberate. In fact, I carefully avoided using the word *value*. Did you notice? Failure to talk about—or even to consider—the value of testing is a common pattern in most of the large organizations that I've worked with.

Identifying the factors of value for testing is an important job that, for now, I'll leave as an exercise for you [11]. If you go through the exercise, though, you'll likely notice that the value of testing is neither easily quantifiable nor quickly realized. Testing's value is in learning about the product, and especially about risks and threats to its value, so that at least some of the risks that we discover can be addressed. Any story about how a risk might have manifested is, by nature, speculative. Ironically, the more effective your development and testing effort, the less you and your organization will ever know about the impact of the problems that testing has helped to prevent. The relatively uneventful transition between New Year's Eve 1999 and New Year's Day 2000 is a case in point. No disasters happened, but what disasters were avoided? At best, we can only guess what some of the consequences of a Y2K failure might have been. Moreover, in cases where a plausible disaster was prevented, people would be unlikely to talk about it because of three cost factors are rarely discussed, and that I've glossed over until now:

> *Psychological cost—Costs associated with handling our mental and emotional reactions to some situation, or to a change in it.*
> *Political cost—Costs associated with the exercise, balancing, and defense of power and reputation.*
> *Cognitive cost—Costs associated with recognizing or adapting the way we think, take in information, impart meaning, and identify significance.*

Software and development projects are *systems*. A system is a set of things in meaningful relationship to each other. In the latter half of the twentieth century, people from many disciplines began to examine general systems—patterns of structure, variation, and behavior common to all systems. Weinberg called general systems thinking "the science of simplification" [12].

One of the basic principles of systems is that any change to some element of a system must cause a change in at least one other element if the system is to remain stable rather than exploding or collapsing. If you decide that you're going to focus on skill in your test group, you will need to hire skilled testers, or you'll need to train and nurture the testers you have. If you decide to reduce the cost of test execution by scripting, you will likely need to increase the cost of preparing and maintaining the scripts. If you decide to introduce an exploratory approach into an organization that already uses a heavily scripted approach, you will increase reporting cost, even though the value of the information being reported is likely to go up.

If you want to reduce the cost of testing in any one dimension, know this: no matter what happens, you're going to destabilize the current system. The system you've got now, as messed up as it may seem, must have been working for somebody at some time, or it wouldn't be as it is. In Kenneth Boulding's famous words, "Things are the way they are because they got that way." When you reduce the cost of development and testing in one dimension, some other dimension (and typically more than one) must adjust. Somebody—and quite possibly everybody—will have to change something about what they do, what they pay, or how they think. There is an enormous psychological cost in dealing with change, even if it's eventually change for the better. Experts are invested in their expertise [13], as McLuhan said, and current expertise is based the way things are now, or on the way they used to be.

The managers of the TellerPlus project had a set of working models that told them that testing is a linear task list rather than an iterative, interactive, social process with lots of loops. They believed that testing is something that happens at the end of the project, at the GUI level, instead of seeing that testing as a process of exploration, discovery, investigation, and learning that continues at every level throughout the project. They believed that "to test" meant "to execute tests," such that testing is essentially piecework and that progress can be easily measured. Their models focused them on easily quantifiable measures of cost that dominated more abstract considerations of value. They continued to invest money in a near-valueless automation project, because the political cost of acknowledging a bad decision and killing the project was higher than the monetary cost of continuing to pay for it until it was completed [14]. When questioned, the managers might have acknowledged that testing isn't really as simple as all that. But what costs would those managers have to pay to trade their simplified model of testing for a set of more complex models?

However you approach some cost reduction, you are going to have to deal with the cognitive, psychological, and political costs of change. For example, a tester might propose a reduction in the cost of system testing by asking management to mandate the programmers to write more or better unit tests. When we ask for programmers to do this, *we are asking them to do more work.* Oh, there's a lot of talk in the books and the magazines and at conferences that more unit tests will result in less work in the long run, and most of that talk is probably true. But good luck in getting the programmers to see it that way, especially at first. Any requirement to do better testing comes with the implicit message that their work hasn't been as good as they might have hoped or imagined. A mandate to change will require many programmers to alter their customary way of working. They will be required to produce running, tested features, which will come at the cost of a perceived drop in productivity. The programmers will be asked to accept responsibility for that and to justify it. Meanwhile, managers have, for years, cheerfully accepted not-running, untested features. Their model of software development says: you gather requirements that cover most of the work that needs to be done; you ask programmers for an estimated schedule, and then mandate them to deliver code to meet aggressive deadlines; you expect code that doesn't quite work (based on requirements that weren't quite perfect); you test the product for a little while; you find a passel of problems; and you fix the most important ones. After that you release the product and wait for problem reports to come back from the field. Managers who follow this model will be dismayed when the programmers start asking for more time to unit test their code. That part of the change won't feel like progress for the managers.

Harder still, the group's investment in more and better unit tests won't pay off for a while. There will be a learning curve and an adoption curve, and there will probably be some backsliding and stutter steps. A body of code that is heavily unit tested now may not be released until several weeks from now. If there's reduction in testing and support costs, those reductions are not likely to be realized until many months from now.

Whenever you try to reduce the cost of testing, the political, psychological, and cognitive costs—and a perception of the slower pace of release—will be experienced immediately by many people. Meanwhile, any benefits of the change take time to work their way through the system. If everything goes well, you'll reap the reward of change later; but you always pay significant costs up front.

NOTES

1. See http://www.developsense.com/blog/2009/08/testing-vs-checking
2. Joel Spolsky, *Joel on Software* (Berkeley: Apress, 2004, ISBN 978-1590593899) p. 124.
3. For a more chilling example of unawareness, see this story about patients being over-radiated by CT scanners: Walt Bogandich, "After Stroke Scans, Patients Face Serious Health Risks," *New York Times* (New York, July 31, 2010). http://www.nytimes.com/2010/08/01/health/01radiation.html?_r=1.
4. Cem Kaner and James Bach, *Black Box Software Testing "Bug Advocacy."* http://www.testingeducation.org/BBST/#tab4.
5. Cem Kaner and Walter P. Bond, "Software Engineering Metrics: What Do They Measure and How Do We Know?" *10th International Software Metrics Symposium*, Chicago, 2004. http://www.kaner.com/pdfs/metrics2004.pdf. My description of

measurement cost here is influenced by Kaner and Bond's definition of measurement: "The empirical, objective assignment of numbers, based on a model or theory, to attributes of objects or events with the intention of describing them."

6. Michael Bolton, "Test Framing". http://www.developsense.com/resources/TestFraming .pdf, May 2010.

7. John Walkenbach, *Excel 2000 Formulas* (New York: M&T Books, 1999, ISBN 9780764546099).

8. Gerald M. Weinberg, *Quality Software Management, Vol. 1 Systems Thinking* (New York: Dorset House, 1991, ISBN 978-0932633729).

9. Michael Bolton, in Fiona Charles (ed.) *The Gift of Time: Celebrating the Work of Gerald M. Weinberg* (New York: Dorset House, 2008, ISBN 978-0932633750). I first named the Relative Rule in this book. I've since then I've added "at some time." I'm particularly indebted to Jerry Weinberg for inspiring this idea.

10. See Kaner and Bond "Software Engineering Metrics" (see Note 5) for a detailed discussion of measurements and models in software engineering. Also see Gerald M. Weinberg, *Quality Software Management, Vol. 2 First-Order Measurement* (New York: Dorset House, 1993, ISBN 978-0932633248). For an excellent discussion on threats to measurement validity, see William R. Shadish, Thomas D. Cook, and Donald T. Campell, *Experimental and Quasi-Experimental Designs for Generalized Causal Inference* (Florence, KY: Wadsworth Publishing, 2001, ISBN 978-0395615560).

11. If you're stuck, the Black Box Software Testing course (see Note 4) identifies a number of dimensions of the value of a test that might help get you unstuck. Other chapters in this book discuss some of the aspects of testing's value, too.

12. Gerald M. Weinberg, *An Introduction to General Systems Thinking (Silver Anniversary Edition)* (New York: Dorset House, 2001) p. 8.

13. Marshall McLuhan and Barrington Nevitt, *Take Today: The Executive As Dropout* (New York: Harcourt Brace Jovanovich, 1972, 978-0151878307).

14. Gerald M. Weinberg, "Overstructured Models of Software Engineering" in Tom DeMarco and Tim Lister (eds.), *Software State of the Art: Selected Papers* (New York: Dorset House 1990).

Part 2

What Should We Do?

7

Test Readiness:
Be Ready to Test When the
Software Is Ready to Be Tested

Ed Barkley

> Doing things right the first time adds nothing to the cost of your product
> or service. Doing things wrong is what costs you.
>
> **—Inspired by Philip Crosby, *Quality Is Free* (1980)**

7.1 A SCENARIO

It's Monday at 8 a.m., and the test team will begin testing at any moment. All eyes are on testing as they expect to be notified that the build is ready. The test manager has assured everyone that the team is ready to proceed when the test environment is up. The release manager finishes migrating the software and gives everyone the thumbs up to proceed. The first tester logs in and receives an access violation error message. Another tester notices the bar code scanner he's testing has a hardware fault. A third tester can't locate a required database. Testing halts while the managers discuss what's going on. The test team takes a break. Several hours later, management announces that a major upgrade must be applied to the test environment. Testing will probably be delayed three days while operations completes the required maintenance.

It's Thursday and everything appears to be ready again. Testing is now three days behind schedule. With the environment problems solved, the testers start anew. One tester receives repeated error messages on an interface; his test cases don't match the expected behavior of the application. The test manager asks the release manager about this, and she indicates she updated the application on Tuesday and didn't communicate this to the test team. The managers stop the testing and the test team spends the majority of the day updating over fifty test scripts. At 5 p.m. everyone goes home.

It's Friday, with the testing schedule now delayed four days, the test team begins again with renewed vigor. Testing proceeds relatively well during the day. The test team reports many errors in one developer's code during the following Monday morning's test status meeting. Everyone points fingers until they notice there are major differences between the requirements the developer used and the version the test team has. After some comparisons, everyone agrees the failed tests resulted when someone changed or eliminated some of the requirements but failed to communicate this to the test team. The team updates the test scripts and reruns the affected tests. This adds further expense since particular testers have to work overtime to get back on schedule.

Many other errors and delays occur because of erroneous data in the databases and the data in the scripts. At critical times during testing, the test manager doesn't refresh the databases correctly and tests are rerun. Things are getting somewhat out of control when the users decide to change the requirements. The test manager is unable to update the databases or scripts quickly and testing is further delayed until everything can be resynchronized.

The company recently installed a new third-party test tool to speed testing. Some of the testers experience difficulties using it and they discover operations did not install a necessary patch. Upon further investigation, management reports that the patch won't be available for several weeks due to a disagreement with the application's vendor. To keep testing on schedule, the test manager decides to work around this difficulty with a manual approach. This will get the job done, at the expense of extending testing in this particular area by one to two weeks.

Given all the delays, the testing schedule is getting very tight. The test manager wants every available tester on board and banging away on their keyboards. It's summer: vacations are coming up and she brings in backups to fill the vacated slots. She soon realizes the new testers aren't familiar enough with the test scripts or the applications. The backups run the tests in the wrong sequence, log erroneous bugs, or miss valid defects entirely. The test manager delays testing while she trains the new testers.

The company recently installed a new bug tracking system. As testers discover issues, they enter them in the system and it generates reports for the following morning's test status meeting. Problems start surfacing several weeks into testing when management asks for improvements to the way the information is being presented. The upgrades cause changes to the information the testers are required to enter and this disrupts the testing process. The test team eventually completes all testing and the release manager migrates the application to the production environment—six weeks past the originally schedule date.

The following morning, the help desk reports a spike in user calls about the application. They don't have enough information to satisfactorily handle the calls. They ask the team to at least provide a list of the known issues, when they would be fixed, and workarounds they could advise the users to take. Without the skills to get this information directly out of the new bug tracker, the project and test managers organize an emergency meeting and work late into the evening to develop a list manually.

During a project retrospective, management points out that in spite of testing having its test scripts prepared and ready to go, other factors outside its direct control impeded progress. Testing did a relatively good job of managing test risks but needed to step back and team up with the project manager to help manage risks to the project as a whole.

7.2 PREPARATION AND PLANNING FOR SOFTWARE TESTING

My past experiences as a quality assurance and test manager (two separate roles) taught me the value of good planning and preparation, especially in managing the risks of unforeseen issues, examples of which we see in the previous scenario. The team experienced problems in the test environment, configuration and change management processes, documentation, data, test tools, testers, and issue management. All of these issues are very real. In my current consulting practice, I see examples of this almost every day. What you do to minimize their impact on your projects can spell the difference between delivering within-budget, on-time quality software and experiencing project delays, cost overruns, and dissatisfied stakeholders.

Good planning can save you money. It's relatively easy to plan test cases to validate the software; it's quite another to address unexpected issues that you don't believe to be your responsibility. Believe this—if it can impact your testing, you've got to be proactive and get ahead of it to minimize this impact. You may not have direct responsibility to manage an area, but you can work collaboratively with those that do to help ensure project success. If it impacts you, guess what? You'll bear the responsibility to help figure out a way around it.

7.3 OBJECTIVES

The objectives of this chapter are to show you

1. seven distinct areas that you need to focus on to identify risks to testing,
2. how to prioritize your efforts on those areas to maximize your effectiveness, and
3. an approach you can take with a simple checklist to manage these risks and control your test costs.

This will take a holistic approach, looking at the whole range of issues you must address to fulfill your responsibilities. If you think you're ready just because the team has test cases ready, look at the range of obstacles the testers experienced in the previous scenario, beyond just the tests they were running. I'll first review the areas you should be concerned with and recommend a prioritization approach. With that background, we'll be better prepared to dive into the checklist approach.

7.3.1 Areas of Concern

1. Environment—The particular system hardware, PCs, monitors, and test fixtures as well as the installed system software that are critical to this project's testing effort.
2. Configuration and change management—The control of changes made to hardware, software, firmware, data and databases, documentation, test tools/fixtures, and test documentation throughout the project's life cycle.
3. Documentation—This is the totality of requirements, test plans, traceability matrices, models, use cases, user stories, test scenarios, cases, and scripts that make up the bulk of any test team's documents.
4. Data—There are two areas of "data" to be concerned with: (a) databases (such as the "golden database"), and (b) the data referenced in

the test scripts. The golden database is explained in further detail later, but basically it's a microcosm of the business's major files against which test cases apply. At periodic times during testing, it is used to refresh the testing environment, thus the term *golden*.

5. Test tools—These can be simple scripting tools such as macros, capture/playback tools used for regression testing, load and stress testing software, simulators, and tracking tools.

6. Testers—One of the most critical areas in testing is the identification, qualification, assignment, and scheduling of testers as well as the training they must receive in the use of the tools and test scripts.

7. Issue management—This area involves tools and processes for the entry and speedy retrieval, viewing, reporting, routing, and resolution of test issues. These can be anything from a simple Excel spreadsheet to any number of more sophisticated tracking and reporting tools.

7.3.2 Recommended Prioritization Methodology

My prioritization approach is to ask the following two questions for each of the seven areas outlined in the previous section:

1. What is the probability of an event occurring in each area?
2. What would be the impact of that event on your project?

7.3.2.1 Probability

For example, in your current organization or for your specific project, how likely is it that you will have environmental issues similar to those in the scenario? Every organization is different. Is your information technology (IT) department well organized? Do they follow industry best practices? For example, IT may be operating at a high CMMI level 5 (Capability Maturity Model Integrated 5) [1], so the chances of an event occurring could be very low. Conversely, everything about the development process may be setting off alarm bells, with high variations both in process and individual performance, thus increasing the chance of issues occurring.

7.3.2.2 Impact

Each area varies in its impact. Are there frequent hardware issues in your organization that shut down development for hours or days? That's big impact! Problems with documentation might not cause as much disruption. The following is my rough ranking of the expected impact by each area, where 10 means the impact is high (you're dead in the water) and 1 means you can probably work around it with minimum impact on the project

Those ranking in at the 10 level are environment, configuration and change management, data, and testers. Testing will be highly impacted in circumstances where the hardware isn't working as expected, software migrations and versioning is out of control, the data is undependable, and testers can't perform as expected.

I estimate the impact of documentation issues at about a 7. This impact can vary. For example, if a requirement is removed early in the development cycle, deleting the respective test cases could be simple. If you discover the problem in the middle of testing and you erroneously report a lot of errors, this can cause quite a bit of disruption and lost time.

The impacts of problems with test tools and issue management come in around 6 in my estimation. Test tools were originally developed to speed testing. Given that you can fall back on manual methods could mitigate impact. The same can be said for issue management. A well-designed spreadsheet can quickly fill in, although not as robust as automated methods.

What to do? You must assess the situation in your organization and then focus on mitigating the risks of those with high impacts combined with high probabilities of occurring.

Hearken to the Philip Crosby quote at the beginning: "Doing things right the first time adds nothing to the cost of your product or service. Doing things wrong is what costs you." Planning ahead and being proactive will help ensure you do things only once. All of the problems in the scenario cost the company not only in time delays but in scarce resources (people and dollars) that could have been applied more productively elsewhere. This is why test readiness can cut the cost of testing!

7.3.3 The Checklist Approach

Let's now delve into the details of this approach using a basic checklist style questionnaire you can use to assess your particular situation. Imagine you're meeting with the project team and you ask the questions in the following sections to determine how risky testing might be. Put a checkmark next to an item if you feel comfortable there's little risk. Enter an X if there's work to be done before testing. After your survey, make note of those you marked with an *X*. You'll need to loop back on these to help determine mitigation action plans.

7.4 ENVIRONMENT

Environmental issues are at the top of your list of concerns. If operations hasn't prepared the environments with all the elements needed for testing, a strong possibility exists that you will not be able to test at all (it's either go or no-go).

_____ Hardware: Are all PCs, terminals, monitors, laptops, keyboards or workstations, printers, servers, routers, tape and disc drives, power supplies, communication devices (landline and mobile phones), security devices, and any other hardware key to your project installed and operational?

_____ Are processes in progress for the acquisition, installation, and testing of any special test devices and software? Will these be complete by the time testing is scheduled to begin?

_____ Are there any long lead times in acquiring and installing hardware and debugging operational software that will challenge the project?

_____ Are there any vendor licensing issues that may impact the project?

_____ Software and operating systems: Is all operational software licensed and up to date? Could any licenses expire during the test schedule?

_____ Code migration: Is there anything that could disrupt code migration between the planned testing environments?

_____ Are the necessary test environments set up, such as unit, systems, integration, performance, stress, user acceptance, and regression?

_____ Power and connectivity: Is there sufficient processing power, data storage capacity, through-put, and network connectivity to perform well in the environments you'll be using for testing?

_____ Remote facilities: If testing will occur at remote facilities, are these set up and running? For example, will testing be performed at the customer's site and is this outdoors or in a factory?

_____ Availability: Will all of the above be devoted to this project and available for the times set out in the schedule? Is anything promised to another project that could impact your testing?

7.5 CONFIGURATION AND CHANGE MANAGEMENT

Configuration and change management are the second most critical areas for you to cover in your questionnaire. Beyond just the risks to testing, even worse is the impact to the entire project of not having a well-managed configuration and change management system to control the code. Throughout the entire testing process, IT will install and migrate new and updated software, and in some cases, hardware. This can be the most chaotic period in the project. Good communications and collaboration help considerably to maintain order. If the test team is "out of the loop," even for a short period, it may miss a critical change or software version release and not apply the correct tests.

An example:

1. A user decides to remove a feature and tells the development manager or the developer.
2. The developer makes the necessary changes.
4. The release manager installs the revised software.
5. No one informs the tester of the change and the tester runs a test case that still expects the feature to be present. The test results indicate an error related to the expected feature.
6. The tester must revise and rerun the tests.

Communication and collaboration broke down and, as a result, rework was necessary. This rework costs you time in terms of project delays and money for the resources who are rerunning tests, thus being diverted from productive work.

_____Requirements: Once the requirements are approved by the business stakeholders, will they be placed under configuration and version control? Are there processes in place to communicate any and all changes to the entire team?

_____Design concepts and vendor agreements: Since changes to any of these documents can impact the project in various ways, will these be placed under configuration and version control? Will changes to these be communicated to the entire team?

_____The test plan: To ensure your test team is always using the most current version of the test plan, will you be able to place this plan and manage it through the configuration and change management process?

_____ The software: Will the software be constantly controlled through the various testing environments, ensuring all components that must work together are moved at the same time? Will there be version control?

_____ Will the reasons why a software component is being changed be documented with traceability back to a valid requester, such as a stakeholder?

_____ Will release management provide an accounting of all software and components being promoted so testing will know what has changed and what to test? Testers must know what versions of software they are testing so they will not use obsolete test cases, thus reporting erroneous results.

_____ Hardware: Will any hardware changes be managed, controlled, and accounted for in the same way so the test team can determine if it must make any changes in the hardware it is using or testing?

_____ Data: Will changes to the data residing in the test environment be under the strict control of the test manager who has sole sign-off for these changes?

_____ Is everyone in the team aware of and do they accept this policy?

7.6 DOCUMENTATION

Documentation is basically anything written down that we expect someone else to read and use in the future. Some examples include: requirements, test plan, models, use cases, user stories, test scenarios/cases/scripts, and traceability matrices.

Need for customization and sizing: No two software development projects are alike, thus the size and scope of documentation must be customized to what is required for each project. For example, some approaches, such as Agile and iterative, value face-to-face conversation instead of a lot of documentation. This is usually at the beginning of the project until more is known about the actual requirements. The team must decide the proper balance for the needs of each project based on the approach used—that is, classic waterfall versus Agile and iterative [2].

Again, you are ensuring things have to be done only once, avoiding waste and rework because of inaccurate documentation.

____Requirements and models: Are the requirements signed off and approved by the stakeholders?

____Are the processes in place to ensure changes to these are communicated to the entire team?

____The test plan: Does everyone involved understand the purpose of the plan and agree to support it? Agreement is essential to ensure accuracy and completeness in testing.

____Use cases or user stories: Do the use cases or user stories accurately reflect the requirements and have they been signed off and approved by the stakeholders? Once the team develops the use cases and user stories, the test team develops the corresponding test scenarios/cases/scripts and traceability matrices.

____Test scenarios/cases/scripts: Does it appear that the test scripts completely and accurately reflect the requirements? Emphasize that these will be critical in determining the number and skill sets of testers necessary to complete the tests in the time allocated. Could testing proceed if these weren't ready? Probably so, but at some level of risk of incomplete testing and missed errors. The problems would probably not surface until user acceptance testing or, worse, in production.

____Traceability matrices: Does each test case have traceability back to a particular requirement? Are there any orphan test cases that are superfluous, meaning there are no requirements for them? Everyone must realize the importance of keeping each test case in sync with the requirements so invalid tests are not run, as we saw in the opening scenario.

7.7 DATA

As briefly reviewed earlier, *data* is defined as:

1. Data in databases set up prior to testing and used repeatedly for interactions with the application's user interfaces
2. Input data specifically referred to in the test cases and scripts

Both are a natural result of test case development in that each case will dictate the data expected to be in the databases that the test will run against and the data the tester enters during tests.

For example, a tester is to enter a new order for a customer. The team must set up a database in the test environment similar to the existing "customer master file" in production. This would contain the name and address of the customer as well as other data needed to process the order. Next, the test script would indicate the order data such as item number and quantity ordered. The tester would use the interface being tested and enter the order. The mock customer database would be updated. Since the database will be updated during testing, it is saved as a golden database prior to testing, so it can be used to refresh the environment for reuse in repeat or regression testing.

All data must be under configuration control and the processes must be set up to enable quick updating by testing if requirements or applications are changed.

_____ Database: What databases are necessary and how do we reconstruct a copy in the test environment?

_____ What processes are available to save the databases as "golden" and then bring them back for a refresh when necessary?

_____ Input data: For each test to be run, what data must we gather and who can assist us in this? If the data used by the testers or for the databases are not ready, you'd probably be in the same situation as if the environment wasn't ready. What would it be worth to run your tests with inaccuracies in the data or data altogether missing?

_____ Expected results: Are the expected results obvious from the requirements or should we consult with the users to determine this? Are these documented in the test cases so the tester can report whether the test passed or failed?

7.8 TEST TOOLS

Test tools do not just magically appear. There are many tools that help testers be efficient and effective. You must ensure you select and obtain approval for the proper tools. This can take appreciable time. You must facilitate the purchase and installation of the tools, diligently coordinating this with the build out of the test environment. Finally, ensure the current test team and, likewise, any new team members that join during the project, are trained. Only then can you assure the team and the tools were ready.

_____ Types of tools: Based on the requirements and test cases, what types of tools are appropriate for this project? For example, do you need: data file, database and file building and extraction software, simulators, file comparison tools, bug tracking, issue management and status reporting software, special tools for managing regression tests, capture/playback, scripting tools, run-time error detectors, test repositories, and load/stress testing software?

_____ Have versus buy: For the tools chosen, are they currently available on site or must they be purchased?

_____ If purchased, are they reliable and what costs are involved? How many licenses are needed?

_____ Capacity to use: Do we have the capacity to manage and use these tools? That is, can we install and put them to good use in the subject environments?

_____ How much training is necessary to use them effectively?

_____ Trade-offs: Finally, can we be effective without these tools? How would not having them impact the project's timeline?

7.9 TESTERS

Testers, like the test tools, don't magically appear. It's a project in itself in ensuring testers:

- Are completely familiar with the application to be tested
- Know how to follow the scripts
- Know how to use the test tools and the bug-tracking application
- Fully understand their roles and responsibilities related to the team
- Know how to collaborate well with others on the project

This is a huge responsibility on the test manager, especially in today's environment where the teams might be separated by geography and time zones. This is another high-risk area that can impact the efficiency and effectiveness of the test process.

Have you:

____ Identified and ensured the testers are qualified to perform the required tests?

____ Assigned and scheduled these testers according to the project and test plans?

____ Ensured they are completely familiar with the applications to be tested and the scripts to be followed?

____ Trained them in the use of the test tools?

____ Trained them in the process of using the tools?

____ Trained them in entering test results in the bug-tracking application?

____ Arranged for the process where they'll be continually updated when changes are implemented that may affect the tests they run?

____ Ensured they are able to harmoniously collaborate with others on the project?

7.10 ISSUE MANAGEMENT

7.10.1 Daily Test Status Meetings

Before testing begins, you must give thoughtful consideration to how testers will communicate their test results to all stakeholders and how the project team will resolve issues. During testing, the quality of the application will be continually on display and you must ensure you have the necessary reports when you conduct the daily test status meetings. It's here where you discuss, prioritize and triaged issues—using "severity levels" (such as showstoppers/must-haves, medium/usability limiting, and low/ minimally impacting issues).

You also assign responsibility for fixes and schedule migration and retesting, including regression tests. You may also need to escalate an issue if it cannot be resolved within the project team. The team must adhere to version control and the change management process as closely as possible. This period can be very hectic, and again test readiness is very important for project success.

_____Does everyone agree to the process of communicating issues to management?

_____Does everyone accept their responsibilities to actively attend the daily status meetings?

_____Does everyone know their roles and responsibilities in fixing issues?

_____Does everyone agree to keep the test team aware of changes that may affect their testing?

7.10.2 Migrating to the Production Environment

Reality being what it is, there are always known issues at implementation time. That is, the stakeholders agree that the application may be migrated to production in spite of errors still existing in the code or tests that were not run due to time constraints or other management directives. You must ensure plans are in place to fix these bugs and execute delayed tests in the near future.

As a part of this scheme, you can provide a list of these known issues to service support (the help desk) to give them a heads-up in the event that a customer calls concerning these issues. Provide service support an explanation for each issue and a miniscript to be used in its responses to the customer. For example: "Yes, that is a known issue and it will be corrected in the next release, scheduled for March 26, 2011."

Additionally, keep service support in the loop concerning issue resolution until all issues are cleared. A real value to this is in the case where you believe you cleared an issue but a customer still calls about it. This is a red flag to IT that the problem still exists, at least for that particular customer at that location and time. This may indicate a breakdown in configuration and change management.

_____Is there a process in place to segregate known issues away from all others so they can be communicated easily?

_____Have you engaged the service support team and agreed on how and when these known issues will be transferred to it?

_____Will service support receive these in time to handle customer calls, which may start immediately after implementation?

_____Is the process in place to be alerted to reoccurring problems once thought to be cleared and their proper prioritization?

7.11 CONCLUSION

At this point do you:

1. Understand the seven critical areas that can impact your testing?
2. See how you can prioritize your efforts by focusing on the areas with the highest probability of occurring and the highest potential impact on your project?
3. Know how to use the results of your checklist survey to proactively show your organization the vital work that must be done before testing begins?

If you do, I've accomplished my objectives and hope this information better prepares you to be ready to test when the software is ready to be tested.

NOTES

1. See the Carnegie Mellon Software Engineering Institute's Web site for an explanation of the CMMI process improvement approach: http://www.sei.cmu.edu/cmmi/index. cfm.
2. There are many groups and Web sites that can explain waterfall and agile/iterative approaches. I suggest you start with the following sites at Wikipedia:
   http://en.wikipedia.org/wiki/Waterfall_software_development
   http://en.wikipedia.org/wiki/Iterative_and_incremental_development
   http://en.wikipedia.org/wiki/Agile_software_development

8

Session-Based Test Management

Michael Kelly

There are a number of different ways to think about software testing costs. You may be someone who thinks that you can't understand the cost of testing unless you first understand the cost of *not* testing. Or you may be someone who focuses on managing budgets and blended rates. Or you may be one of the few who thinks that the costs associated with testing are a tax on other software engineering activities—they're process or tooling inefficiencies.

I think about testing cost a bit differently. I think about waste when I think about the cost of testing. I've worked on projects regulated by the Food and Drug Administration where people collected reams of needless paperwork. I've worked at insurance companies where automation teams wrote suites and suites of long-running and hard-to-maintain automated regression tests. And I've worked at startups where developers spend hours exploring and experimenting with tools that will help them automate tests, only to throw it all away six months later for the next new thing.

I don't think documentation is bad, and I love test automation, continuous integration, mocks, and test harnesses. But I do think that as an industry, it's easy for us to lose focus of what's important when it comes to software testing. And when we lose that focus, I find that our costs tend to go up.

For me, the two most important aspects of testing are risk and coverage. How do I know if I'm addressing the right risks, and to what extent have I addressed them? Risk and coverage are the two most difficult problems to understand and solve when testing. Those two dynamics—risk and coverage—are what drive my testing costs. Testing as a discipline is the application of a number of different techniques and approaches geared toward understanding and mitigating product and project risk. The way that I qualify my understanding of risk, and how much I've mitigated those risks, is through my understanding of test coverage.

8.1 HOW RISK AND COVERAGE DRIVE THE COST OF TESTING

It's risk and coverage that drive how much I spend on testing and what I spend it on. If I don't feel there is a lot of risk associated with change over time, I likely won't develop extensive regression test suites. If I don't feel there is risk in scalability or other aspects of load, I likely won't invest in extensive performance testing. If I don't feel there's much risk in the adoption of a design, I likely won't invest in usability testing. My concept of risk informs what tests I should and should not perform.

I measure how much risk I've addressed with coverage metrics. As a testing community, we commonly talk about code coverage, feature coverage, requirements coverage, data element coverage, and traceability. We develop models and metrics that give insight into when we might have covered enough, or when we might need to create additional tests. We invest a lot of time and money in tools that simplify the tasks around understanding coverage: code coverage analyzers, integrated test management suites, and homegrown spreadsheets that list hundreds of test criteria specific to the products on which we work.

As an industry, if we fail to effectively capture and efficiently manage our risk and coverage criteria, our testing costs go up. Most projects suffer from two pathologies: (1) they do too little—not accurately capturing the right risks, or not covering them enough; or (2) they do too much—overtesting for certain risks, or providing excessive levels of coverage. For as much as we talk about "right sizing" our testing practices, experience tells me we do very little of it.

There are software projects where someone in the formal role of a "tester" may not need to be involved. There are software projects where the project team can't be too careful because people's lives are on the line. But there's also the reality that for all software development projects, for all companies, cost is an important project factor.

8.2 THE EXPLORATORY APPROACH TO TESTING

I'm going to make an assumption that if you're reading this book, you're at least familiar with the concept of exploratory testing. There are numerous definitions on the topic, and more than a couple of paradigmatic examples of how and when it might be useful. If you're not familiar with exploratory testing, here are some excellent introductory resources for developing an understanding of what exploratory testing is and can be:

- James Bach's article "Exploratory Testing Explained"
- Cem Kaner's 2006 talk "Exploratory Testing after 23 Years"
- Cem Kaner's 2008 Quality Assurance Institute tutorial on exploratory testing [1]

By making test design and execution a more real-time process, exploratory testing places at its center the concepts of risk and coverage. It's impossible to perform exploratory testing without understanding those two concepts, although the same cannot be said for heavily scripted test processes. Someone performing exploratory testing *must* have mental models of what risks they are trying to address. They *must* also have mental models of test coverage. Exploratory testing is the exercise of designing a series of tests that allow you to address the identified risks with some acceptable amount of coverage.

It's this closeness of the tester, the person executing the testing activities, to the central ideas of risk and coverage that enable the exploratory testing approach to be so cost effective. Instead of test design and execution being separated by iteration or team, with each test executed the tester learns more about the product and uses that information to design the next best test to be executed. It's a process that allows the tester to respond to each test in a way that should maximize focus on the most relevant risks.

To manage risks and coverage, exploratory testers leverage frameworks and techniques for structuring and managing their ideas [2]. They have to be experts at generating test ideas while testing and tying those ideas to test techniques. That process starts with developing the ability to identify missing information and considering multiple possibilities and probabilities for explaining what they've found based on the information they have. It requires that they identify the relevant dimensions, variables, and dynamics, and use those to build and work with mental models of the software they are exploring.

When alternating between learning, test design, and test execution, testers are switching among different activities and perspectives. Like the programmers on the team, they are working quickly, focused on testing the most important features at that moment and building out coverage as they go. As they work they continuously take feedback and use it to extend, refine, refactor, and correct their testing. They have tools (mental and physical) that allow them to produce, manage, abandon, and recover test ideas. This allows them to work fast with confidence.

Exploratory testers are also skilled at controlling how they interact with the world. They know that collaboration can be more productive than working in isolation. They are good at obtaining the tools and information needed to support their testing efforts. Above all, they are continually focused on improving their ability to interact with the software they test: understanding its business purpose, the technology and how it's configured, and establishing procedures for better control of experimental conditions. They collect different kinds of data and look at different aspects of the software than the programming staff might.

Exploratory testing gives you real-time control of risk and coverage while testing, and session-based test management (SBTM) gives you control of the exploratory testing process. Session-based test management is a technique for managing exploratory testing [3]. Used properly, session-based test management can provide rapidly evolving visibility into what risks *currently* affect your project and how much you're covering them. For me, session-based test management is primarily focused on providing a way to provide metrics for measuring progress (sessions) and quantifying coverage.

8.3 USING SESSION-BASED TEST MANAGEMENT FOR EXPLORATORY TESTING

I find that one of the most difficult aspects of software testing is coming up with good test ideas [4]. It doesn't matter how I'm doing my testing: scripted versus exploratory, manual versus automated, or performance versus functional. It's not enough to be able to follow the technology and understand the business context for the problem I'm trying to solve; I need to be able to turn that understanding into questions that I can ask the software in the form of tests.

The quality of my questions, or tests, is often one of the key determining factors in how good my testing is ultimately going to be. If I'm not asking the right questions, or running the right tests, then it likely won't matter how many tests I run. Session-based test management introduces the idea of a test charter to help testers better manage those test ideas, so your next test executed is always the next *best* test to run.

When performing session-based test management, my basic unit of work is the test session, and sessions are organized around test charters. Each of my sessions is time boxed (typically forty-five to sixty minutes) and each charter for my sessions outlines the basic testing mission for that session. So when you look at a list of ten of my charters, you should see ten distinct testing missions equating to around eight to ten hours of heads-down testing.

8.4 GENERATING TEST IDEAS USING SESSION-BASED TEST MANAGEMENT

When I generate a test charter, I start with a basic mission, like test adding items to the shopping cart. Once I have a mission, I start to list all the coverage areas and risks I can think of related to that mission. For example, if I were to test adding items to a shopping cart, I might specify the following:

Coverage
- Adding items
- Removing items and adding them again
- Updating existing items
- Number of different items in the cart
- Quantities of items in the cart
- Saving items for later (or adding to a wish list)
- Adding gift wrap to an item
- Very expensive and/or very inexpensive items
- Items with very large (or small) names or descriptions
- Etc.

Risk
- Accuracy of information displayed about items (name, description, price, etc.)
- Accuracy of quantities displayed
- Accuracy of calculations performed (totals, savings calculations, estimates around shipping)
- Accuracy of displayed recommendations (or other adds)
- Slow performance as you add more items
- Ability to change price (hacking local cookies, URL hacking)
- Etc.

As you can see, as I list out the various features I can cover and the different risks I can think of related to my shopping cart, I quickly outgrow my forty-five-minute time box. That's by design—that's *why* I list all those test ideas out in my charter.

It's at this point that I would pass my list around for a peer review. So for this example, I passed these lists to Jason Pitcher (a fellow exploratory tester) for a quick review and he pointed out that I was missing charters for session management (having multiple windows open while I add to my cart), out-of-stock items, and testing with a shopping cart linked to an account. Those are blatant oversights on my part and should clearly be tested.

After I get the feedback from peer review, it's time to refactor. Obviously, even with the coverage and risks I came up with while writing this chapter, I already have more than forty-five minutes of work testing my shopping cart. That means I need new charters.

After refactoring I might have the following charters:

- Test adding items to the shopping cart
- Test shopping cart calculations
- Test shopping cart recommendations
- Test shopping cart session management
- Test shopping cart behavior with an integrated account
- Performance-test adding items to the shopping cart
- Security-test adding items to the shopping cart
- Etc.

Then I get the fun of repeating that process for each and every one of those new charters. This process continues until each charter is no more than forty-five to sixty minutes of work, and all of my test ideas (and my peer reviewer's test ideas) have been captured at least once.

8.5 MANAGING TEST IDEAS USING SESSION-BASED TEST MANAGEMENT

Once I have a large listing of test charters, the next step is to prioritize them. That doesn't necessarily mean force-rank them (although if I had a small enough list I might do that). I typically use three levels for ranking:

- A—This charter must be executed before I know enough about the feature to make a recommendation related to production. Or more simply, "We need to run this charter."
- B—This charter represents a good set of test ideas, which could uncover issues that might prevent us from going to production. Or more simply, "If we have time, we should run this charter."
- C—This charter represents a set of test ideas that might be valuable at some point. Or more simply, "It's a test, and we could run it, but likely there are better uses of our time."

When I start my testing, I pull first from the pool of A-level charters. After each session testing, I add any new charters I can think of as a result of my testing and then reprioritize the remaining charters.

For example, after I execute any given charter I might:

- Add some number of new A-, B-, or C-level charters
- Reprioritize existing A-, B-, or C-level charters (up or down)
- Make no changes

Run a test, capture the new test ideas generated by your testing, and reprioritize your existing tests based on your new knowledge of the product. The process outlined earlier illustrates the exploratory testing tactics of overproduction, abandonment, and recovery [5]:

Overproduce ideas for better selection—Produce many different speculative ideas and make speculative experiments, more than you can elaborate upon in the time you have. By capturing all the test ideas in a charter (even the C-level ideas you know you might not execute), you increase your chances that you've got all the options on the table. That increases the likelihood that the next test you run is likely one of the best tests you could be running.

Abandon ideas for faster progress—Let go of some ideas in order to focus on and make progress with others. By downgrading charters as you learn more, you're adapting your testing to focus on the most important risks and the areas that require the most coverage. You know you likely can't run all the tests you'll think of, so you put a process in place that helps you abandon ideas gracefully, so you can recover them later if needed.

Recover or reuse ideas—Revisit your old ideas, models, questions, or conjectures. Discover ideas by someone else. By keeping your B- and C-level charters handy, you're ensuring that you've got them ready to be used later as needed. In addition, as you get better at chartering, you'll find that old charters become great sparks for developing test ideas in the future as well. And peer reviews are another way of saying discover ideas by someone else.

8.6 TRACKING CHARTER VELOCITY

Velocity is the key metric I use to track day-to-day work and to predict when my testing will be done. On a daily basis, I look at how many charters the team is creating and how many charters a day the team is executing. These measures can be based on charters per day, per iteration, per tester, per charter priority (explained in more detail later), or per area (also explained in more detail later).

For a basic look at charter velocity, let's look at the following data from my first nine days of testing on a hypothetical project:

	Charters Created	Charters Executed	Remaining Charters
Day 1	10	9	20
Day 2	8	8	21
Day 3	9	7	21
Day 4	6	8	23
Day 5	5	7	21
Day 6	7	9	19
Day 7	4	6	17
Day 8	5	7	15
Day 9	3	8	13

On this project, we start with twenty charters from our initial look at the testing, and on our first day we discover ten new charters we hadn't thought of initially and execute nine charters out of our pool. That gives us twenty-one charters on the start of the second day. That process of creating new charters and running charters out of the pool continues for the next few days.

Two patterns typically emerge from this type of data. First, you'll likely find that over time the number of new charters you create each day starts to go down. Second, you'll notice that you tend to average around the same number of charters a day as a team (give or take a few depending on what else is going on within the project).

If you were to chart the data, it might look something like Figure 8.1. At this point, I might add a trend line to help me predict when I might be finished with my testing. As you can see from Figure 8.2, based on my testing to date, I might be finished with my testing as early as three days out. On large projects, with a lot of measures of charters by area, priority, or some other criteria, I've found simple charts like these to be predictive of what the team will actually do. It's normally not correct down to the exact day, but it's normally within the week (for small- to medium-sized projects).

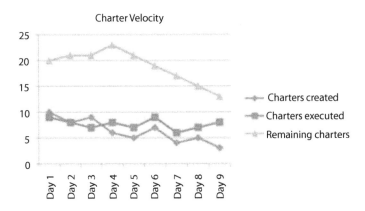

FIGURE 8.1
Charting test velocity.

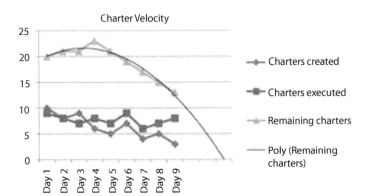

FIGURE 8.2
Predicting completion with a trend line.

8.7 TRACKING THE LEVEL OF COVERAGE ACHIEVED

As stated earlier, when I create my charters I prioritize them into three levels:

- A—We need to run this charter.
- B—We should run this charter if we have time.
- C—We could run this charter, but there are likely better uses of our time.

I did this to allow me to easily map my charter coverage to the coverage metric James Bach outlines in his low-tech testing dashboard [6]. In that dashboard, Bach provides four levels of coverage:

- 0—We have no good information about this area.
- 1—We've done a sanity check of major functions using simple data.
- 2—We've touched all functions with common and critical data.
- 3—We've looked at corner cases using strong data, state, error, or stress testing.

This gives me the ability to do a direct mapping of charters to coverage. When my level A charters are done, we've completed our basic sanity tests. When our level B charters are finished, we've hit all the common cases we could think of. Same for level C. What's interesting about this is that if we're at level 2 or 3 coverage, as soon as one of the testers identifies another level A charter we go back to level 1. It means we missed something—likely something big.

8.8 UNDERSTANDING THE FEATURES, AREAS, AND RISKS COVERED

As with any testing effort, with session-based test management I'm always watching what we're testing. I look at the number of charters by feature or by area of the application. I'm trying to answer questions like:

- Do we have at least one charter per story (or requirement, depending on your methodology)?

- Do the areas of the application that are historically more complicated or more error prone have more charters than those areas that are easier or more stable?
- Are there certain areas or risks where we need a high level of coverage (level 3 coverage or priority C charters)? Do we have that coverage planned or executed?

Keeping an eye on coverage from multiple perspectives (story vs. area vs. risk) can help make sure you're getting a good balance. For example, if I'm only looking at coverage for my current stories or requirements, then while I might have great requirements coverage, I might miss areas that need regression testing. If I'm only looking at areas by feature set, then I might miss testing for performance, security, or some other quality criteria. In general, I try to get at least two different views on coverage per project.

When thinking about how to break up an application by area or risk, I'll often start with subsystems and work out from there. For example, if you look at an e-commerce site, you'd have something like search, item browsing, shopping cart, checkout, e-mail and messaging, order lookup and tracking, account administration, and help documentation. You might also include performance, security, internationalization, and usability. For a given iteration, you might track coverage across those areas, but then using a separate view of the data, also look at coverage by feature or story for that iteration.

8.9 TRACKING AVERAGE SESSION EXECUTION TIME AND PERCENT COMPLETE

One of the things I try to measure when running a project using session-based test management is how long it takes to run charters. If you remember, each session is time boxed (typically forty-five to sixty minutes). Once you have this information, you can then sort and filter the data to better understand how much time your team is spending executing tests by functional area, by feature or story, by type of testing (functional, performance, security, etc.), or by tester.

Capturing this metric gives me feedback:

- It tells me how good we are at estimating when we do our initial chartering. With this information, I know when I need to work with the team or individuals on the team, and when to help them improve either their time estimates or help them better manage the scope of their charter missions.

- It tells me how much time we're spending on specific areas or features of the application. With this information, I can better manage where we are spending our time to ensure the most important areas of the application are getting the most coverage. It can also be an indicator of which areas of the application are more difficult to test than others. That can be useful in future planning and training.

- It tells me how much time we're spending on specific types of testing. With this information I can better understand how much time we spend testing various quality criteria and work with the team to make sure when we charter our work we're giving proper attention to areas like usability, security, performance, or supportability—areas we might be ignoring without being aware of it.

8.10 TRACKING PERCENT OF TEST EXECUTION COMPLETE

A big aspect of session-based test management is that testers have the freedom to add and remove charters as needed to be successful. That means, one day you might have twenty more charters to execute until you're finished. Depending on how your testing goes, the next day you might have twenty or fifteen. My experience tells me that many project managers are uncomfortable with that idea. Most project managers want a predictable, always going up, never going down, measure of percent complete.

The measure of percent of test execution complete is the number of charters you've executed divided by the total number of charters you have for the interval you're measuring. While you likely won't get a nice predictable increase day after day like you might get on projects where all the test design is done up front, there is value in measuring your percent complete by iteration or release. I don't use percent complete to predict when I'll be done (I use velocity for that), but I will use it to help me remain focused on the end goal. It's one macrolevel measure of when our testing might be complete.

8.11 TRACKING OTHER DETAILED SESSION METRICS

In his article "How to Manage and Measure Exploratory Testing," Jon Bach outlines session metrics he commonly uses [7]:

- Percentage of session time spent setting up for testing
- Percentage of session time spent testing
- Percentage of session time spent investigating problems

The capturing of detailed session metrics like those Bach outlines in that article is quite common in the session-based test management community. In the article, Bach outlines the details of setup, testing, and problem investigation.

Test setup measures the time it takes to get ready to run the first test. Test execution and design measures how much time is spent thinking of tests conditions and running those tests. And bug investigation and reporting looks at the time that gets spent researching issues identified and logging them in your defect-tracking tool.

These measures help tell a different story about your testing. For example, knowing how long your testers are spending on setup can be helpful in letting you know when you might need to pay more attention to automating setup tasks, focusing on making data more available, or providing training. And knowing how much testing is done per charter is useful in helping understand how much coverage you actually got out of a session. If someone ran a sixty-minute charter, but only did ten minutes of design and execution, you might take some extra time to ask if they really fulfilled their mission. Did they lose too much time during setup? Or did they get sidetracked investigating a specific issue?

8.12 REDUCING COST BY MINIMIZING HEAVY DOCUMENTATION

One of my early experiences in session-based test management took place at a company that was working completely ad hoc [8]. By ad hoc, I mean a team that claims to be Agile only to find it was using the concept as a shield to avoid discipline. The project was an interesting mix among research and development on a new product, a migration of a legacy product to a new platform, and implementing ad hoc marketing requests. This made nailing down the testing scope very difficult and that in turn resulted in a lot of busy work for the testing team.

When I arrived on the project the testing team was organized around heavy scripted manual testing using IEEE 829. However, the development team was largely working without requirements. This meant that for the methodology the testing team members were using to work, they needed to write the requirements themselves, hope they matched what the development team was coding, and then execute their tests. Shortly after I joined the team, we decided to move from IEEE 829 to exploratory testing.

Integrating session-based test management into an ad hoc process turns out to be quite easy. You are, in effect, only really changing your own process. All you have to do is identify what information people are asking you for—defects, basic progress metrics, and so forth—and make sure you can still provide those after you've made the change. As you'll see, as the number of outputs grows, the complexity of implementing a process change goes up. This is what you would expect.

In this case, the testing team changed how they documented their testing—cutting most of the documentation—increased collaboration with those outside of the testing team, and continued to deliver high-quality defects and metrics [9]. The testers focused on making sure the quality of the defect reports went up, while the test manager made sure the measurement needs of the management team were met. He actually developed a great dashboard for this that I still use today.

8.13 REDUCING COST BY CAPTURING TESTING FEEDBACK BEFORE DEVELOPMENT "ENDS"

On another set of projects, I integrated session-based test management into Scrum. The team I was working with initially structured the work so that development work would be completed in sprint N and test execution would take place in sprint N + 1. Since sprints were two weeks in length that meant chartering tests for the stories currently being developed and testing the features that were developed in the previous sprint would occur over a two-week period.

This process worked OK, but it was not as effective as we initially thought it would be. Code that was leaving sprints was buggy. It covered basic happy paths but not any of the edge cases. And defects we found weren't fixed in a timely manner. Because the programmers had already moved on to the next sprint and next set of stories, they didn't have time to go back to fix the code they had written in the previous sprint.

After a few months, we made the decision to consolidate programming and testing into the same sprint. With this in place, no story was "done" until all defects related to the story were fixed. This consolidation pressured the team to move faster. For this to work, programmers would need to finish stories in the first week. Testers would need to have initial chartering and setup work done before the story was completed. Defects would need to be logged early in the second week of the sprint so that programmers had time to turn them around for retesting.

This approach has the advantage in that it produces a high-quality product. Programmers get rapid feedback on their software, and if they need to fix bugs, the code is still fresh in their minds. It also creates a shared objective: done means tested and all bugs fixed. Everyone knows it, so everyone works towards it. There's little back and forth on bugs, and decisions are made swiftly and acted on more swiftly.

On the other hand, it creates tremendous pressure in the last few days of the sprint. Any story of reasonable size needs to be completed early in the sprint, else there isn't enough time to run tests or fix bugs. That means the team members need to be on the ball when it comes to estimation, and they have to be smart in the way they structure the sprint. Everyone makes mistakes, so as you can imagine, in this setup, there are a lot of sprints that have complications late in the sprint.

8.14 REDUCING THE COST OF TRACEABILITY

The IBM Rational Unified Process (RUP) is the most common project methodology I've worked in. I've seen it implemented a number of different ways, from small waterfalls to something that represents iterative development. And I've worked on everything from the small ten-person RUP project team to a large three-hundred-person project. One thing that's been true of every RUP project I've worked on, whether it's been in a regulated industry or not, is that people who manage RUP projects want requirements traceability.

Although I don't see traceability as the holy grail of testing that some see it as, it has its place. On regulated projects it's a requirement of the process. And even on unregulated projects, it can be one of many helpful tools in tracking test coverage.

So how, you ask, do you take an inherently chaotic practice like exploratory testing and make it traceable? Well, it should come as no surprise that session-based test management can help [10]. In fact, I've even implemented requirements traceability on Agile teams using session-based test management. The simplest way to do this is to outline what requirements you plan to cover in a coverage section of your charter. Then, wherever you track your charters, you add a mechanism to tie those charters to the requirements they cover. On past projects I've done this using Excel, IBM Rational TestManager, IBM Rational Quality Manager, and HP Mercury TestCenter.

Regardless of the tool, you simply need a listing of requirements tied to a listing of charters that cover them—just like traditional test scripts. Then, after you execute your testing, when you debrief your session with your test manager, you simply correct any changes in coverage. If you didn't get to a specific requirement, unconnect that requirement and charter. If you decide to add additional coverage for a requirement, simply link the new charters you created for that additional coverage.

My experience has been that on the projects where I do exploratory testing and track requirements traceability in this way, I get better coverage than I do with traditional testing. In traditional testing, because debriefs seldom happen, there isn't much revisiting of the requirements covered or the test cases that cover them. It's more about building the traceability artifact than it is about the actual testing coverage.

8.15 A FINAL LOOK BACK AT RISK, COVERAGE, AND COST

At this point, I hope I've successfully illustrated how I think risk and coverage drive testing costs. Testing omissions happen because of misunderstood risk or inadequate coverage. And more effective and efficient testing happens when risk and coverage are both adequately understood and are both *actively* managed. Session-based test management is the tool that I use to actively manage risk and coverage. You can manage those two variables in other ways, but I've yet to find a more real-time method or one that brings me closer to the details of what's happening in the project and with the product.

If you're interested in getting started with session-based testing, try picking a single feature of a product you're currently testing and apply the structure I've outlined in this chapter. Generate an initial list of test ideas, charter those ideas, prioritize them, and work them using sessions. After each session, practice debriefing with your test manager and determine what the next step is for your testing. Use the information you learn after each session to build a more informed risk model, and make sure you're actively managing coverage and not just running a charter because you thought it was a good idea at some point.

NOTES

1. James Bach, "Exploratory Testing Explained" (first published as a chapter in *The Test Practitioner* [2002]), http://www.satisfice.com/articles/et-article.pdf; Cem Kaner, "Exploratory Testing after 23 Years" (presented at the Conference of the Association for Software Testing, 2006), http://www.kaner.com/pdfs/ETat23.pdf; Cem Kaner, "A Tutorial in Exploratory Testing" (presented at the Quality Assurance Institute QUEST Conference, Chicago, 2008), http://www.kaner.com/pdfs/QAIExploring.pdf.
2. James Bach and Jon Bach, "Exploratory Testing Dynamics," http://www.satisfice.com/articles/et-dynamics.pdf.
3. Jon Bach, "Session Based Test Management" (first published in *Software Testing and Quality Engineering*, November 2000), http://www.satisfice.com/articles/sbtm.pdf.
4. This chapter includes a number of excerpts and examples from a series of articles on session-based test management first published on SearchSoftwareQuality.com. These excerpts and examples are used with permission. For more on the original works, see http://searchsoftwarequality.techtarget.com/.
6. James Bach, "A Low-Tech Testing Dashboard" (presented at *STAREast*, 1999), http://www.satisfice.com/presentations/dashboard.pdf.
7. Jon Bach, "How to Manage and Measure Exploratory Testing," (Quardev, 2006), http://www.quardev.com/content/whitepapers/how_measure_exploratory_testing.pdf.
8. Kenn Petty, "Reflections on the Use of Session-Based Exploratory Testing as the Primary Test Methodology for Software in an Agile Environment" (presented at the Indianapolis Workshops on Software Testing, April 2005), http://www.indianapolisworkshops.com/docs/Reflections_on_the_use_of_Session-Based_Exploratory_Testing_in_an_Agile_Environment.doc.

9. Kenn Petty, "Transitioning from Standard V&V to Rapid Testing Practices in a Chaotic Project Environment" (presented at the Conference of the Association for Software Testing, 2007), http://www.associationforsoftwaretesting.org/documents/Kenn_Petty_Transitioning_from_Standard_V&V_to_Rapid_Testing_Practices.pdf.
10. Bill Wood and David James, "Applying Session-Based Testing to Medical Software," *Medical Device and Diagnostic Industry Magazine,* May 2003, http://www.mddionline.com/article/applying-session-based-testing-medical-software.

9

Postpone Costs to Next Release

Jeroen Rosink

How wonderful it is to deliver working software used by many and founded on the experiences of its users. Sometimes the experience and skills required by the software do not match the users' expectations and experiences. The mismatch between perceived and delivered functionality colors the value perception of the system. Do requests usually have a date of immediately? Is this reasonable? What will the impact be on the agreed-upon deadline? Deadlines are often scheduled without discussions around or concerns for the system as a total solution but instead based on a few issues of functionality.

In previous projects I learned that delivering value through the number of satisfied requirements is less important than delivering on time. Incomplete functionality, be it a bug fix or new feature, can be scheduled for the next release. This shift of focus from delivering value at the expense of schedule to delivering on time is often made by identifying remaining risks and considering the deadline urgency. The main concept underlying this chapter is that the costs associated with a release may be postponed to next release by shifting requirements. By postponing functionality and costs to the next release new benefits may be discovered, like the ability to group sets of similar changes.

This chapter discusses:

- General phases of a test process
- Balancing business value and risks as guidelines for test depth
- Translating business value and the technical solutions to test types
- Mapping discovered issues to impact on the system
- Translation of a mixture of these activities using examples from own experience

On a previous project I tested two core concepts, the first of postponing and the second of demanding solutions to known issues. To truly value the provided examples you will want to understand the reasoning used in the decision-making process. This decision making was a game of collecting, valuing, and sharing information. I learned that immediately solving the problem is not always the best solution. Testing was cheaper by waiting until the next release to provide solutions. In this case the delivery of remaining issues was postponed until the next release and accepted the risk of known issues in production was accepted. Limiting the time spent on problems that would have previously needed an immediate solution left additional time to work on functionality that provided higher business value.

Before I started testing these concepts I tried to fit all necessary activities into a process model. I divided the testing process into certain phases. Let me explain further.

9.1 PHASES OF TESTING

A phase in testing can be seen as a period of time with a definite start and end in which related activities create structure and transparency in a project. Testing phases have similarities whether a waterfall or Agile approach is taken. This also relates to the well-known circle of Deming: plan–do–check–act. In my experience in software testing the majority of time is spent on activities that can also be structured in phases that are described by TMap Next as plan and control, infrastructure, preparation, specification, and execution [1]. Each of these activities consumes time and skills and therefore resources. Examples of these activities include collecting and reviewing documentation, defining test-scripted test cases, creating test data, and executing tests. These are only a few of the many activities that could be assigned to these phases. A method of working based on identified importance of requirements, impact, and risks that associates the activities to these phases to maximize use of time, money, and resources to deliver the correct functionality.

Although other phases could be recognized, the more repetitive activities lie in *preparation, specification, and execution.* Many activities and actions must be performed to support the testing process. Testing goes far beyond simply performing the test to see if the system meets expectations.

Gathering and understanding both data and the system are also valuable. These phases will be used to explain the relationship between requirements, risks, and value and how the moment of delivery impacts the cost. Each phase is explained next alongside its significant resource-consuming activities.

9.1.1 Preparation

In the preparation phase testers focus on collecting information about the test objects. This is essential, preparatory work performed before test execution. The output of this is a decision about whether enough information is present to start preparing the test cases. Although this phase is often performed implicitly, understanding its presence helps to realistically balance activities and weigh their costs against time and resources.

The preparation phase consists at least of the following activities:

- Collecting information about issues and requests for changes (RFCs)— For example, issue description, test results, functional designs
- Reviewing information
- Assigning testers to the test objects
- Defining the test case definition requirements based on risks

Unfortunately, proper information is not always in place. When sufficient or proper information is not available, it affects the other phases and makes performing the activities in following phases harder. Although these actions can be performed implicitly while specifying test cases, I learned that performing these actions explicitly allows for the gleaning of additional insights about the components under test. These insights help model the test approach. An explicit preparation phase helps identify both gaps and strengths and allows better control over their impact in following phases.

9.1.2 Specification

After determining whether sufficient information is available the question of how to test must be answered. In this phase you decide at which level of detail you will specify your test cases. Will they be fully scripted, or is there some room left for exploring the application? In the specification phase you think about the tests you want to perform. The main activities in this phase are:

- Defining test cases
- Preparing test data
- Defining regression tests

The development approach and activities of the time shape how this phase is defined. A related decision is whether to start activities in parallel sessions. When the specification phase has ended the actual execution of test cases often begins.

9.1.3 Execution

In the execution phase issues become apparent. Different processes for testing RFCs and issues may be present. RFCs can often become part of a future release instead of the current release.

Several activities form the execution process:

- Performing an intake (sanity) check on the test environment
- Executing test cases
- Changing, adding, or updating tests
- Logging issues
- Retesting issues
- Performing regression tests

The output of this process is measured functionality and a list of complete and incomplete issues.

9.2 BUSINESS VALUE

Business value is one of the main goals of software delivery, if not the only goal. To deliver the appropriate business value different processes must be aligned. The organization should decide whether to pay attention to requirement verification, validation, and improvement. How often is there a claim from business that everything is important and that everything must be delivered? Under these conditions everything would merit being tested at the same depth. Although this is sometimes inevitable, depth of testing is often not a rigid requirement. The appropriate stakeholder can weigh the risks functionality may have in production with respect to actual needs. When objects are valuable and have high risk they may need extended or extraordinary testing. When both the feature's risks and the costs of testing-related activities are understood the best possible decision may be made.

In this section explanation will be given as to which types of risks there are, and how to reflect them against the MoSCoW principle (which stands for must have, should have, could have, and would like to have). Is it acceptable to spend time and money on high-risk changes for low value business requirements? Using tables like this helped me to talk with business how to value requirements. For the business everything is important, perhaps the question to be asked should be is it important compared to risks.

The next step is to make a model of the functionality with respect to its business value and technical risk. A final step is to place the issues discovered into a model that allows the relationship between business value, frequency of use, and issues preventing its delivery to be visualized. I call this issue maturity.

9.2.1 Requirements versus Risks

To control and monitor risks within a product, different types of risks should be differentiated [2]. The following definitions help differentiate between product and project risks.

> *Product risk—A risk that is directly related to an information system and that may be covered through testing*
> *Project risk—A risk that relates to the setup and control of a (test) project*

Testing mainly focuses on product risks. Reducing product risks ensures that provided functionality provides business value. Each product risks can often by related to a specific requirement. The MoSCoW principle helps classify the different risks, which provides an overview upon which decisions can be based. One thing often forgotten is that the late delivery of functionality to meet requirements results in later-stage project risks. Therefore, both product and project risks, as guided by the MoSCoW principle, should be considered. Just like product risks, project risks may be defined or classified by preparation and specification and effort involved.

After a risk-requirements assessment is performed, a provisional test strategy can be defined and used by involved parties to agree upon how requirements will be tested. Not every piece of functionality must be tested as extensively as others. As issues are discovered in certain areas, this decision may need to be reevaluated and the strategy reapplied.

	Requirements			
Risk	Must Have	Would Have	Could Have	Nice to Have
High	Extensive early testing, impact of issues is possibly high	Extensive testing, impact of issues is possibly high	Cases should be considered important to be executed if functionality is delivered due to high risk	Avoid delivery?
Medium	Extensive, early testing, issue dangers the usability of the RFC	Extensive testing, impact of issues is possibly high	Testing the symptoms	Avoid delivery?
Low	Easy gains, less testing, quick gains	Testing the symptoms or basic changes	Testing the symptoms or basic changes	Less testing? Need to test?

Experience teaches that some requirements are easy to fulfill and some are more complex. When complexity is involved risk of failure is also increased. Risks can be avoided or reduced by classifying then against MoSCoW principles. Should a nice-to-have "requirement" truly be required when there is an extremely high implementation or usage risk? Stakeholders should define where on the requirements spectrum it lies and accept the test approach that matches the risk assessment given to that functionality.

Issues related to project risks are of another order. Costs involving project risks should be aligned with product risks and the impact on delivering value.

9.2.2 Technical Impact versus Business Gain

After classifying requirements and defining the associated test approach requirements may be aligned against business gain and technical impact.

This alignment helps refine test strategy. Why should the easy, less risky items be considered and tested before the technical, complex items that have higher risk and increased chance for failure or other problems? Keep in mind that even "simple" functionality can result in complex or risky issues.

One question that should often be asked as a part of this alignment is what impact will it have on the test process if an issue is discovered later in the project and how will it impact value delivery. The answer to this helps define the required early involvement and test depth.

The following list shows how technical impact helps define the initial testing approach. While answering the aforementioned question, technical impact and business gain must be considered distinctly.

> Technical impact—The change's coded impact related to its complexity compared to the size of function, component, module, and the chain of functionality
>
> Business gain—Outcome of benefits in money, time, or resource usage related to the functionality

For example, technical impact could be measured through

- Lines of code needed for changes
- The number of functions impacted
- The number of modules impacted
- Relationships with other complex functions or modules
- Developers' knowledge of the change part of code

Business gain could be measured by

- The function's frequency of use
- The number of involved customers
- The impact of not implementing the feature
- Business experience with the related functionality

In the following table you see an example how test effort can be allocated in certain testing types. Depending on impact and value, you might measure risks by testing intensively. Keep in mind that testing more results in higher costs. I used this table to explain to managers that choices must be made between "testing it all" or testing it wisely.

Business Gain	Technical Impact		
	Low	**Medium**	**High**
High	Functional test, integration test, informal/formal testing techniques, error guessing	Unit test, functional test, integration test, informal/formal testing techniques	Unit test, module test, functional test, integration test, formal testing techniques
Medium	Functional test, integration test, informal testing techniques, error guessing	Unit test, functional test, integration test, informal/formal, testing techniques, error guessing	Unit test, module test, functional test, integration test, formal testing techniques
Low	Error guessing	Unit test, functional test, integration test, informal/formal testing techniques, error guessing	Unit test, module test, functional test, integration test, formal testing techniques

The same approach should be handled when issues are found. As issues are discovered consideration should be given to where they lie on the technical impact verses business gain spectrum table. Does delivering with known issues produce a net positive business gain when compared to the risk of solving it? Solving issues requires code changes, which introduce new project risks.

- What are the risks of remaining issues?
- Can RFCs be shipped to production?

As issues are discovered this table and these concepts can be used to identify which, if any, tests may be needed. Overall business gains may be made by not testing all affected functionality.

9.2.3 Value of Issues

The value of issues changes during a project. When a project starts all issues discovered seem to be equally important and must be solved. Near the end of a project an issue's value is more contextual and depends on where in the software and development process the issue is discovered.

In the beginning of a project issues that block certain test cases from being executed may be extremely important. At the end of the project they may be less important than missing functionality that needs to be created for or migrated to the production system. Classifiers such as severity and priority are often used to describe these relative priorities. These classifications can be used to help schedule solution delivery. To judge the impact, and more important, the risks, more information may be needed.

The maturity of discovered issues may adversely affect business value, which itself affects the impact on testing. If both business value and complexity are high, then the likelihood that extensive testing must be done is high.

The following table illustrates the relationship between the value of discovered issues and business processes.

Business Gain	Value of Discovered Issues		
	Low	**Medium**	**High**
High	Important functionality supporting the major business processes	Complex functionality that supports the majority of the business processes	Complex high-risk areas, which result in heavy regression testing
Medium	Functionality that is identified to be important and has no huge impact on other processes; issues have emotional value for business	Functionality that supports a major process or some general processes	Functionality that is identified as important and has huge impact on other processes
Low	Small processes are using this functionality, possibly with workarounds	Important for some people, not for processes	Obvious small changes that impact the output of a majority of processes

Cost can be calculated in several ways; most of the time you know only afterward the actual cost. The value of a found issue can be calculated by its position in the process. How many times is that specific functionality used? By whom is it used and are there workarounds available? Another point of view is to value it also against the usage in the test process. If the functionality is used often in the test cases, then a lot of retest might be scheduled as part of a regression test. For certain business processes it might be a low impact issue to solve although the solution might have more impact on the test execution.

To avoid deliverance of changes or solutions during testing in a later stage you should assess the issues based on business gain and its location in the business process with respect to the test impact. This should make the relation between testing and the business process visible.

Here is another table-formatted example:

Business Gain	Value of Discovered Issues		
	Low	**Medium**	**High**
High	Correct names and addresses on letters sent to customers	Supporting reports based on legal terms	• Errors on billing and invoices • Errors in voice logging with legal importance • Processes are blocked and no workaround available
Medium	The hotkey to start the printing	Certain processes are not executable directly but a workaround is available	Under certain roles functionality is not available, four-eye principle (user is able to work with functionality, manager is not and cannot grant users work) cannot be guaranteed
Low	Textual, on-screen errors	Authorization management	New input value in dropdown box resulting in new variants in processes

Early in a project the test and technical focus is high; at the end the business focus becomes higher. Because of the relationship between the time when an issue is discovered and its cost, the time an issue is discovered impacts preparation, testing, execution, and their related costs.

9.3 DELIVERY OF TEST OBJECTS

Test objects can be delivered by adding them to a release or creating a new project for them. Either way functionality is often tracked by a certain identifier. In some organizations these identifiers are called tickets. In others they are referred to as defects or issues. I prefer to use the term *tickets* in the following examples. A distinction can be made between issues and

RFCs. Although different definitions for the terms *issue* and *RFC* exist, I use the following thoughts to keep the two terms separate: an issue is solved when unexpected and incorrect symptoms are removed; an RFC is delivered when all corresponding test cases are successfully executed.

Herein lies another business opportunity. The business should be able to accept RFCs when an RFC is delivered with missing functionality or known issues. An RFC is accepted after taking into consideration business gain, remaining risks, and required test effort. RFCs are initiated when a business case shows that the change will provide additional gains or value for the business. In other words, will this feature or request for change provide gains to or prevent losses for the business?

Let me explain using an illustrative example. Given an RFC or issue, translate issues and test work to some actual cost and value for the business using the mentioned phases and activities. Example of business gain of a specific RFC: An RFC is expected to deliver €300,000 of profit over the next eight months if implemented within the next two months. The RFC is expected to cost €110,000, including testing. The release consists of the RFC above in addition to several other RFCs and bug fixes. The following numbers represent sample data on testing this specific RFC.

- RFC testing will require about seventy test cases
- Phase: Test preparation
  - Preparing and reviewing test documentation: Four hours per FTE (five FTEs)
- Phase: Test specification
  - Test case design: Twelve hours
  - Reviewing test cases: Two hours per test case (two FTEs)
- Phase: Test execution
  - Test data preparation thirty-five hours (one FTE)
  - Test execution fourteen hours (two FTEs)
  - When implementation is completed within four weeks of test preparation and specification, the test execution will take sixteen hours as additional calculations need not be performed. When implementation exceeds four weeks, test preparation and specification must be redone as the data becomes stale due to billing and schema changes. If issues are delivered later, test preparation must be fully redone.

- The RFC may be moved to production in pieces based on business gain, possible risks, and whether the majority of test cases are successfully executed.
- Postrelease regression testing will be defined based on risk, solution complexity, and where in the source code the fix would be necessary.

The costs can be estimated when we assign activities per phase and consider the effort required for those activities. When situations occur that make it impossible to deliver the solution on time, rework can be calculated against those activities.

When a new issue is discovered, an impact analysis considering business gain and testing costs will help determine whether the solution should be implemented during the current release or postponed. The following section explains how these decisions affect the costs.

9.4 COSTS PER PHASE

Costs should not always be equally balanced across a certain phase. By considering the costs per activity per phase it may become evident that under certain conditions it may be worth postponing parts of the solution to the following release. Business value can be provided by delivering tested functionality after business case acceptance.

The following examples describe how decisions can be made and costs affected. Some fictitious values are used to help show the difference between delivering value now or in the next release. These examples are based on experience with a SAP implementation project. This project delivered small releases every two months and a major release every six months. Each release delivers the business working functionality including implemented RFCs and bug fixes.

I will explain with one example the effect of delivering at different points during the release. Another two examples explain decisions to postpone functionality to a following release. The purpose of these examples is to explain how our understanding evolved and we discovered that focusing on test effort alone is not always the way to go. Business value, which varies per issue and release, must always be considered.

9.4.1 Within Current Release

When the remaining functionality is expected in the current release certain predeployment activities have to be assigned and compared against their value and the additional costs.

9.4.1.1 Example 1

When issues and RFCs are delivered in the same release, retesting is needed. Depending on the solution's impact it may be desirable to perform some or all test cases. It is important to identify the benefits to the business and compare them to the required testing efforts. To help make these decisions I identify per phase the reoccurring activities.

9.4.1.1.1 Phase: Preparation

Although lots of testing literature speaks about reusing tests and test data, it can be beneficial to investigate restarting all test cases from preparation phase to execution phase. Test management must rethink about executing all test cases and defining a new approach. It is often easy to claim everything must be tested again, but it is wiser to make an assessment based on priorities, impact, technical impact, and risks. When it is decided to proceed, the objective is to define which test cases should be executed based on the earlier matrix related to risks, business gain, and issue maturity. The outcome should be a well-defined set of test cases to reexecute. If other functional changes are involved, other functionality must also be retested.

Given the aforementioned scenario, the necessary preparation and review can take two FTEs least two hours each. These hours also need to be considered when calculating costs and making a decision.

9.4.1.1.2 Phase: Specification

Even after selecting the set of test cases necessary to cover the identified risks, you are not ready to start testing. Test cases may need to be changed, adapted, or added. Careful attention must be given to make sure that test data can be reused. In this phase effort is expended setting up the test data for test cases. Besides checking the new solution, necessary regression tests are selected. This should be done based on the impact to the system, the accepted risks, and the solution as it relates to the business. Again, additional costs are accrued. Per the RFC example given earlier, four hours are required for test case design, one hour for test case review, one hour to identify old test cases that need regression testing, and about two hours to adapt the regression tests to the new features. Test execution may begin as soon as the new features are available in the test environment.

9.4.1.1.3 Phase: Execution

When the execution phase is started I suggest starting with a small intake test. During this intake test you spend a small amount of time checking if the delivered functionality is in place and if the test environment is suitable for full testing. If suitable, the selected test cases, including any additional regression tests, are executed. For this phase you have costs related to intake-test execution, test-case selection, regression tests, and any remaining test cases. None of these values are fixed values. Also keep in mind that new issues may be discovered when executing test cases, which might result in extending the release date.

9.4.2 Within Next Release

A good alternative I found is postponing solutions to the next release. In the following two examples I will explain how early deliverance of a partial working product enables business to earn on new functionality and how to deal with it in testing.

9.4.2.1 Example 2

An option I worked with is shipping issues to a next release. In this example I use a release that contains multiple RFCs and issues. "Everything we tested" following a defined strategy and met our standards with the exception of one important RFC. The RFC is delivered with about 90 percent of desired functionality. This means that when delivering this RFC now to production and business accepts certain parts are not yet ready for usage and also not disturbing the process, they can start earning the value from this RFC.

For this release we almost reached the deadline. We had the choice to force development to deliver a solution, although this development and testing and also the regression testing time will extend the deadline. For this RFC it would meant that instead of eight months that were left to earn the investments back, the delay would equally reduce earn back time. You might say that the value of the remaining 10 percent of functionality is less worth the loss of money due to delay. It is easy to draw conclusions based on these figures. I suggest being careful and also assessing this decision. Again you assess based on the business gain in combination with technical complexity; a decision can be formulated to deliver. It is not your decision to make; it is the management who has to consider the location of the remaining issues in the process, the maturity of the issue. If the result of the assessment is that value for business is less significant after the release moment, for example, due to low usage by customers, an option is to extend the remaining functionality to the next release. It might even be cheaper than extending the release date.

Before you postpone the solution to the next release you can calculate the additional test work. It will help management to make decisions. In this example I use a solution that results in standalone test activity; test activities cannot be combined with other RFCs.

9.4.2.1.1 Phase: Preparation

In the preparation phase you preserve the cases that are not executed successfully; these test cases are reusable. As a result of the isolated characteristic of the remaining functionality, you don't have to do additional work on preparation for the next release. This means all test cases can be reused by the team as the impact analysis is already done on the original release. This doesn't mean you have to do nothing right now; you should spend special care for preserving test cases and test data for the next release. I calculate that the process preserving data in this case as one hour.

9.4.2.1.2 Phase: Specification

In addition to one additional preparation needing to be done, no test specification is needed as the cases were already prepared. The solution was already defined only not yet implemented by the team. The test cases remain valid. Additionally, you might consider extra investigation into how these cases could influence other test cases from new tickets/RFCs that already are assigned to a next release. In this situation it is important to position the value of remaining functionality of this RFC compared with the gains and test depth based on complexity. Information about relations must be done before the decision is made to postpone it to the next release. I expect the time involved here is about five hours between two FTEs.

9.4.2.1.3 Phase: Execution

The final step would be calculating the cost of execution in the next release. Keep in mind that you perform the execution as a standalone test. We defined the sequence of testing based on impact and priority. If the outcome is complex, my advice is to test everything again to make sure that no new issues are introduced.

The benefit we learned from this approach is after delivering the maximum possible value at that moment agreements are made with business. According to those agreements we scheduled the deliverance of remaining functionality in the next release. This helped us create transparency for all stakeholders. Transparency is what is delivered, what needs to be done, by whom and when. It also provided insight in the additional costs and risks.

The business was able to make money out of the provided functionality and work on reaching the department's goals.

9.4.2.2 Example 3

Another option we choose for a specific situation was preserving the testware by definition in front of a regression test set. Based on the remaining functionality that was not delivered yet, management chose to make it part of the future release and there are opportunities for testing. We decided to make a selection of tests that also covers the remaining functionality part of the standard regression tests. The reason for this was avoidance execution of the same actions twice. In this example it is cheaper for testing to delay the functionality and test later on similar actions that are already scheduled.

For this specific change it was cheaper to ship issues to the next release so delivery of an RFC is granted and business gain can start earning back the RFC costs, especially when the test execution can be spread over the cases of newer RFCs in the next release.

9.4.2.2.1 Phase: Preparation

If the issue is of lower priority and impact, the decision can be that the testing will become part of another RFC in the same area. Instead of testing the RFC as a whole, it is tested in combination with new defined test cases. This will result in additional reading and investigation instruction of new RFCs. The test cases based on new functionality might be extended.

9.4.2.2.2 Phase: Specification

The additional cost of this approach within this phase consists of the investigation of old test cases and matching this with the new cases. Remaining issues will become an addition on the test basis. Based on the maturity of cases and also the impact and gain on functionality, a test approach must be defined. There is a change that the approach of new functionality must change due to higher impact of remaining issues that will be tested accordingly.

As new functionality is hard to schedule when the current release is not yet deployed, it is important to identify the remaining risk on project level. What is the change of disturbing a new test process? If it is cheaper to test the RFC separate, then reusage of test cases can be done. These are additional costs. These costs must be lower than the costs in missing savings of delivering late.

9.4.2.2.3 Phase: Execution

During the execution phase, the test cases become part of the new test cases. This means that it will be harder to identify the costs of solving remaining issues. Management has come to the conclusion that the importance of identifying costs to the original RFC is less compared to delivering value. As the strategy is not yet defined when this decision is made, there are several options with their own costs. Possible options to test remaining functionality are

- Test together with other RFCs
- Test only the failing test cases, and combine the regression test with the other regression tests
- Test all cases based on impact, complexity, business importance, and maturity
- Test in the proper test phases (unit test, system integration testing [SIT], user acceptance testing [UAT]), and make a combination of the above

9.5 CONCLUSION

It is not wrong to deliver functionality in a next release. Important here is that we get agreement upon the approach on valid arguments. The relation between the complexities of functionality in combination with the effort it takes at specific moments should be understood. This understanding can be created by splitting the test process into several phases. Using these phases might help us to understand the specific activities and the impact on it when certain parts are delivered late or not at all before the testing time is over. It is not up to the tester to make these decisions. The tester can make it transparent and even should note the impact changes have on their process. This information should be compared against business value and possible risks when the solution for issues or RFCs is delivered later then the moment the system is shipped to production.

When changes and issues are assessed properly you might find other options to help the organization. It is an option not to claim that everything must be delivered properly. The option is that what is delivered should be working as accepted with minimal and accepted risks. Using assessments as mentioned earlier might help to uncover the hidden costs in testing. This helps management make decisions concerning when certain parts should be delivered.

NOTES

1. Tim Koomen, Leo van der Aalst, Bart Broekman, and Michiel Vroon, *TMap Next, for Result-Driven Testing* ('s-Hertogenbosch, The Netherlands: UTN Publishers, 2007).
2. Iris Pinkster, Bob van de Burgt, Dennis Janssen, and Erik van Veenendaal, *Successful Test Management: An Integral Approach* (Berlin: Springer-Verlag, 2004).

10

Cost Reduction through Reusable Test Assets

Karen Johns

With over thirty years of industry testing experience, I have struggled with the long hours and late nights from rework due to constant changes, difficulties keeping a regression test bed viable, and all the testing pressures to get it done faster and cheaper so the software can be released. Does this sound familiar? You are a testing manager charged with testing a new version of the company's ordering software. With the new version, the login processing and the item numbering have changed. The developers have converted the test database to the new item numbers.

You meet with your test team to plan the testing. Adam, the new test automation engineer on the team, asks Mary and Mark, the two manual testers, for help identifying the scripts that need modification. They say they are too busy and they are not very familiar with the details of the automation. Adam says he can just start running the automation and see what pops up. Mary and Mark are concerned that the automation will not be available. Without the automation they will need to recreate the regression tests manually and their plate is full developing the tests for the new functionality. They will need to leave the regression testing to as time allows. They decide to split the needed testing between them.

You ask about the test data. Mark says he has a developer buddy who created a tool for gathering new order numbers. Mary says her developer friend created a query to pull item numbers for her, and Adam says he developed his own query. You mention the tight target date and the issues with the regression test bed. You ask if there are ways we can work as a team to improve the testing process to avoid these issues and reduce the testing time and effort.

The answer is yes and the answer is through reuse. We are already seeing the costs of not working in a reusable manner. If the item numbers had been centrally maintained as reusable data, and the login processing had been centralized as reusable components, Adam's work would be easy and straightforward with little need to bother the testers. If the manual tests had been originally defined and captured as reusable assets that could be directly automated, Mary and Mark could still execute the regression tests manually until the automation was ready. Maintaining and managing the new item numbers centrally as a shared asset would have simplified the update to the new numbers and would avoid the duplicate work while minimizing any potential conflicts. And rather than dividing the work and testing separately, Mark and Mary could leverage existing reusable manual tests to speed the test development and work together to create new reusable tests for the new release.

Does this sound too good to be true? Read on. This chapter describes:

- The opportunity for reusability in your testing assets
- Existing industry practices for reusing tests
- How test data can also be managed as a reusable asset to enable Full Reuse™—reuse of your manual tests, automation scripts, and test data
- How Full Reuse provides significant savings through fewer shared test assets and minimal maintenance

10.1 THE OPPORTUNITY FOR REUSABILITY

Testing is a prime candidate for reuse. Let's look closer at the testing process to see why. Testers usually start with a test plan to establish the foundation for the testing effort including scope, responsibilities, environments, tools, approaches, procedures, and so forth. The testers then proceed to analyze the system requirements to identify the tests needed to verify the system. These tests usually consist of

- Actions that input data or perform some interaction with the system
- Expected results against which the system is verified

So a tester defines an individual test composed of steps describing the tester's conduct during the test, and test data describing the specifics of any values being input into the system or expected from the system. For example, Figure 10.1 illustrates a test case to test the sign-on process for an application.

Sample Test Components

Scenario Name: Enter Valid Sign on		
Description: Sign on to the system		
Test Case	**Input/Action Description**	**Expected Results**
1	Enter **TTE STER** User ID	User ID Field displays **TTE STER**
2	Enter "**PT9summer**" Password	Password field contains **Asterisks**
3	Click Logon Button	Sign on is accepted and Menu Appears

FIGURE 10.1
Sample test case with test actions and test data.

The test case includes actions to sign on with the data TTESTER as the user ID entry and "PTSummer" as the password and then click the Logon button. From these actions, we expect the entered value to be displayed in the User ID field, asterisks in the password field and sign-on accepted resulting in the menu appearing when the Logon button is entered.

Note that to test this function thoroughly you would repeat these steps with varying user IDs and passwords, and you would also execute the sign-on processing for many different test flows. Most testing actions involved with testing efforts are largely redundant. Testing by its nature exercises a system repeatedly with varying sequences of actions and specific data to find defects. Let's look at another example. Suppose we were assigned to test an intranet order site. Let's take a look at the functional testing. The first functions we would need to test are

- Search for an item
- Review the search results
- View the product details
- Add a product to your cart
- Check out

Following checkout, we would need to test the log-in processing followed by a series of windows to enter shipping, billing, and payment information before reviewing and submitting the order. For example, Figure 10.2 illustrates three testers beginning to test the site. Each tester defines a test case that searches and reviews results. Then testers 2 and 3 begin developing test cases that repeat the cart filling and order processing. Do you see how the testing would redundantly test through this processing trying various searches, multiple cart configurations, and various billing, shipping, and

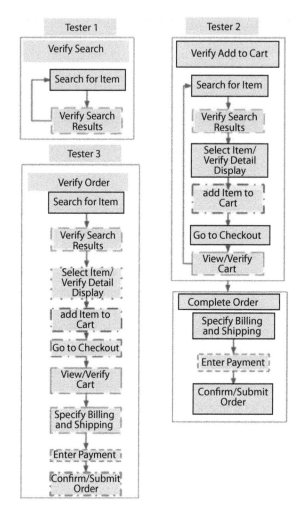

FIGURE 10.2
Four sample test cases for an intranet ordering site.

payment options? In our example, if each test case was defined and shared across testers, we would create nine test cases in place of twenty. Even with just this small sample, the savings are significant.

Structuring the various testing steps as reusable test actions greatly reduces the number of tests that must be created and maintained. The testers can then use these reusable tests to accomplish the needed testing by combining them into various sequences and system flows.

The other test component is the test data. Test data also offers ample opportunities for reuse. Let's look at our intranet order site example again.

We have a test to search for an item. What data do we need? The item name, description, price, and so forth would be required for the test. Then we create a test to verify putting an item in the shopping cart. What data is required for that test? The item name, description, price, and quantity are needed. Next we test the ordering process; again we need the item name, description, price, and so forth along with address and payment information to confirm the order. Then let's do a test case to verify the confirmation e-mail; now we have the item name, description, price, quantity, and so forth. And then the packing slip, but I think you get the idea. Most systems move, manipulate, and process similar data through the system so the testing likewise uses similar test versions of that same data. Organizing and reusing test data offers significant savings.

10.2 TECHNIQUES FOR REUSABLE TEST PLANNING

Several industry approaches are taking partial advantage of the test reusability opportunities. The term *partial reuse* is to contrast with the potential of Full Reuse that this chapter is proposing. The partial reuse in the industry is focused on reusing test actions (specified user conduct during a test). Keyword-driven testing gathers the actions as keywords that can be shared and reused across many different tests. This approach offers the added benefit that automated scripts can be developed for the keywords to enable automation of the manual tests. So with keyword-driven testing, the testers can create test cases using the keywords to specify shared actions offering advantages of reusability, maintainability, and also ease of automation.

You can implement this keyword approach with a high level of reusability with tools like HP Quality Center. Or you can set up the process using MS Excel or MS Access as shown in Figure 10.3. As the figure illustrates, you can achieve reusability of the keywords and associated scripts as the testers use the keywords for their testing. The problem is the test data. The test data is bound to each use of a keyword making the individual usage of the keyword and the test data nonreusable and also difficult to maintain. So in our first example, if keyword testing was used with the item numbers imbedded in each test, we could have hundreds of tests to find and correct.

Full Reuse requires reuse of both the test actions and the test data. As soon as data is included or bound to a test case, the test case loses its reusability. Every use will accomplish exactly the same testing with the same

Action	Input/Verification Data	Restart Point	On Error	Comments
Select Search Area	Books	Y	NextScen	Select Search type
Enter Search Item	Cookbooks	N	Errscript	Enter search criteria
Click Button	Go	N	Errscript	Perform search
Click Item Link	The Healthy College Cookbook	N	Errscript	Select item
Select Item Quantity	2	N	Errscript	Select amount
Click Button	Add to Cart	N	Errscript	Add item to cart
Click Button	Proceed to Checkout	N	Errscript	Checkout
Enter e-mail address	tester@gmail.com	N	Errscript	Sign in with e-mail
Enter password	Password1	N	Errscript	Enter password
Click	Sign in using our secure server	N	Errscript	Sign on to proceed with checkout
" "	" "			

FIGURE 10.3
Keyword-driven testing sample.

data. Although this repeatability is needed at execution time so the test can be reproduced and any defects can be fixed, it tends to be inefficient during test planning because the planned test is not reusable. To achieve the needed reusability, we need to architect the tests so that both the tests and the test data can be managed as reusable assets.

10.3 REUSING YOUR TEST DATA

Most testers today manage test data by assembling the data for each test in a data sheet. They may develop the manual tests with reusable components, but then they pair the test with one or more spreadsheets that supply the necessary test data. In a similar fashion, the automation engineers then drive their automated tests by attaching data sheets or data tables to each automated script. Attaching a data sheet with multiple instances of the test data may make the test initially reusable but this reusability is usually short-lived as the attached data becomes stale making the test unusable. In addition to maintainability issues, the data in each data sheet is often redundant since the tests manipulate the same data through many different scenarios. Figure 10.4 illustrates

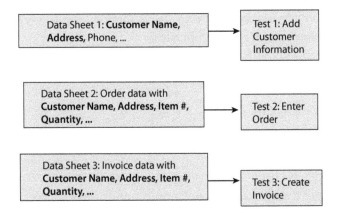

FIGURE 10.4
Three sample test cases with individual data sheets.

the potential for reusability. In this example, three testers are testing an order processing application. The first is testing the add customer functionality, the second is testing order entry, and the third invoicing. The individual data sheets would have a lot of similar if not identical data and the testers would go through similar activities to create customers, items, and orders for testing.

You can gain two cost savings by taking steps to reuse the data. The first is a reduction in the actual cost to define and manage the test data. By recognizing the redundancy and working as a team to develop and share test data, you can dramatically reduce the number of data sheets and data items needed for testing. With fewer sheets, and data created once and used multiple times, testers can reduce their test development effort.

The second saving is through improved maintainability. Most test data does not remain stable. The data in the test cases must be in sync with the test databases. The test databases can change due to system changes, date changes, environment changes, or the system processing itself. Test databases are often refreshed frequently so that they include these changes. For example, as in our initial example, if item numbers change, the testers may need to update tens to hundreds of data sheets that include item numbers. With reusability, we can consolidate the item numbers with little to no duplication, greatly simplifying the maintenance effort.

Treating test data as a reusable asset shared across testers offers large benefits, but how is it done? You can take three steps to start organizing your test data for reuse:

1. Consolidate the test data into sheets representing the types of data the system under test manipulates
2. Develop standards for the data sheets to enable sharing
3. Maintain the data sheets in a database

Let's look at each of these.

10.3.1 Consolidate the Test Data by Types of Data

As a first step, we need to reconsider the data sheet concept. Creating one data sheet per test can result in potentially hundreds of sheets with largely redundant data. Instead of a data sheet per test, we can consolidate the data needed by the tests into data sheets representing the types of data that the system under test manipulates. To differentiate the shared data sheets from the individual sheets, we call the shared data sheets data templates. The term *data template* indicates that the sheet serves as a form for the category of test data that the data template represents.

In our intranet order site example, we might set up data templates for users, items, orders, billing and shipping address, and so forth. Each template would then contain the field values for the type of test data represented. For example, the user data template may have user name, e-mail, password, and so forth, whereas the item data template would have item number, name, description, and so forth. Tests requiring users and items can then reference the appropriate instance in the data template and test cases using the same item can then share the test data. Grouping the data by type rather than test not only enables a framework for sharing the data, it also dramatically reduces the number of data sheets and enables maintainability by minimizing redundancy.

Figure 10.5 illustrates the three test cases with individual data sheets reworked to access shared data templates. In this example, the types of data needed (customers, items, and orders) are organized into separate, accessible data templates. As the example illustrates, each type of data needs to be defined only once so if the three test cases use the same customer, the customer data can be shared across the tests. Also from a maintenance standard point, if item numbers change on the test database, the tester can update a single data template to effect the change.

10.3.2 Establish Standards

Along with rethinking how the data sheets can be organized into data templates, the testers should also establish standards. Reuse requires

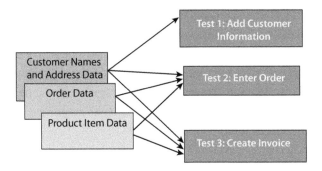

FIGURE 10.5
Three sample test cases with data templates.

consistent deliverables across testers. A uniform naming standard and a standard format for the data sheets is necessary for effective reuse across the team. You can structure naming standards to provide a unique yet meaningful name for each data sheet. For format the easiest approach is to standardize on maintaining the test data in the rows of the spreadsheets.

Along with standard formatting, you can use standards to specify one or more metadata fields before the actual data in each row. These can be used to help share and control the reusable data. A description field to describe the data condition in each row should be mandatory. Other popular metadata examples are owner or locked to allow testers to communicate when a set of data is used and should not be modified. Cross-reference fields are another example to allow data from multiple data templates to be logically related. For example, claim data may be related to the policy data with which the claims are associated.

Figure 10.6 illustrates a sample customer data template. Note that the examples in this chapter use a data sheet stored in MS Excel, but the benefits of organizing the data as reusable assets applies to other test data representations as well. Notice in this example that there are several metadata

Customer Data						
ID	Description	XREF Acct	Cust ID	Customer Name	E-mail	...
010	Valid New Cust	ACCT_010	123450987	Fran Newbody	fn@gmail.com	...
011	Valid Repeat Cust	ACCT_025	999999999	Joe Many	many@yahoo.com	...
012	Invalid ID Cust	ACCT_311	0	Fred Boss		...

FIGURE 10.6
Sample data template.

fields preceding the actual test data instances in each row. This includes an ID field to identify each instance of data so it can be referenced by the tests using the data, a description to describe the data condition in each row, and in this case a cross-reference field to cross-reference the customer to his or her account data in the account data template. These fields are then followed by the actual customer test data such as customer ID, customer name, e-mail, and so forth.

10.3.3 Maintain the Data Sheets in a Database

Now that we have reusable and sharable data, the final step is to move the data sheets to a database to enable effective sharing and maintainability. It should be mentioned that even stopping here and maintaining the data templates in MS Excel in a controlled folder according to standards is superior to maintaining individual data sheets, which are also typically organized in MS Excel. Even with MS Excel, defining data templates and sharing them dramatically reduces the number of data sheets created, supporting improved maintenance and saving test data management time.

Moving the data templates to a database significantly increases these benefits. With the power of a database environment, multiple testers can easily access and share the data. A database also provides the full capabilities to locate and search the data. Finally, a database provides improved opportunities for maintaining the data over time as the test databases change, even opening possibilities for automated maintenance of the test data. If you are already using a database or other repository, looking at the potential for increased reusability of your test data assets can provide additional benefits.

10.3.4 Achieving Full Reuse

This chapter has described how you can plan reusable actions to drive the test planning and also how you can define and manage test data as a reusable asset. The result when we combine the two is Full Reuse. Full Reuse is achieved when a tester defines his or her tests in terms of reusable actions and in place of data sheets points to data templates. This process can be done in many tools, including MS Excel and HP Quality Center. Figure 10.7 shows an MS Excel implementation—a reusable scenario with a data field to specify the data templates for a reusable test.

Reusable Super Scenario (SS)			Executable SS	Executable SS
Super Scenario Name: Check out Non Prime Known Billing	**SS ID:** QS 104_checkout_ WObill_Wship_nonprime		QS 104_checkout_ WObill_Wship_ nonprime_001	...
Author: Dan Debug	**Objective:** Test checkout processing with regular existing user with known billing and new shipping addr		Verify Checkout of one Item order— MasterCard with US address and 2-day shipping	...
Date: mm/dd/yyyy	**Setup:** Cart has one or more items and Proceed to checkout clicked		Exec OS 103_one_item_ cart_001	...
Test Scenario ID	**Description**	**Data Template(s)**	**Data Profile(s)**	**Data Profile(s)**
QS SI GN 001_ valld_signon	Sign on Valid User	QDUSR_users	DUSR_users_003	...
QS AD DR001_ ender_shipping	Enter a Shipping Address	QDCSHP_cust_ ship_address	ODCSHP_cust_ ship_address_003	...
...	...	...	...	...

FIGURE 10.7
Sample reusable scenario.

This example describes the steps to test the entry of the customer information as a reusable scenario with generic data pointing to a data template containing customer shipping address data. This scenario as written is highly reusable. You can use it to test multiple orders with both valid and invalid data. This is the case since, to make it more reusable, the commit key is outside the scenario. The steps to enter the shipping address are identical for valid and invalid data until the commit key is entered. The scenario is also reusable because you can pair it with any number of valid and invalid customer shipping addresses.

When the reusable scenarios are ready, the tester can then sequence them together for execution, and can assign data from the needed data templates. Figure 10.8 illustrates an MS Excel implementation of an executable super scenario, a name for a sequence of reusable scenarios constituting a test run. On the worksheet, the tester can plan the sequence of reusable scenarios and then specify columns for different combinations of data conditions by indicating the instances in the data template to use for the execution. We call each instance of data within a data template, a data profile. In other words, the data profile points to the row of data in the data template.

As Figure 10.8 illustrates, reusability can be maximized by delaying the assignment of test data until execution time. In fact, the super scenario or

Scenario Name: Enter Shipping Address		HLR(s): 1.0 Capture Customer Information	
Scenario ID: QSADDR001_enter_ship_address		ILR(s): 1.1, 1.2	
Description: Enter a Shipping Address		Test Automation:	
Date: mm/dd/yyyy		Setup/ Base State:	User has non-empty cart and has proceeded to checkout and signed on. Website is displaying the Shipping and Payment Screen
Author: Dan Debg			

TEST CASE #	INPUT / ACTION DESCRIPTION	EXPECTED RESULTS	DATA TEMPLATE
1	Click on Full Name field, enter Full Name and press the tab key	Full Name entered is displayed and cursor is positioned on the Address Line 1: text box	QDCSHP_cust_ship_address
2	Enter Address Line 1 and press the tab key	The Address line 1 entered is displayed and the cursor is positioned on the Address Line 2: text box	QDCSHP_cust_ship_address
...	...	...	...
8	Enter the phone number	The phone number entered is displayed	QDCSHP_cust_ship_address

FIGURE 10.8
Executable super scenario.

test flow itself is reusable because you can rerun it with multiple sets of data conditions. The columns to the right represent test runs ready for execution where test data instances from the data templates are finally assigned.

Full Reuse simply requires treating the testing deliverables as testing assets. Thinking in terms of reusability, testers can define the reusable actions underlying the tests that they need. These can be defined in a test repository and then the testers can use them to define their tests. Benefits from the reuse can be achieved immediately, and as new releases are ready for testing, the repository can continue to grow, enabling more reuse.

As the testers develop the reusable tests, they can also define the data templates that they will use to organize the test data needed for the testing effort. The reusable tests can reference the appropriate data templates. Prior to execution, the tester can identify the actual instances of the data templates to enable execution. With the reuse, the cost savings can be collected.

10.3.5 The Benefits of Full Reuse

Reusability provides numerous benefits. First, the reuse reduces the cost of planning the needed tests. With Full Reuse, fewer components need to be developed. Data costs are cut with data templates shared across testers and significantly fewer data sheets. On the testing side, fewer scenarios reduce test development costs. As an example of the savings, we implemented forty reusable scenarios for a financial application in place of one hundred sixty test cases. On the data side, only fifteen data templates were required to support one hundred tests. This level of reuse is not unusual.

A second and often more noticed benefit of Full Reuse is the reduced automation costs. Reusable scenarios and test data position the manual tests for test automation. Automation engineers can quickly develop automation scripts from the manual actions with little to no rework, minimal required application knowledge, and minimal dependency on the manual tester's time. Automation resources are freed from data creation time; the test data defined for the manual testing can be directly used for the automation. This is a practical and efficient automation approach with improved use of resources.

Reusable manual tests minimize maintenance costs of test data and automation scripts. Application changes can be focused on a few reusable actions and scripts that, once updated, propagate the change to all affected tests. Data updates can be focused on the impacted templates rather than across multiple data sheets. And with the power of a database, regression test bed data updates can be automated with even more costs savings.

10.4 CONCLUSION

Reusability is a natural way of increasing testing efficiency and significantly reducing testing costs. Testing by its nature tests application flows repeatedly in different sequences and with varying test data. By recognizing this inherent tendency toward redundancy and moving test teams to work more in mutual support, we can capitalize on the reuse and share the test development to produce fewer, less costly components while increasing coverage. Once the manual tests are reusable, we can capitalize more efficiently on test automation. Then, with fewer components to maintain, we can create the cost-effective test beds necessary to efficiently cover the risk management needs of our applications over their life.

So back to our original example. If Full Reuse had been implemented, Adam could come on board and edit the reusable scripts associated with login and then simply work with the manual testers to update the item numbers data template. Mark and Mary could leverage the reusable test bed for both their regression testing and for creating tests for the new release. Seeing these benefits, the test team works to move to Full Reuse. Adam begins pulling out reusable components as he corrects the automation to reduce maintenance going forward. Any new automation is then structured with the reuse. Mary and Mark share responsibility to consolidate the item numbers and other data into reusable data templates sharable with both the manual and automated testing effort. This allows Adam to use these item numbers as he updates and further develops the automation. Mary and Mark then work to create reusable components and data for the new functionality. With this approach, the testers are able to react more quickly to overcome the changes and efficiently test the current and upcoming releases.

11

You Can't Waste Money on a Defect That Isn't There

Petteri Lyytinen

As the introduction to this book stated, there is a constant need in the information technology (IT) world to be faster, to accomplish more with less, and to generally be more effective. Some practices, such as taking technical debt, may be fully OK in the short-term while being seriously harmful in the long-term, if not kept under control and properly addressed in time. Some people may even regard these practices as beneficial since they might not be problematic right away. Rather, they slowly develop into real problems over time. As a side effect, through this delay the people responsible for creating the problems may even appear effective at the time for coming up with a quick solution that solves a particular issue. The problem, obviously, is that although the quick solution may address an immediate need, it does so in a way that completely disregards any future needs. This kind of short-sighted thinking is not healthy as it favors quick, seemingly effective, solutions that, in reality, can be seriously damaging and actively ignore the negative financial impacts they will have. I am sure everyone in the IT world has heard a nightmare story or two about a project going way past deadline, going way over budget, and being in real trouble, quality-wise.

Although there are excellent chapters elsewhere in this book covering the topic of *how to directly reduce the cost of testing*, in this chapter I will focus more on reducing the costs indirectly by preventing defects, making the defect fixing cycles faster, and by improving the development process in a responsible, sustainable way as a whole. There are several possible ways to accomplish this, but I decided to concentrate on test-driven development, continuous integration, and some simple techniques borrowed from Lean software development principles. None of the methods I write about are new in any way, but everything I have read on these subjects has mainly concentrated on the technical side while only mentioning the cost-saving aspect briefly in passing, if at all. This chapter tells the same story but from exactly the opposite direction: I will only briefly cover the technical basics in a generalized and simplified manner and concentrate on the cost-saving aspect in more detail.

The methods and practices I write about in this chapter mainly originate from the Agile world, but there is no reason why they could not be just as effectively applied in a noniterative environment. For example, striving to minimize waste, which is borrowed from lean principles, is simply just a good idea and not bound to any specific project model or development approach.

11.1 TEST BEFORE YOU DEVELOP

As unintuitive as it might sound, by far the best way to reduce the cost of testing is to help your developers improve. I am not ignoring the importance of having skilled and experienced testers, but bear with me for a while. The reason behind this is really simple: every defect has a price tag—that keeps increasing over time—attached to it so the fewer defects that get introduced in the application, the fewer costs they will accumulate. This could potentially be achieved by sending your developers on coding courses to improve their technical skills but an even better way might be to help them change the way they approach the whole development process in general by training them to create code that is testable and tested from the very beginning. It is not so much a technical change than it is a shift in perspective.

Test-driven development, or TDD, is a development approach introduced by Kent Beck in the late 1990s [1]. In TDD, the functional requirements of a particular code module are defined first and then the actual module is developed to meet those requirements. This is done in the form of small pieces of code, or the so-called unit tests, that make assertions about the output provided by the module. The idea is that first you write a test that fails since the assertions made by it are not met. Then you write just enough code to make the test pass. Then you write another test and, again, just enough code to make that test pass. Then you keep doing this until the whole module is completed and you move on to the next module. In addition, TDD requires constant refactoring to make the code as clean and as elegant as possible, before anything is passed on to testing.

In defect prevention, TDD is an invaluable asset, mainly for the follow-ing reasons:

1. Since each module is developed against a clear set of requirements and only accepted as *done* once all of those requirements are met, the internal functionality of each individual module is guaranteed—provided the requirements themselves are correct.
2. As unit tests are a natural by-product of the approach, TDD helps ensure very high test coverage—especially when compared to an environment where no unit tests are written at all—even when the size and complexity of the code base increase over time. TDD also guarantees that all of the developed code is testable by definition.
3. As found out by Chip Groder in 1997, nearly 90 percent of all defects caught by TDD were discovered during the creative process of writ-ing the tests and the modules [2]. In any real-life development project this is likely to translate into a significant number of defects pre-vented from ever being passed on to testing. This should also easily justify the effort spent on learning and using TDD—even if the unit tests never revealed another defect afterward.

Note: The definition of *done* is no trivial thing, as Michael Bolton writes in his blog entry titled "Done, the Relative Rule, and the Unsettling Rule" [3].

Doing TDD can also save time on other levels of testing. Consider build-ing unit tests that go on the integration level, for example. Or, save time and effort by doing some calculations via unit tests that you would normally test through the user interface (UI) during system testing. Also, there is a confidence-building advantage here. More about that in the next section.

11.2 DEPLOY AND TEST CONSTANTLY

Continuous integration, or CI, refers to a development practice in which all new code committed to a source code repository, typically a version control system, is immediately built and deployed to a server where the new features and functionalities are tested right away [4]. When combined with TDD, a direct result of this practice is the confidence it offers devel-opers to commit even major changes to an application. This is because running all unit tests against each new build will immediately reveal if the recent changes broke anything. This also allows doing a quick roll-back if necessary. Obviously, the single biggest advantage of CI is instant feedback.

When the unit tests are complemented with an automated smoke test set, which refers to a limited functional test set covering the most important features and functionalities across the different application components, it frees up the testers to concentrate on manually testing the most recent changes and their integration into the already existing system. This not only contributes to higher test coverage but also leaves more time for the testers to improve on test automation and, maybe more important, to do exploratory testing—to think of new ways in which the application might be made to work incorrectly, inconsistently, erratically, or made to crash entirely.

Immediately discovering that a recent change broke the build also has the advantage that it minimizes the risk that developers continue writing new code on top of a broken module. This is important due to the fact that doing so would create a dependency on the defect being there, or in other words, if the original defect is detected and fixed later on, all of the code written on top of that module needs to be fixed as well. In large-scale projects this could result in several man-days of rework that could have been avoided entirely if the developers had been aware of the defective module sooner.

The negative financial impact of finding defects late—after product launch at worst—is clearly shown in a number of studies [5], all of which reached the very unambiguous conclusion that the longer it takes from the point of introducing a defect into an application to the point of discovering it, the more money and effort it will cost to fix it. Because of that, defect prevention as well as quick discovery and fixing cycles are among the best ways to reduce the costs associated with defects and, hence, testing.

However, no amount of testing, or builds deployed, or automated test sets executed will make an application completely defect-free, so beware the "all tests passed, there are no defects" thinking fallacy. Your build may come out with a green light, but still contain severe problems. As E. W. Dijkstra noted: "Program testing can be used to show the presence of bugs, but never to show their absence." Even Murphy's law states: "Nature always sides with the hidden flaw." You can rest assure: there will be defects, so don't fool yourself thinking otherwise. That would be a waste of time and could lead to even more severe problems.

This leads me to my third main point: small changes to eliminate—or at least mitigate—waste.

11.3 OPTIMIZE YOUR TIME MANAGEMENT

Eliminating waste is one of the key points in Lean software development [6], and, as with TDD and CI, it is possible to apply the principles in any kind of organization and project environment as all three are really just simple things many might consider plain common sense.

One of the worst cases of waste that I have personally come across in the projects I have participated in is waiting to be able to do something productive—for example, waiting for a fix after reporting a defect through a defect management system or waiting for a reply to an e-mail asking for clarifications. Fortunately, in many cases, the simplest way to reduce this waiting time is direct personal interaction with the people involved.

For example, it would be a good idea to seat your whole team in the same place so that when a tester discovers a defect he does not need to file a ticket in a defect management system, wait for a developer to notice the ticket, fix the issue, and then assign the ticket back to the tester for retesting. Instead, the tester can just tap the developer on the shoulder, describe the defect to him or her, and then have the developer notify the tester as soon as the issue has been fixed so he can verify if the fix really solves the problem. If not, the tester can immediately report further findings related to it. If required—for example, due to customer demands—the defect can be reported in a defect management system while waiting for a developer to fix the issue.

If it is not possible to physically seat the team in the same place, for example, due to offshoring, then the second best option is to use some kind of near-real-time communication method like instant messaging. The key point here is to minimize unnecessary waiting overhead as this overhead may interrupt the flow of information and cause value-generating work to stop. Reducing it helps the team members keep focused and spend less time twiddling their thumbs wondering how to spend the weekend. This is important due to the simple fact that idle employees are still generating costs while not producing anything valuable in return, which, by almost any definition, is waste. Of course, everyone needs a bit of slack every now and then in order to stay in a good working condition, but that is beyond the scope of this book so I will not go any deeper into that.

Another huge source of waste is trying to cover everything with testing, which is impossible [7]. Test cases and test automation scripts are generally good, up to a point, where you hit diminishing returns, that is, adding more test cases adds less and less value compared to the effort required to prepare—and maintain—them. There are a number of ways to try to optimize the amount of test cases prepared, and one helpful way could be to try combinatorial testing. In combinatorial testing the purpose is to find the most effective combinations of test input in order to reach maximum coverage with as few test cases as possible. For more information about combinatorial testing, read Chapter 14 in this book by Justin Hunter and Gary Gack.

Another way that I have found working is to only give just enough information in the test cases you prepare. Over the years, I have developed a personal approach that I call iterative test development. In practice it means that when I read a user story, a use case, or a part of a technical specification, depending on the project, I write down a few brief lines about what I think needs to be tested. At this point, those lines are just potential test case names. When developers start coding the features, I add some high-level content to each test case but will not go into too much detail yet. Then, once a feature implementation is complete, I will not only start testing it but also fill in the exact details for all test cases related to that feature. At the same time, I keep constantly comparing the implementation with the requirements.

Advantages of the approach are that developing test cases this way:

1. Helps me truly understand each feature
2. Works as a way to recheck the requirements
3. Saves time as I will not write more than is absolutely necessary to be able to test each feature

So far, this approach has worked quite effectively. In addition to saving time and effort, it works as a way to help control the costs without concentrating on the costs (see Chapter 1 by Matt Heusser and particularly the quote by John Seddon). Also, I have found it useful to apply the same approach to test automation, or in short: do not automate what you do not plan to test manually. Manual one-time throwaway tests are often useful but think twice if it really is worth the effort to write throwaway test automation scripts. In some cases those may be justified, for example, when you have a lot of test data to process in a test, so do not abandon the idea entirely.

11.4 SUMMARY

The goal of this chapter was to point out some simple approaches and practices that can effectively be utilized to help make a team's work more effective and reduce the costs related to defects as a positive side effect.

Whereas other chapters in this book will give you more practical, hands-on advice on how to achieve cost reductions by doing things in a more professional way, I am hoping to nudge people toward a more responsible direction. These two aspects, professional and responsible, should naturally go hand in hand but that does not always seem to happen. Your mental disposition is no trivial issue—you could have all the best tools available and all the best experts working for you but you could still fail if you are not committed to success in a responsible, sustainable way.

The bottom line is do not make short-sighted decisions that will save you ten thousand dollars right now but cost you fifty thousand dollars over the next six months. Do not allow the amount of technical debt to grow uncontrollably hoping somebody else will pay the price for your irresponsible decisions, and so on. Irresponsible actions like that are guaranteed to generate unnecessary extra costs. Be responsible.

NOTES

1. Kent Beck, *Test-Driven Development: By Example* (Boston: Addison-Wesley, 2003).
2. Cem Kaner, "Avoiding Shelfware: A Manager's View of Automated GUI Testing," 1998, p. 5, item 4, http://www.kaner.com/pdfs/shelfwar.pdf.
3. Michael Bolton, "Blog: Done, The Relative Rule, and The Unsettling Rule," 2010, http://www.developsense.com/blog/2010/09/done-the-relative-rule-and-the-unsettling-rule/.
4. Paul M. Duvall, Steve Matyas, and Andrew Glover, *Continuous Integration: Improving Software Quality and Reducing Risk* (Upper Saddle River, NJ: Addison-Wesley, 2007).

5. Johanna Rothman, "What Does It Cost You to Fix a Defect? And Why Should You Care?" 2000, http://www.jrothman.com/Papers/Costtofixdefect.html; RTI, "The Economic Impacts of Inadequate Infrastructure for Software Testing" 2002, pp. 1–13, table 1-5, http://www.nist.gov/director/planning/upload/report02-3.pdf.
6. Mary Poppendieck and Tom Poppendieck, *Lean Software Development: An Agile Toolkit* (Boston: Addison-Wesley Professional, 2003).
7. Gerald M. Weinberg, *Perfect Software: And Other Illusions about Testing* (New York: Dorset House, 2008).

Part 3

How Should We Do It?

12

A Nimble Test Plan: Removing the Cost of Overplanning

David Gilbert

One of the simplest ways to lower the cost of testing is to avoid unnecessary testing and testing-related tasks. I have often seen clients spend an unreasonable amount of time and resources creating long-winded test plans. This not only represents an initial waste of resources, but it entraps rather than empowers. It can cause people who are beholden to the plan to do things that are increasingly inefficient as time goes by. By keeping our test plans lightweight and focused, not overplanning and being responsive to change along the way, we can make our testing efforts more efficient and less costly.

12.1 WHAT IS A NIMBLE TEST PLAN?

A nimble test plan is a point of departure. Years ago a young engineer on the *USS Alexander Hamilton* said to me, "A plan is simply a point of departure." He knew nothing about software testing, yet in that simple statement he expressed more understanding of exploratory thinking than many testers of today. He understood that a plan tells you what you *believe* you are going to do, not necessarily what you *are* going to do. He understood that things change over the course of time and that being able to adapt to that change is far more effective than being locked into a plan that was created earlier. He understood that the value of a plan was not to govern one's actions, but to focus one's intention. Accordingly, a test plan focuses our intention for testing; therefore, it stands to reason, if we base that plan on some really good ideas for testing, we should end up with a really good plan.

Consider the concept of "exploratory" in an historical context. Explorers of old were sent out to sea with ships, provisions, and a basic mission. Although these missions were often altruistically justified, they were in reality mostly meant to expand the financial strength of the backers, typically the king and queen. However, the king and queen were smart enough to know that they could not dictate to the explorer anything like this:

- For two days sail due west
- Turn left and then for two months sail due south
- Turn right and then for four months sail due west
- Turn right and sail due north until you hit the North Pole
- Map your route so everyone else can learn it

The problem is if you spell the route out in advance, then there is no value in exploring to learn it, since you already know it. The real problem however, is not that you already know the route, but that you *think* you already know the route. A more likely plan to be handed to the explorer would look like this: Take these ships and provisions and sailors, find a new southwest route to the North Pole, map it out, and bring it back to us.

The autonomy and decision making is now left in the hands of the seafaring explorers. If we need structure, schedules, and accountability, a more formal plan may look like this:

On Sunday, report to the docks and take command of your four ships. From Monday until Friday, stock them with provisions, interview prospective sailors and appoint officers beneath you as you see fit. On Saturday, given the weather is accommodating, sail forth on your appointed adventure. Every Sunday, send a carrier pigeon back with your location and a summary of how the voyage is going. If you need anything, let us know. If you find friendly ports along the way, let us know so we can begin conducting trade with them and make alliances, which may be politically beneficial. If the weather is so foul you cannot continue, let us know and turn back. Godspeed.

In addition to the original description of the mission, we have a schedule, a reporting process, the ability to make good use of incremental progress, and exit criteria. This sounds a lot like a test plan. The plan still does not dictate the actual exploration, the schedule is sufficiently open ended to allow the explorers to do their job, and the goals and criteria are voiced in such a way as to not breed fear of failure (which may ultimately lead people to obfuscate truth). Although the communication in this simple example is fairly one sided, it still provides value to the customer as quickly as possible and there is some feedback for changing the plan in process. Our modern nimble test plan will have efficient face-to-face communication and feedback built in, and it will be a living document that changes as new information unfolds to better support the needs of the customer.

A nimble test plan is a point of departure from which we begin to learn those things about the application that we wish to know and those things that we have not even considered but may find valuable. It should provide support and an appropriate degree of formalism and structure, without constraining the effort to the point of stagnation. It should clearly accept the fact that whatever you believe you already know, you understand that you do not know everything; some of what you think you know will ultimately be proven wrong and that the process of discovering what you do not already know will take time and effort, which simply cannot be accounted for and scheduled fully in advance. A nimble test plan is nimble.

Dictionary.com defines *nimble* as:

- Quick and light in movement; moving with ease; agile; active; rapid: nimble feet
- Quick to understand, think, devise, etc.: a nimble mind
- Cleverly contrived: a story with a nimble plot

Therefore, for a test plan to be nimble it must be small, lightweight, adaptable to change as the project unfolds, and easy to read and understand. It contains only useful information about important aspects of the system and is completely focused on the goal to deliver value to the customer. The opposite of a nimble test plan is a cumbersome test plan: huge, difficult to change, not focused on customer needs.

The nimble plan changes and evolves as time progresses based on customers', needs which may change over time, based on the information we provide and other outside influences. Our test plan should be nimble enough to respond to those changes rapidly.

A nimble test plan uses good ideas from many different disciplines. A nimble test plan gets good ideas by borrowing from many different disciplines as required by the changing needs of the customer, not necessarily adhering to all of the tenets of any of them.

Exploratory testing, rapid software testing, Lean testing, and Agile testing are four evolving schools of thought in the software quality assurance universe, each bringing its own unique perspective and application to the table.

James Bach, author of *Exploratory Testing Explained* (http://www.satisfice .com/articles/et-article.pdf), defines exploratory testing as follows:

> I've tried various definitions of exploratory testing. The one that has emerged as the all around favorite among my colleagues is this:
>
>> Exploratory testing is simultaneous learning, test design and test execution. In other words, exploratory testing is any testing to the extent that the tester actively controls the design of the tests as those tests are performed and uses information gained while testing to design new and better tests.

Later, Bach describes critical thinking as one of the characteristics of a good exploratory tester:

> Critical Thinking. Excellent exploratory testers are able to review and explain their logic, looking for errors in their own thinking. This is especially important when reporting the status of a session of exploratory tests, or investigating a defect.

By expanding our concept from exploratory testing to exploratory thinking, we can apply these ideas to any part of the testing process, including the creation of supporting documentation.

Rapid software testing (RST) is a concept developed by James Bach and Michael Bolton that seeks to teach and improve core testing skills rather than impose a methodological system of prestructured testing. In RST, the test plan is defined as the set of ideas that guides your test project. It is the combination of strategy and logistics:

> Strategy—The set of ideas that guides your test design
> Logistics—The set of ideas that guides your application of resources to fulfilling the test strategy

According to Bach and Bolton, a good test strategy should be product specific, practical, risk focused, and diversified.

The National Institute of Standards and Technology defines Lean as "a systematic approach to identifying and eliminating waste through continuous improvement, flowing the product at the pull of the customer in pursuit of perfection."

Lean processes fit nicely into a nimble test plan because Lean is obsessively focused on eliminating waste. Lean is very customer centric, with the value of a Lean process pulled by the customer. Lean is also more strategically focused than other Agile methodologies and has a very practical sense to it. Lean software development is based on the following seven principles:

1. Eliminate waste
2. Amplify learning
3. Decide as late as possible
4. Deliver as fast as possible
5. Empower the team
6. Build integrity in
7. See the whole

Agile is a software-specific theology focused on providing rapid and continuous value to the customer in a software development environment. Although Agile was designed to guide development, we can still look at how to apply it to nimble testing, to help us drive cost out of testing.

In the book *Agile Testing: A Practical Guide for Testers and Agile Teams,* Lisa Crispin and Janet Gregory provide a straightforward list of ten principles of Agile testing:

1. Provide continuous feedback
2. Deliver value to the customer
3. Enable face-to-face communications
4. Have courage
5. Keep it simple
6. Practice continuous improvement
7. Respond to change
8. Self-organize
9. Focus on people
10. Enjoy

12.2 RULES FOR CREATING A NIMBLE TEST PLAN

We have briefly discussed how various theologies of testing provide good ideas that we can use in creating more useful test plans. The challenge is to put as many of these various ideas as possible together into a single, cohesive whole and create our new beast: the nimble test plan.

Following are eight tenets or rules for creating a nimble test plan, followed by a brief summary of how each applies.

1. Keep it light
2. Make all content goal oriented
3. Commit to as little as possible
4. Keep it practical
5. Empower the team
6. Create fast feedback loops
7. Iterate often
8. Communicate face to face

12.2.1 Keep It Light

Exploratory thinking says we cannot know all the tests in advance and write them in a plan; rather, we will come up with new and valuable ideas along the way and have the freedom to explore, then prove or devalue them. There may be little to no value in some of the ideas along the way, which is fine. With exploratory testing, we discover lack of value quickly and that idea will be set aside for other more valuable ideas to explore. The value in this concept is that an idea not thought of in advance may turn out to be important. Given that this potential value exists, when creating a test plan, be careful not to craft a document that would curtail exploratory practices. If the test plan completely dictates the scope and detail of the work to be done, then little new information will be learned in the process. The test plan should provide proper guidance for the scope of testing, but should not dictate the act of testing.

Agile tells us to keep it simple and this may be the single greatest contribution from our list of Agile principles. Test plans (especially test plans written by committees) by their very nature want to expand and expand. There is so much to test and no one wants to have to admit to forgetting the one thing that blew up. Everyone also wants to cover his or her political posterior, which means building in as much plausible deniability for responsibility as possible. Fight these things as much as you can. They are not practical and they do nothing to empower good testing. Minimize at every opportunity. Simplify to the point that it is painful.

Lean processes dictate that everything not adding value to the customer is considered to be waste. This includes unnecessary code and functionality, delay in the software development process, unclear requirements, bureaucracy, and slow internal communication.

Although unnecessary code and functionality are a bit outside the scope of this chapter, all these other elements may bear directly on the content of our test plan. If we consider automated test scripts to be code, or for that matter, testing to be functionality, then that bullet applies as well.

Remember the test plan is our point of departure for moving forward. There really is no place in it for history, theology, politics, architecture, and other technical design considerations, or fortune telling beyond what can practically be understood at the beginning of our testing journey. Those things simply bloat the document, making it unwieldy and practically guaranteeing no one will ever use it. Light is approachable. Light can be quickly read in its totality, understood completely, and altered appropriately as events unfold. If this does not describe your test plan, it is not nimble. The test plan is about moving forward on good, practical testing. If an idea does not specifically and realistically support and drive actionable, good testing, it should not be in our test plan.

12.2.2 Make All Content Goal Oriented

One of the primary concepts taught in rapid software testing is heuristics, a rule of thumb that works well most of the time. Since we are already employing the concept of exploratory thinking and allowing for the epiphany of the previously unknown over the course of our testing, the concept of creating a plan based on an imperfect understanding should not bother us. Remember, the plan is a point of departure. It provides structure and guidance, but if reality changes along the way it is also adaptable and changeable.

RST is full of useful heuristics, but the one I recommend most for test plans is the San Francisco Depot (SFDPOT): structure, function, data, platform, operations, and time. SFDPOT is a simple way to remember the content structure you should be looking for in a nimble test plan. While each of these elements has an entire list of heuristics beneath it, for the purpose of our nimble test plan I would simply use these as elements to be explored (with a small amount of context-specific description to support whatever real information may be known about the system we are testing). If you plan on testing these areas of a system and actually execute that plan, you will already be far ahead of many of the testing efforts I have witnessed.

So often, we allow documentation to become the repository of useless information. Any part of a test plan that is not making a specific statement about how we are going to move forward with our testing to our stated goals is by definition useless and should be pared out.

12.2.3 Commit to as Little as Possible

Exploratory testing says that we cannot know all the tests in advance and write them in a plan; rather, you will come up with new and valuable ideas along the way and should have the freedom to explore, then prove or devalue them.

Lean methodologies also teach us to decide as late as possible. This concept seeks to keep your options open as long as you can. Do not make decisions and plans now for something you cannot do for a long time. You can never be certain about how things may change in that time.

The test cycle, especially in environments that are waterfall, gets squeezed for time. If the time for testing gets squeezed, the scope of testing will also get squeezed and simple good sense dictates some testing that was planned may not get done. How much time, energy, resources, and money have already been invested toward that testing that now cannot be done in time? Rather than locking into a complete "we will test all of these requirements and we will do it this way" philosophy, be more flexible. Organize requirements or test cases into testable groups based on some agreed upon criteria such as risk. Outline the projected approach to testing the groups and invest in tools, research, systems support, and so forth, as needed for each group as that group gets close. When the realities of time and rework and technical difficulty dictate that some testing will not be done, there will be no need to have last-minute meetings to try to redo the schedule, explain away the problem, or justify time and expenses already sunk. Simply decide which options from the plan are realistic and proceed.

This is not a call to laziness. Rather, it is a call to rationality. Exploratory testing teaches us that the next test we execute should be influenced by the results of the last test we executed. Keeping that in mind, there is therefore a finite and quite short limit to how far into the future we can reasonably expect to see. Do not commit to anything beyond that. Doing so will only make the entire team feel obligated to adhere to decisions made in a state of ignorance—and may very well obligate time, money, and resources of the organization in wasteful ways. The fast feedback loops and quick iterations we build into the plan later will take care of any perceived shortcomings of such an approach. Committing to as little as possible for each of those iterations helps to ensure the most nimble execution of our plan.

12.2.4 Keep It Practical

Rapid software testing teaches that our test strategy should first be product specific. One of the major causes of poor test plans is the practice of reusing an old test plan for a new project. This is often done to make test plans look uniform. However, after just a few iterations of this, test plans end up with entire pages of irrelevant content, which has become so generic that it no longer empowers or supports the current project. Rather, it becomes a general statement about the corporate policies regarding testing at large. Although this information may be useful in some context, it simply does not belong in the test plan. It fails to provide strategy and logistics of the actual testing and does nothing to empower or support that process. It diminishes the document's focus and lowers the plan's effectiveness. The way to avoid this is quite simple: start each test plan with a blank sheet of paper. If you must conform to some corporate standard, then try to limit it to a simple outline.

Second, it should be practical. Above all else, our nimble test plan is about empowering the team to do good testing and returning good information to the customer. Anything that is not goal oriented should not be included in our plan. As you add content to your test plan, continually ask, "How will this help the test team do good testing?"

Third, it should be risk focused. RST also incorporates risk as a powerful tool in the tester's arsenal. Among other things, it provides a practical way to focus on the most important parts of a system. With that information, we can prioritize which parts of our model need the most attention and in what order. A risk matrix is an excellent addition to any test plan and is easy to create. You can do it in a group meeting or just by talking with stakeholders individually. Ask them what parts of the system or functionality worry them the most and how bad it would be if that part of the system did not work. Compile their answers and give them a relative weighting of high, medium, and low. Then, put all of that into a table and plan on testing in that order. As a working guideline, it is an excellent starting point for prioritization and as such should be a staple in a nimble test plan.

Lean teaches us to build integrity in. Recall that although the plan is a point of departure and a means of empowering the team to do good testing, it is also a champion of our intent. As such, we want it to be a professionally written document of integrity.

To say that our test plan should have integrity means that the document's separate sections work well together as a whole with balance between flexibility, maintainability, efficiency, and responsiveness. This could be achieved by understanding the problem domain and solving it at the same time, not sequentially. The feedback to the stakeholders is received in small batch pieces—not in one vast chunk—with preferable face-to-face communication and not a lot of written documentation. The information flow should be constant in both directions—from the test team to the development team and back, thus avoiding the large stressful amount of information after long periods of testing in isolation. By clearly stating our intentions to operate in this fashion and then following through, our nimble test plan becomes a document people will have trust in, rather than an exercise in bureaucratic wordsmithing.

A test plan should be a document of action, not a theoretical treatise. We have already stated that the content should be goal oriented, but even goal-oriented content can sometimes become unrealistic if our goals are not firmly grounded. Grandiose goals lead to grandiose plans. When grandiose or unrealistic plans get foisted off onto the backs of those responsible for implementing them, there is a sense of powerlessness and defeatism that can hinder or even completely paralyze progress. Keeping it practical leads directly to our next tenet: empower the team.

12.2.5 Empower the Team

This sounds more in line with implementing the plan than with creating it. However, if you do not explicitly empower the team in the test plan itself, the likelihood of their being empowered throughout the implementation of said plan greatly diminishes.

One of the concepts we pull from Agile is self-organization. In the context of testing, the simple definition of self-organization is "that property of a test team that allows them to respond to changes and challenges in the testing process by calling upon the skills of different individuals—and allowing those individuals to direct the efforts of some or all of the team as those skills are needed." Once that challenge is solved and the next one arises, a totally different team structure may emerge as other skills are needed. Management must step aside for this internal evolution and intervene just enough to keep the team on task. This type of management focuses on removing roadblocks to progress and facilitating information transfer in and out of the team.

Agile also teaches us to focus on people and seeks to rapidly create value for the customer. In order to do that you must understand what the customer values. One way to do this is through face-to-face communication. Software development is a people process. People gather the requirements, people write the code, and people test the code. While stacks of documentation may contain a wealth of information, understanding what is really important requires interacting with people. As you write your test plan, do not lose sight of this fact. Focus on roles, relationships, and ways that information will be communicated.

Finally, Lean tells us to empower the team. Empowering the team motivates people to do good work by making them responsible for that work. When creating a test plan, one of the simplest ways to do this is through proper task management. If you have a task that requires a specific skill set and a team member with that skill set—for example, some custom development of a test harness and a team member who has strong development skills—then assign that task to that team member.

Remember that the primary goal of our test plan is to empower good testing. The next goal is to communicate to other stakeholders how we are going to empower good testing—which sometimes means stating what is obvious to us, the test team, but may not be obvious to the stakeholders. It is common for test plans to have a roles and responsibilities section. Consider listing the team members and then make a short statement to the effect that you employ a diverse team and that different members will fulfill varying roles as needed to conduct the testing.

However, empowering is more than just task assignment. There is an old saying: "Do not make someone accountable for something they are not responsible for." When you assign tasks, transfer ownership and responsibility for that task as well. Let people do the job the way they believe it needs to be done, as long as the job is done responsibly and meets objectives (strongly reminiscent of the self-organizing principle). State clearly they are the primary point of contact and own the task and its associated processes. This sends a clear and highly motivating signal that will inspire them to step up to the plate and deliver.

Although this may not be noticeable the first time you do it, after a few times it will become energizing to the team. This has an immediate self-organizing effect, empowering everyone on the team to have a greater sense of control and understanding (even if they do not explicitly own any particular task).

12.2.6 Create Fast Feedback Loops

One of the keys to making a nimble test plan work is the creation of fast feedback loops. For the plan to evolve properly, feedback must find its way back to the project teams in a timely manner.

The Agile concept of deliver value to the customer is really at the heart of what we should be seeking to do as testers, and in our nimble test plan we want to document how we are going to deliver that value quickly.

The Lean concept of deliver as fast as possible applies to all aspects of the system development life cycle (SDLC), including testing and the test plan. Aside from the fact that people are impatient, delivering as fast as possible is key to avoiding one of the biggest problems with a non-nimble test plan: that you must decide everything before doing anything. Nonnimble test plans say "we will do this and this and this and we will do it this way and that way," which means you have to make a lot of big, expensive decisions up front, without the benefit of knowing how things evolve over time. Yes, you can adapt, but at a high cost. This directly violates our earlier principle of deciding as late as possible. It also violates the principle of eliminating waste.

Instead, plan to do a little testing, get the results to the development team (amplify learning) and decide (as late as possible) what further testing is warranted and in what order. This only works, however, if the results of those tests are delivered as quickly as possible. If the feedback from the testing you are doing is delayed by bureaucracy or technical impediments, then the development team will not have the trust to allow the plan to work. It will push to include more of what it considers critical work in the initial round of testing, thereby making the design larger and more complex (ergo, more expensive and more wasteful), making more commitments up front (violating the decide as late as possible principle), and naturally pushing to a less nimble process.

Strive to plan on short iterations with a fast, personal feedback loop, with follow-on iterations of optional testing that can be picked up or not as deemed necessary based on the results of the original testing.

When designing your nimble plan, it is absolutely vital that you communicate as much as possible with the development team. By committing to as little as we can and keeping documentation to an absolute minimum, we leave many things unsettled during critical parts of the project—and it is easy to fool ourselves into thinking that things have been settled when they have not. Constant, clear communication is important rather than leaving that communication to chance. Communication must be part of the plan from the beginning. A good weekly meeting where test results executed so far are reviewed and risks and issues are addressed will provide much better benefit than an arbitrary line in the sand six months out where the total results of all testing are expected to be magically provided.

12.2.7 Iterate Often

Build into the test plan a commitment to iterate (to take critical information from the test team to the development team and vice versa) often. This commitment should include the methodologies and personal assignments to manage iterations. It means we need to have a written process that allows critical information to drive iterative team activities without creating feelings of resentment, powerlessness, or loss of control or ownership. An iterative process should look something like the following:

- Quickly stop testing based on critical information found from testing
- Put the project back into development
- Have the development make critical changes to design and implementation
- Get the project back to testing
- Possibly also make adjustments to the test goals and designs

In Lean methodologies, the amplify learning concept tells us we should seek to shorten and personalize whatever feedback loops we can from the test team to the other stakeholders. For instance, do not create a plan that says you will do all of your testing and then create a huge written report to deliver that contains all of the defects you found. Do your testing in short iterative loops and supply feedback to the development teams as quickly as you can. Document how these loops will be scoped and defined and how you will supply the feedback to the development team, hopefully face to face.

Agile also teaches us to practice continuous improvement and the basic idea behind this is pretty straightforward: you do something for a bit, then you check it to see if it is going well, then you make adjustments to improve it. "For a bit" is the key. You do not want to do so much that you become heavily invested in a bad process that harms the project before you make adjustments, but you also do not want to stop and check so often that it impedes forward progress.

A simple weekly check-in meeting where suggestions can be brought up and considered can work very well. Find what fits for you and your team, but be sure it is incorporated both in your plan and in your schedule. By making it a point to say, "Part of what we do is a constant sanity check on what we are doing," this important element will be less likely to fall through the cracks and your test plan, as well as your testing, will become more nimble.

12.2.8 Communicate Face to Face

Two more points from Agile—enable face-to-face communications and have courage—support our last nimble tenet.

Face-to-face communications are vital. There is so much to communication that is nonverbal such as body language, facial expression, breathing patterns, nervous ticks, laughter, speed, and tempo. There is an energy flow when two people ask questions and answer them, and the answer leads to the next question by its illumination of previously unknown information. That simply cannot happen in asynchronous written communication.

It does not have to be a formal weekly meeting. It can be lunch or a late afternoon wind-down session. Just be sure you include in your test plan a regular means to be with the other stakeholders to discuss how things are going. It will pay great dividends.

How does having courage apply to writing a nimble test plan? Courage allows you to withstand challenges to the ideas you present in your test plan. Many of the things I advocate in this chapter may be challenged. The bottom line is that this is not corporate standard test planning and you will have to stick to your guns to get such a thing accomplished.

12.3 CONCLUSION

A plan should not dictate. It should hold out a collection of ideas and foundational agreements that will drive the actions of teams toward a common goal. It should do so with a minimum of wasted time and effort, and without creating unbeneficial documentation along the way. After reading this chapter, you would likely agree that it would seem ludicrous for me to now dictate exactly how you should create your nimble test plan. I do not even know your context. However, the guidelines and comments presented, along with their more detailed information, should serve you well to determine how to create a nimble test plan that is appropriate for you and your organization.

Beginning with the end in mind is a great axiom for planning such adventures and so as we reach the end of this chapter, let's go back to the beginning to see if we have come full circle. I began by telling a tale of explorers headed for sea and the instructions provided to them by the king and queen for their voyage.

- Those instructions were short, sweet, and to the point. (Keep it light)
- They were focused on exactly what the king and queen wanted done and did not bother in any way addressing other issues such as how to find fresh food and water along the way. (Make all content goal oriented)
- They provided only the guidance and provisioning needed to get the adventure started, but clearly stated that they would address additional needs as they arose. (Commit to as little as possible)
- The goal was grand, but the specifics of execution were not micromanaged or grandiose in nature. (Keep it practical)
- Although in this example there was really only a team of one captain, he was empowered with making decisions regarding execution of almost all details. (Empower the team)
- A simple, effective feedback mechanism was put into place, which not only kept the stakeholders abreast of the status of the adventure but also allowed them to take quick advantage of early successes, allowing them to revise the plan and supply additional assistance as needed. (Create fast feedback loops)

- The schedule for that feedback was set and was relatively rapid, so that the two-way flow of information was clearly established and met the needs of all involved. (Iterate often)

Alas, our example fails on the tenet of communicate face to face, as it is somewhat difficult for our intrepid explorers to be back in front of the king and queen every week for a new report while the explorers are out discovering a new route to the North Pole. However, this is fine because the goal is not to create the perfect test plan but rather to create a nimble test plan, to thereby greatly reduce the man-hours and direct cost of creating that plan in the first place. Then continue to reduce cost by reducing the amount of inevitable rework as events unfold and adjustments need to be made.

Many modern organizations could benefit greatly and reduce costs appreciably by adopting such practices. Not only would the immediate costs of creating the plan be greatly reduced and the long-term costs of maintaining it reduced as well, but the positive aspects of setting standards and expectations up front in such a positive and proactive fashion would pay immeasurable long-term benefits. Lowering the cost of testing is not just about reducing headcounts and billable hours but about creating more efficient organizations from the ground up.

13

Exploiting the Testing Bottleneck

Markus Gärtner

Testing is the bottleneck on software development projects. That's what some people say. Managers may wait for the software to be ready while testing is still ongoing. More often this perception is wrong. The requirements were not as thorough as they should have been, the architecture did not scale up as it ought to, the code was not as well written as it could have been, and all of this is piling up until the last step in the project, which is testing before delivery. In order to reduce the cost of testing, we have to look at the whole project for optimizations. In *The Goal,* Goldratt refers to this as exploiting the bottleneck (Goldratt, Cox, and Whitford 2004).

In this chapter, let's take a look at testing on an ideal Agile project. Testing helps to remove the impediments that exist in more traditional projects. This may sound like a fable to you. It is not.

Before we start, we need a few definitions. In the following, *software development* means every aspect of creating software products: the act of trawling requirements, the act of conceptualizing a software product, of designing it, of programming and testing it, alongside with the necessary documentation and training for the users of the product. The according discrete work products evolve while the project runs and are therefore parts that are *developed.* I will mention *programmers* for the activity of coding, and *testers* for the activity of testing, *developer* means any part of the whole team with all the roles required for the particular product.

Agile projects use *iterations* between one and six weeks in length. Some compare these iterations with the heartbeat of the project. After each iteration, the team delivers a *shippable product. Shippable* means that it is ready to use, deployable on a Web server, or ready to run through the DVD press. *Shippable* also means that we can ship the product but not that we necessarily will. At the end of the iteration, the team *demonstrates* the working product to the customer. The team *plans* each iteration in and on its own. Since the business priorities may change, iterations let us adapt to fit customer needs.

There are a few roles defined. Scrum defines a *product owner*. Other Agile methodologies provide comparable roles. The purpose of these roles is to provide the team answers on a continually basis. Otherwise open questions would block the team.

In Agile methodologies the team creates *acceptance tests* on the level of a user story. The terms *acceptance test* and *story test* are used interchangeably.

At the time of this writing, Scrum is the most widespread Agile approach. The terms used are mostly based upon Scrum. Other Agile methodologies like XP or Crystal have similar mechanisms in place.

13.1 PREPARING AN ITERATION

Testers get involved right from the start. They provide estimates during the planning of the iteration. They help the customer to identify acceptance tests. They help to tackle the risks in the software. Compared to traditional software testing, these activities directly reduce testing efforts before we even start to think about it.

13.1.1 Iteration Preparation

The product owner maintains the product backlog. The product backlog consists of prioritized, estimated user stories. Usually the work items are written down on index cards. The most popular approach is to use story cards to track individual user stories.

In the planning meeting the team members discuss which stories they think they can finish during the iteration. The associated story cards are pinned on a commonly visible board, so that everyone on the team, as well as any stakeholder, knows about the scope of work for the current iteration.

Any time a new requirement is identified, the product owner creates a new story card. To identify the priority of the feature, the product owner will check with a programmer how much effort this feature may take. The programmer will then provide a story point estimation for the individual story. Sometimes the programmer misses some aspect of the story that has high impact on testing it. That programmer then checks her estimate with a tester.

On some teams, the product owner invites testers and programmers to an estimation meeting. In the meeting testers and programmers clarify stories and estimate them collaboratively. So testers are involved in planning and estimating right from the start.

Testers help the customer define basic acceptance tests for any user story. Cohn (2004) suggests to track these on the back of the card. Usually these tests consist of simple happy paths together with some corner cases that are relevant for the business rules. Testers help the customer on this by bringing in their talent as critical thinkers.

Testers help the customer and the programmer to think about critical conditions, which may not have been thought about initially. Since testers are not the only ones contributing, a wide variety of viewpoints helps to collaborate in getting a first set of tests before development has started. The team communicates right from the start about problems in the underlying rules, rather than deferring critical conditions until the end of the project. The customer decides about the trade-offs. Some corner cases might be treated more thoroughly, thereby the feature gets more expensive, or the implementation may be left as is in a suboptimal state, or to have it now as is, but pay for improvements in a later iteration.

For example, consider a user story for signing up to courses of an online university. The product owner and the programmer have written the story. Students want to sign up for courses for the next term. As basic happy path test cases they identify that a student should be able to enroll in a new course for the current and next term. The tester asks what should happen if the course is currently full. The customer explains that the student is put on a waiting list. As the team works on the story, they notice the story is too large to estimate and plan.

They break the story into the enrollment part and the waiting list part. The product owner decides that a suboptimal of just the enrollment is a first step, but by putting up the second story of a waiting list for enrollment to full courses, she indicates the willingness to pay for improvements later.

In this example, the tester's feedback reveals the missing case of a full course. Calling out that new case was very important: Had the team started only consulting the tester at a later point in time, this would have been hidden until late into the project.

13.1.2 Release and Iteration Planning

During planning, testers help the team see the impact on testing. As stories are chosen for implementation, testers contribute in the planning meeting with their view on the testability of features. They may occasionally help the team trade-off a simpler implementation with a more testable implementation of the same feature. Testing costs can be reduced right before any implementation is done. Since Agile teams follow the principle to postpone hard-to-change decisions as late as possible, the whole team can decide upon different alternatives to testability problems.

During Planning Poker the team sits together to estimate the size of a user story ("Planning Poker" n.d.). Each participant takes a card holding his or her estimate, and places it facedown. When everyone is ready, all cards are turned. If the estimates differ from each other, the differences are discussed before a new round is played. Since programmers as well as testers participate in this activity, estimates include the insights from both. In addition, since differing estimates are directly discussed, the team reaches a common understanding of the effort needed. Programmers become aware of difficulties testing a given implementation. Testers may get aware of difficulties and boundaries for implementing an easy-to-test story.

The most effective way to plan and prepare an iteration is to use workshops focused on specifications. Gojko Adzic (2009) calls them specification workshops and describes advantages from this approach in his book *Bridging the Communication Gap*. By bringing together programmers, business analysts, customers, and testers in a focused meeting, problems regarding customer expectations derived from unclear communication are prevented right from the beginning. He explains the success he had with identifying requirements using unambiguous test descriptions in these workshops. By turning them later during the iteration into executable tests, the amount of rework resulting from misunderstood specifications is reduced. Testers can spend more time on testing activities, instead of maintaining and rerunning tests.

Peter M. Senge (2006) points out another benefit of this collaborative approach in his book *The Fifth Discipline*. Since the team gets together early in the project, they start to build a shared mental model. This supports the team-building process and reduces misunderstandings based upon vague verbal descriptions. Having all participants work out of a shared mental model is a first step in the team-building process. Along with that, it helps to overcome language barriers. The shared mental model creates a joint energy toward delivering the software.

13.2 ONCE UPON AN ITERATION

Imagine working on an Agile team. What may happen during an iteration? After having set up the common goal in terms of user stories to be completed in a time-boxed iteration, the team starts to work on them. The practices the team chooses make a clear difference. Collaboration between testers and developers as well as testers and customers, the daily meetings, and testing as an integrated activity are the key points that help the whole team.

13.2.1 Collaboration

Agile practices rely heavily on collaboration. Pair programming and daily standup meetings are two opportunities for this. Testers on Agile projects contribute by pairing with another tester, a developer, or a customer. The shared mental model created earlier is thereby maintained even when the iteration starts and things may change daily. When the whole team sits together, testers get a more thorough understanding of the problem by the benefits from osmotic communication (Cockburn 2006). Testers contribute greatly just by overhearing the team's talk. They can then step up and help the pair understand the particular acceptance test or bring in a viewpoint from the larger picture of the application.

In his book *Agile Software Development: The Cooperative Game*, Cockburn (2006) shows that having people placed in different offices decreases their productivity. Each time a developer wants to ask a question, he has to make the decision to stand up, walk to her place, and see if she is not there. If she is not there, the probability of the developer asking a different team member decreases dramatically.

You can compare this to the basic trust babies are born with. Initially babies trust everyone everywhere. Gradually being disappointed, this basic trust is turned into mistrust over time. Likewise a developer trusts that everyone on the project is available to help her out on a difficult problem.

Sitting together not only enables team members to ask for help right when it's needed, but they also develop a sense whether the potential conversation partner is currently busy or not. Team members not only get the choice to help each other, but also to receive help from the whole team, and to decide whether to disturb or interrupt other colleagues. This optimizes the communication flow on the team, and thereby raises productivity as well as respect for colleagues on the team.

For example, consider the enrollment story. A pair implementing this story discusses whether to allow double course enrollment. The tester overhearing the communication joins them and explains that a double enrollment should not be permitted, as the course could get filled up by just one multiply enrolled single student.

Thereby the collaboration setting of the workspace enables the team to make relevant decisions quickly. In addition, that tester might have just finished the tests for that same story and show them to the programmers, so they know what that feature should look like. On the other hand, if the tester has problems automating her tests, she may ask for help on the test automation part.

The tester will gradually learn the difficulties of programming, while the programmer will gradually gain respect for the work of the tester. Over time, the programmer will get a sense for the other roles included in the software project. He may be able to inform the testers on probably negative side effects up front as well as to get a sense for hard-to-test design decisions in the code. This finally leads to less rework for the tester to keep up the pace with the new developed features.

13.2.2 Daily Standup Meeting

The exchange of progress and obstacles at the daily standup meeting is another source of building trust among team members. When a tester has a problem with the software, the issue is picked up after the meeting, and traced down to a solution in the software, or a different approach for the testing. When the team takes up the responsibility to deliver the features they agreed with the customer at the beginning of the iteration, everything is possible. Testers do not hide problems in their progress, but discuss them openly, while getting the support from the whole team—every single day of the iteration. Testers are no longer left alone with the problems and impediments they face. Rather, the team contributes to solutions of individual problems. Team members optimize the whole software development process rather than just their spot between the walls.

Testing the application is a team effort. Having a storyboard spreading the progress on the whole team makes problems visible. If some testing tasks get behind the schedule, this is directly visible at the daily standup meeting. The team may decide a programmer should work some time on testing-related tasks; maybe the product owner joins in, too. Thereby, testing becomes a vital and integrated part of the software project. The team will spend its time and energy on those tasks that need support right now. As these may be testing tasks as well as programming or documentation tasks, the team is put in the position to decide what to do about the problem rather than suboptimizing the workflow and throwing work products over the wall.

Consider a standup meeting where one developer speaks about yesterday's achievements. She states that she implemented the most critical story for the current release together with another developer. They found out they forgot to consider changes to an area of the application that seemed unrelated, and she is going to work on it today. Unfortunately, she does not know about the tests associated with this area. Peter, who worked on the tests for the last iteration, speaks up, and they decide together to pair up to get this impediment out of the team's way.

13.2.3 Testing

During an iteration we still have to test. Brown bag as well as lunch-and-learn meetings help *everyone* understand other approaches to solve problems. Team learning enables the team to go beyond its scope of expertise and learn new things. The team decides to sit down and learns something about exploratory testing or programming in a coding dojo. Setting aside dedicated time to learn new things is a great way to prepare for possible future problems and keep the team flexible.

An Agile team does multiple testing activities. Developers use test-driven development to implement the current set of features. Testers may use acceptance-test-driven development to implement the story tests. Ideally the first set of tests is written during a specification workshop together with the customer. Right before the end of the iteration, the set of implemented features is explored using an exploratory testing approach. Since previous automation steps might have left some problems in the developed code, this is the final step before an iteration can be marked as complete.

Testing is an integrated part on Agile projects. Reaching the final *done* of the iteration therefore includes all of these testing activities. Having a feature done means that it is implemented, tested, and explored. Since developers are implementing the feature with test-driven development, *implemented* means using Kent Beck's red—green—refactor cycle multiple times (Beck 2003). *Tested* means the team discusses acceptance tests before the iteration, develops and automates them, and shows them to the customer. *Exploring* a feature means to discover the functionality in an interaction with the product, decide whether that is the desired functionality, and act accordingly. To summarize:

- Done means implemented, tested, and explored
  - Implemented means red—green—refactor
  - Tested means discuss—develop—deliver
- Explored means discover—decide—act

Let's walk through an example on this. Right before the iteration begins, the team members sit down to discuss the next stories. While they do so, they talk to their customer about the acceptance criteria and corner conditions of the business rules. They discuss the stories in the forthcoming iteration. After the iteration planning meeting, the team has agreed upon a subset of stories to implement over the course of the next few weeks. During the iteration, the team members develop the stories they previously discussed.

The development includes the act of implementing the user stories using small steps with test-driven development as well as automating the acceptance tests. The programmers implement a failing test for the next functionality to be put into the code, "see the red bar," indicating that it is failing. Then they implement just enough to make that small test pass, thereby making the bar green. In the end they take a step back and seek opportunities to refactor. This is how they drive the design.

When the story is implemented and the automated tests pass—both unit tests and acceptance tests—a tester explores the application for missing functionality. In a time-boxed session, she starts to discover knowledge about the product as it is implemented. When she finds something unexpected, she decides whether the discovered behavior is OK, or should be marked as defective according to the business rules, or whether to mark the feature or story as defective. Finally, the tester acts according to the decision. This may include exercising some follow-up tests to discover more about the behavior, or this might include writing a story card marked with a defect sign (i.e., a red dot).

At the end of the iteration, the team members present the product to the business stakeholders. They show the acceptance tests and their additions during the iteration. They agree to explore the delivered functionality together with the customer, and to find out new knowledge about the usability of the product. The product owner and customer may reprioritize the stories for the next iteration based upon this new knowledge.

13.3 ITERATION DEMO AND REVIEW

The iteration is finally wrapped up in a customer demonstration to get feedback about the just-developed features, and a reflection workshop that helps the team to improve how it works. During an iteration demo, the just-developed features are presented to the stakeholders. Since the features are shown in the working software, the development team receives direct feedback from the customer about progress.

Depending on the length of the iteration, the team gets feedback for a week up to one month of work behind them. After this, the team sits down and reflects on their course. During this reflection the team can decide to adapt their course. Since all team members are included in the reflection, testers also have a voice during this step toward process improvement. The team owns the process in that it is responsible to take necessary course corrections.

The iteration demonstration serves as a direct feedback mechanism. Programmers and testers learn from the feedback what they missed during the iteration. Since the features were specified right before the iteration and were continuously discussed during the implementation, there is little risk that something was missed. In the rare occasions where this is the case, the final demonstration to the stakeholder will reveal any misunderstanding. During these meetings testers can learn about their users and which aspects they missed so far. In the next iterations testers can then bring in this new knowledge to help discuss a feature or to test the product. This will greatly reduce rework.

In the adaptation step, the iteration retrospective, the whole team sits together to review the course of the past few weeks. Testers bring in their unique vision here. Even if the most important issues for testers are not handled in the first iteration, in a few weeks there will be another reflection. If the topic is still relevant, it will be raised again, and the team gets to decide how to act upon it. Testers being a fully integrated part in this reflection will raise the awareness to improve the practices the team uses or to bring in their own critical thinking abilities. Since the team adapts their own process, over time it finds a way to optimize programming and testing work.

Consider an iteration review after an iteration where the team delivered less stories than they planned. The team gets together to identify the problems they were facing. The programmers state that they missed crucial feedback from the testers about their stories. The testers start to explain what they did and why. The session facilitator has a hard time keeping everyone mindful of one another's position. Eventually the coach turns the meeting around, and the team agrees upon the following steps:

- Switch pairs more often
- Testers and programmers pair on test automation

In addition the team agrees to commit to fewer story points for the next iteration. At the next reflection workshop, the team sees the benefits of pairing a tester with a programmer. Since the team is able to provide a stable safety net from the automated tests, the team is able to move faster. It even pulled in new stories from the next iteration. Unfortunately during the review session with the customer, problem areas were identified. The team decides it wants to spend some time refactoring the old code base, so that adaptations to the business rules can be more easily made. Since the test automation now provides a solid safety net, the team has the flexibility to keep up with the upcoming business rule changes from the customer.

13.4 PRACTICES AND PRINCIPLES OF AGILE TESTING

In her talks, Elisabeth Hendrickson identifies eight practices and five principles for testing on Agile teams. Having seen them in practice, we are now set to take a closer look.

13.4.1 Acceptance-Test-Driven Development

Acceptance-test-driven development is a way to trawl requirements for the current iteration [1]. Since the team and the customer agree upon these business-facing tests, they also represent the expectations from the business perspective. So, rather than writing a test case for an unsupported or outdated platform (e.g., Commodore 64, Internet Explorer 3, Java 1.2), the resulting tests are meaningful. The waste of running meaningless tests during the iteration is avoided right from the start.

As we saw earlier, the team gets together with the customer to discuss upcoming stories. They identify acceptance criteria and denote them on the back of the story card. Over the course of the iteration, while the team members work on a story, they also automate the tests they identified with the customer. Seeing them passing gives the team the indication that this story is potentially finished to ship. During the iteration review together with the customer, the team shows the passing test but is also able to explore further conditions in the product. The customer and the team get the direct feedback about the product. As a by-product the team creates a fully automated test suite. This test suite provides the safety net for future iterations.

13.4.2 Automated System Tests

With acceptance-test-driven development, the identified examples are automated as acceptance tests during the iteration. As a result the team has a large number of relevant tests that are automated and can be run at the press of a button. Instead of thorough descriptions of the test cases that need to be run—either manually or automatically—the tests are put into a single repository from which they are automated. Over time the team creates reliable tests that are run continuously.

The acceptance tests that the team creates initially together with the customer serve as a basis for further tests. A tester working on a story can come up with additional tests that were previously not considered. The tester then automates not only the acceptance tests but also the additional tests she may think of. Ideally the automated system tests are run on a continuous basis in the continuous integration framework (Duvall, Matyas, and Glover 2007), thereby providing the whole team the feedback when something is not right.

Also, having automated system-level tests provides the team with quick feedback. No daunting test scripts are executed manually and in a time-consuming manner. The team gets results from unattended test execution runs. Since most of these tests pass all the time, the team is able to see broken functionality instantly and take necessary actions to correct their course.

13.4.3 Test-Driven Development

Though the name test-driven development might indicate that it has something to do with testing, its primary mission is to drive the design of the underlying code. The refactoring step in the red–green–refactor cycle enables flexible code. This avoids the trap of the big redesign that might be necessary over time on more traditional projects. As the code base grows, the code keeps this flexibility.

Developing code in a test-driven way makes sure that the most relevant parts of the code—the lower-level modules—are testable and tested. Rather than having unit tests postponed until the last feature is working, inevitably being abandoned to time pressure for the delivery, developing code with a simple test first in tiny increments helps the individual programmer and the whole team know what the code does and what it does not. For some great examples on test-driven development, Shore and Warden (2007) and Beck (2003) walk through the process practically.

13.4.4 Automated Unit Tests

When using test-driven development, automated microtests are a by-product [2]. Since every single new line of code is tested even before it is written, a large base of microtests is created as the code gets written. On more traditional projects the unit tests are often postponed until the last moment, which practically means they are not written at all. With test-driven development, automated microtests are developed up front. They express the intent of the code to the next programmer that needs to adapt it, and they run in a fragment of a second. This leads to unit tests that are actually run by the developers before submitting their code.

In combination with continuous integration, these automated microtests also provide instant feedback. A pair of programmers having finished their work on the next piece of code for the story, run the microtests locally as well as the acceptance tests. When they pass, they check in their piece [3]. If the build environment differs between the programmers' desktop PC and the production environment, the continuous integration build will notify the team about this problem. (Examples for this are different path separators, different localization settings, or simply different time zones for time handling.) The automated microtest suite provides nearly instant feedback in case some functionality does not pass these tests.

13.4.5 Collective Test Ownership

Everyone on an Agile team tests. There is no dedicated testing team that defines the tests. Instead, the customer is involved in defining meaningful tests right from the start. Everyone is encouraged to reflect the current understanding of the product in the tests. Since automated unit tests as well as the automated system-level tests are kept in the same version control system, every change to a test is traceable. When in doubt the particular developer can be asked about the particular change.

Working in this way overcomes most of the things found on traditional projects that can be considered as waste in the sense of Lean software development (Poppendieck and Poppendieck 2003) and should be eliminated. This includes traditional test case documents, which are now kept under the same version history as the production code itself. Similarly, bugs no longer need to be tracked. When a problem occurs, there is a failing test, either on the system level or on the unit level—most of the time on both. Fixing the bug then becomes a matter of changing the code to make the test pass.

For example, suppose a recent check-in broke one of the story tests from the previous iteration. A tester and a programmer get their heads together to find out what caused the trouble there. The programmer identifies the faulty change in the version control history; the tester revisits the acceptance tests. They discuss the problem and find out that parts of the code changes for the current story had side effects to the story from the previous iteration. They discuss the approach together with the onsite customer representative and identify that the changes to the code are fine, but they missed to adapt the story test from the previous iteration. The programmer and the tester pair up to fix that test, and in a matter of minutes, the fix gets back into version control.

13.4.6 Continuous Integration

All the automated unit- and system-level tests are run very often. Continuously, a tool checks version control for new changes. If something has changed, it triggers a build and test run. The results are made public to the team and even other stakeholders. The team avoids "it runs on my machine."

For tracking the project progress, management can check the dashboard of the continuous build system and see the number of unit tests and the number of passing acceptance tests steadily increasing. Since it's human to err, whenever a build does no longer pass, the team puts immediate efforts to get a stable build again. Therefore integrating source code from the developer's machine to the version control system becomes as simplistic as possible. A failing build is a potential problem for anyone who wants to use the latest version from the repository, so it gets immediate attention. Less time is spent with lengthy builds that do not pass their tests in the end (Duvall, Matyas, and Glover 2007; Shore and Warden 2007).

For example, when a programmer checks in a piece of code that breaks previously existing functionality, the build server will compile the code, execute the unit tests, and execute the automated system tests. When the build fails because an automated system test stopped passing, the team is automatically informed. They jump in to locate the problem. Since the team is working in small increments, there are just a few changes that could have caused that build to fail. The problem is immediately fixed before more and more problems pile up based upon it.

13.4.7 Exploratory Testing

As a final step, before each story can be marked as finished, it needs to be explored. Beyond the scope of the automated tests, a human starts up the system and explores it. Difficulties with the alignment of the user interface become apparent, which have not been in the scope of the automated tests. Exploratory testing simultaneously enables the tester to learn about the software, design tests, and execute them. The feedback from a test just run informs the decision about the next test to exercise. Jon Bach (2000) describes in his article "Session-Based Test Management" that test charters for a time-boxed exploratory testing session should be used to focus the areas of interest in the product. These charters for exploratory testing should be put into version control together with the automated tests.

A tester sets up an exploratory testing session on a user story after it has been marked as complete by both testers and programmers. Since the automated build process would fail if any test was broken, the tester can directly start. The tester initially brainstorms a charter for the session.

For an online course enrollment system the tester starts to take a closer look at the usability of the pages, or the ordering of the workflow. Everything that comes to mind is put into a test charter for the session. During the session, the tester works through her list and takes notes of the session. Debriefing with the product owner she goes through her notes and provides new information. The product owner may want to take little corrections or to put the story card back to implementation after choosing additional test cases.

13.4.8 Rehearse Delivery

Since Agile teams deliver early and deliver often, the act of polishing a product for delivery gets immediate attention. Rather than having to polish the installer five minutes before planned delivery, the team pays attention to the tiny things that would usually be kept unfinished until the last possible moment. Additionally, the team gets the direct feedback from the users about blind spots in their software. These are the tiny bits that can be forgotten, and then quickly made available in a first patch of the product.

The team regularly exercises various tools, like scripts for transforming available production data or an installation procedure. Since the team is delivering early and often, it gets the immediate feedback. The team gets to know what could possibly go wrong while installing or deploying the product.

13.5 BACK TO REALITY

This concludes the journey of an Agile team. Now, consider the most painful area in your project. Consider if you were working on an ideal Agile team. What would be different? How would this problem be tackled? What do you need to make this happen? What's the tiniest little thing you can bring into your team today? Does it reduce the cost of testing? Does it reduce the cost of testing now or in the long run?

The principles underlying Agile testing are well founded in the methodologies themselves. Many of the concepts underlying Agile software development serve to minimize management overhead. Team collaboration and responsibility help to involve everyone and see beyond their own technical field. In the long run this enables Agile teams to reduce some of the costs of testing and the costs of development overall. Locally optimizing the costs of testing does not necessarily serve to deliver a valuable product to the customer. Instead the whole project needs to be taken into consideration: the customer, the context, the development team, and the technical practices used. As a by-product, testing costs will get reduced, but this shouldn't be the only purpose.

Many approaches to reduce software testing costs exist. Most of them, however, consider just a small portion of the whole project. Agile software development reduces the costs of testing by making the whole team responsible for testing and quality.

NOTES

1. The term *acceptance-test-driven development* is a misnomer. As Michael Bolton points out, we don't know that we may ship our product when acceptance tests pass. But we know that we certainly must not ship when one of them fails. Bolton suggests calling them rejection tests instead. Lacking a better alternative, at the time of this writing the term *acceptance-test-driven development* was widespread, so that I decided to use it.
2. *Unit tests* are a misnomer as well. To prevent misunderstanding, I will refer to unit tests when I refer to more traditional unit test approaches, whereas I will refer to microtests when referring to tests in an Agile context.
3. Mike Hill pointed out that he usually checks in when the code passed all its microtests, since executing all story tests takes too long. For faster-executing story-level tests, however, you want to execute all of them before checking in.

REFERENCES

Adzic, Gojko. 2009. *Bridging the Communication Gap: Specification by Example and Agile Acceptance Testing.* London: Neuri Limited.
Bach, Jonathan. 2000. "Session-Based Test Management." http://www.satisfice.com/articles/sbtm.pdf.
Beck, Kent. 2003. *Test-Driven Development by Example.* Boston: Addison-Wesley.
Cockburn, Alistair. 2006. *Agile Software Development: The Cooperative Game* (2nd ed.). Upper Saddle River, NJ: Addison-Wesley.
Cohn, Mike. 2004. *User Stories Applied: For Agile Software Development.* Boston: Addison-Wesley.
Crispin, Lisa, and Janet Gregory. 2009. *Agile Testing: A Practical Guide for Testers and Agile Teams.* Upper Saddle River, NJ: Addison-Wesley.
Duvall, Paul M., Steve Matyas, and Andrew Glover. 2007. *Continuous Integration.* Upper Saddle River, NJ: Addison-Wesley.
Goldratt, Eliyahu M., Jeff Cox, and David Whitford. 2004. *The Goal: A Process of Ongoing Improvement* (3rd rev. ed.). Great Barrington, MA: North River Press.
"Planning Poker." n.d. http://www.planningpoker.com/.

Poppendieck, Mary, and Tom Poppendieck. 2003. *Lean Software Development: An Agile Toolkit*. Boston: Addison-Wesley.

Senge, Peter M. 2006. *The Fifth Discipline*. New York: Doubleday.

Shore, James, and Shane Warden. 2007. *The Art of Agile Development*. Sebastopol, CA: O'Reilly Media.

14

Science-Based Test Case Design: Better Coverage, Fewer Tests

Gary Gack and Justin Hunter

14.1 SYNOPSIS

This chapter describes an approach to test case design using a proven statistical method known as design of experiments (DoE). Benefits and costs quantified by a study comparing effectiveness of a manual test case design approach to effectiveness of DoE-based test case selection methods are described. In the interest of balance, we discuss counterarguments and limitations. We illustrate use of this method with examples and a case study.

14.2 DESIGN OF EXPERIMENTS (DOE): AN INTRODUCTION

DoE is by no means a new idea. Indeed, according to Wikipedia (http://en.wikipedia.org/wiki/Design_of_experiments#History_of_development), an early example occurred in the British navy in the eighteenth century.

In 1747, while serving as surgeon on HM Bark *Salisbury*, James Lind carried out a controlled experiment to develop a cure for scurvy. Lind selected 12 men from the ship, all suffering from scurvy, and divided them into six pairs, giving each group different additions to their basic diet for a period of two weeks. The treatments were all remedies that had been proposed at one time or another. They were:

- A quart of cider every day
- Twenty-five gutts (drops) of *elixir vitriol* (sulphuric acid) three times a day upon an empty stomach
- One half-pint of seawater every day
- A mixture of garlic, mustard, and horseradish in a lump the size of a nutmeg
- Two spoonfuls of vinegar three times a day
- Two oranges and one lemon every day

The men who had been given citrus fruits recovered dramatically within a week. One of them returned to duty after 6 days and the other became nurse to the rest. The others experienced some improvement, but nothing was comparable to the citrus fruits, which were proved to be substantially superior to the other treatments.

As illustrated by Lind's application to scurvy, DoE is a controlled experiment that focuses on pairs (in this example, pairs are defined by treatment and subject). In other examples, pairings may involve three-, four-, or *n*-way combinations of factors. This method has been widely applied over the years to drug testing (e.g., clinical trials), engineering design (e.g., optimal wing design), and many other areas. More recently this approach has been adapted to software test case design and embodied in easy to use tools. The statistical methods and algorithms underlying tools that implement DoE are outside the scope of this article—knowledge of those methods is not required to use DoE tools effectively. Think of DoE-based test case design tools as a "black box"—given appropriate inputs they generate optimized test cases—knowledge of internal workings is not required.

14.3 BENEFITS OF DOE IN SOFTWARE TEST CASE DESIGN

In essence, application of DoE to software test case design provides three principal benefits. First, it guarantees any desired (user specified) level of "coverage" of factor interactions—for example, it ensures all two-way, three-way, or *n*-way interactions are included in the set of test cases generated by the method. In complex test situations, such as those found in many software systems, this method will always ensure full *n*-way coverage of huge numbers of potential interactions.

Second, it ensures coverage is achieved with a minimum number of tests, which means test execution effort will necessarily be reduced. DoE tools do not necessarily generate the absolute theoretical minimum number of cases as that may require excessive compute time, but they always come quite close and result in dramatically fewer test cases than are typically created by manual methods. A recent article in IEEE *Computer* magazine reported the results of a ten-project empirical comparison of DoE-based testing to "business as usual" methods [1]. On average, the DoE-based method found 2.4 times more defects per tester hour and 13 percent more defects in total.

Consider a real-world test problem [2]:

- Sixty parameters
- Each with two to five value choices that trigger business rules

This would require 1,746,756,896,558,880,852,541,440 tests if we wanted to test all possible combinations of the inputs we've identified. To put that into perspective, at a rate of one test case per second, 6 billion people could execute "only" 189,216,000,000,000,000 tests in one year.

It takes just thirty-six tests to achieve 100 percent two-way coverage. Achieving that with conventional (manual) test design approaches is extremely difficult and almost never certain.

The third benefit is because the process used to generate the necessary inputs is highly structured and repeatable, the effort necessary to provide the required inputs and generate the test cases is significantly less than that typically needed to create test cases manually. Pilot projects conducted by a major outsourcing firm on average realized 30 to 40 percent reduction in test planning and execution effort. Larger gains are expected with future releases of software systems under test as the DoE test planning process leads to highly reusable test inputs.

14.4 WHY FACTOR INTERACTIONS MATTER

The IEEE article mentioned earlier [1] reports results of several retrospective studies of the characteristics of software defects that "escaped" into systems released to customers.

Defect "Trigger"	Cumulative % of Defects		
	Minimum	**Maximum**	**Average**
Single parameter value	30%	70%	60%
2 parameter values	70%	95%	86%
3 parameter values	88%	99%	91%

Many fewer defects arise from four- or five-way interactions, and six-way interaction defects are exceptionally rare. The key takeaway: *over 90 percent of all software defects are, on average, triggered by interactions between three or fewer parameter values.* Hence any sound test plan should guarantee at least 100 percent coverage of two-way interactions. Applications with high reliability requirements, such as medical devices or avionics, should guarantee a minimum of 100 percent coverage of three-way interactions. That is extremely difficult to achieve without DoE-based test case design tools.

14.5 DEFINITIONS: PAIRWISE, COMBINATORIAL, ORTHOGONAL

Pairwise, combinatorial, and *orthogonal* are often used interchangeably. Pairwise implies only two-way combinations, whereas combinatorial suggests *n*-way combinations. An orthogonal array has the balancing property that for each pair of columns all parameter-level combinations occur an equal number of times. This is a fine distinction vis-à-vis two-way and will in practice generate slightly more test cases.

14.6 COUNTERARGUMENTS AND LIMITATIONS

James Bach has taken issue with designating DoE-based and combinatorial methods as best practices [3]. He points out, we think quite rightly, that

A SIMPLE TWO-WAY COMBINATORIAL EXAMPLE

Given these parameters and (values): OpSys (XP, W7, Unix, Mac); Browser (Firefox, Opera); User Type (Admin, General)

	OpSys	Browser	UserType
1	XP	Opera	Admin
2	XP	Firefox	General
3	W7	Opera	General
4	W7	Firefox	Admin
5	Unix	Opera	Admin
6	Unix	Firefox	General
7	Mac	Opera	Admin
8	Mac	Firefox	General

We can ensure 100 percent two-way coverage with eight tests as illustrated here. One hundred percent three-way coverage in this example would require sixteen tests. As the number of parameters and values grows the advantage of this approach grows exponentially as we will see in upcoming examples.

this method is not a solution to every testing challenge. Michael Bolton, although generally positive, has also expressed reservations [4]. However, most experts will agree that it is at least a good practice that has an important place in many testing scenarios. We believe this method merits far wider adoption than currently is the case.

Specific limitations of DoE-based methods include the following:

1. As with any approach to test case design you need the input of intelligent and thoughtful test designers. Using DoE-based methods will not turn incompetent, inexperienced testers into prodigious bug killers.
2. Testers can and will forget to include significant test inputs. If a test designer fails to include inputs that should be tested, tool-generated test cases will also fail to include them.
3. You should not rely exclusively on DoE-based methods as a single approach for all of your test cases. These tools may well generate the vast majority of tests that should be run on an application, but you should consult subject matter experts to see if they would recommend supplementing with additional tests.

4. DoE-based methods are generally not appropriate for unit or white box testing. The degree of benefit you can expect rises dramatically with scope and complexity of the application under test.

5. DoE-based methods are generally not well suited to find "race" conditions in multiprocessor configurations.

6. DoE-based methods won't necessarily find sequential dependencies—for example, a failure occurs only when a certain combination of inputs occurs in a specific sequence (we find it only by chance).

7. DoE-based methods (and other methods as well) won't necessarily find unexpected side effects—for example, when testing Word a combination of configuration parameters appear to achieve the expected result but lead to document corruption.

The general characteristics of situations in which these methods are more or less likely to be cost effective are illustrated by the following:

Testing Challenge	Larger Benefit	Lesser Benefit
Constraints	Simple constraints handled by "invalid pairs," e.g., Hardware = Mac + Browser = IE8	Complex constraints, e.g., if P1 = B and P2 = C, then P3 cannot be x or y unless . . .
Branches	Steps in a process flow are independent, i.e., choices in each step do not influence later selections	Many different branches; may require a series of different combinatorial test plans rather than a single plan
Number of parameters and values	Many parameters, relatively few values for each; equivalence classes may be used to reduce length of the values list	Few parameters, each with many essential-to-test values (few equivalence classes), e.g., two parameters (state and product) to calculate shipping charges—50 states × 20 products = minimum 1,000 two-way tests

As with any approach to testing, limited experience and limited analytical skills in the test team present severe challenges.

14.7 LEVELS OF ABSTRACTION

DoE-based methods can be applied at a high level of abstraction in the early stages of testing to explore the application. One might think of this level as very similar to exploratory testing strategies advocated by a number of experts. The underlying thought process is quite similar—we think about what the application does at a very high level and we take a test drive through the more common paths the system under test may support. Let's explore this conceptually (actual navigation is not shown).

Often we begin by enumerating any relevant configuration options (e.g., PC and Mac; Firefox, IE 6-7-8, and Chrome). Next we think about the major functions of the system; for example, in Amazon we can find a book or a CD, we can add or remove items to our cart, and we can checkout or cancel. If we wanted to explore all potential combinations of this limited set of parameters we would need $2 \times 5 \times 2 \times 2 \times 2 = 80$ tests. That might be a bit more tests than we want to execute simply to explore. Alternately we can explore every potential two-way pairing (e.g., PC + Chrome + Find book + Add item + Checkout) with only ten tests. When we do this we learn more about the application, we find things we want to explore more fully, and we get an initial smoke test that may reveal any glaring problem areas (e.g., we find can't search successfully with Mac or Chrome). The ten tests generated are shown in Table 14.1.

Using DoE at this level of abstraction differs from free-form exploration in that it involves a degree of formalization of our exploratory venture. We make a simple but explicit map of the territory we plan to explore. We might think of it as structured exploration. This has several advantages over a less formal approach: (1) if we are interrupted we need not rely on memory to pick up where we left off, and (2) we cover a lot of ground with a minimum of effort, and we know exactly what has and has not been explored.

TABLE 14.1

Exploratory Test Cases

Hardware	Browser	Find	Cart	Finish
PC	Firefox	Books	Add item	Checkout
Mac	Firefox	CDs	Delete item	Cancel
PC	IE6	CDs	Add item	Cancel
Mac	IE6	Books	Delete item	Checkout
PC	IE7	Books	Delete item	Cancel
Mac	IE7	CDs	Add item	Checkout
PC	IE8	Books	Add item	Checkout
Mac	IE8	CDs	Delete item	Cancel
PC	Chrome	Books	Add item	Checkout
Mac	Chrome	CDs	Delete item	Cancel

Often, exploratory testing leads us to recognize areas of the applications that are most interesting and deserving of a deeper dive. Taking this illustration one step farther, we might decide we want to test the checkout function more fully. To do that will need to navigate the following screens. In the sign-in screen we'll assume we're an existing customer, and we want to ship to the same address we used last time.

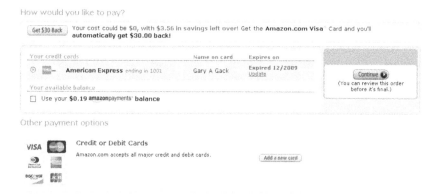

Next we choose a shipping method.

Choose a shipping speed:
- ⊙ Standard Shipping (3-5 business days)
- ○ FREE Two-Day Shipping with a free trial of AmazonPrime™ (Learn more)
- ○ Two-Day Shipping (2 business days)
- ○ One-Day Shipping (1 business day)

We then select a payment method; in this example one already on file.

At this point we have several options: we can change the method of payment, we can change the shipping address, or we can place the order.

Payment Method:
Change
American Express : ***-1001
Exp: 12/2013

Billing Address: Change
Gary A Gack
1641 Pinecrest Dr
Fleming Isle, FL 32003
United States
Phone: 9045791894

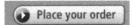

In the interest of brevity, our example does not fully explore every possible branch but is perhaps sufficient to illustrate our point. This set of possible inputs (clearly only a small subset of the complete application) leads to 512 potential combinations if all possibilities are to be tested. Two-way coverage can be achieved in only eight tests as illustrated in Table 14.2. In this example 100 percent three-way coverage can be achieved with thirty-two tests. The statistical methods used to generate these test cases are "smart" in that tests are generated in a sequence that leads to a large percentage of desired coverage with a comparatively small number of tests. As illustrated in Figure 14.2, 80 percent coverage of three-way combinations is achieved with only thirteen tests. Obviously this is very valuable when schedule constraints force an early end to testing. In most cases the Pareto principle (the 80/20 rule) will apply; relatively few tests will find a disproportionate percentage of defects.

TABLE 14.2

Deeper Dive Test Cases

E-Mail Address	Password	Ship to	Ship Method	Payment Method	Change Payment Method	Change Billing Address	Place Order
Valid	Valid	On file	Standard	Existing	Yes	Yes	Yes
Invalid	Invalid	New	Standard	New	No	No	Cancel
Valid	Invalid	On file	Free 2-day	New	Yes	No	Yes
Invalid	Valid	New	Free 2-day	Existing	No	Yes	Cancel
Valid	Valid	New	2-day	New	Yes	Yes	Cancel
Invalid	Invalid	On file	2-day	Existing	No	No	Yes
Valid	Valid	On file	1-day	Existing	No	No	Cancel
Invalid	Invalid	New	1-day	New	Yes	Yes	Yes

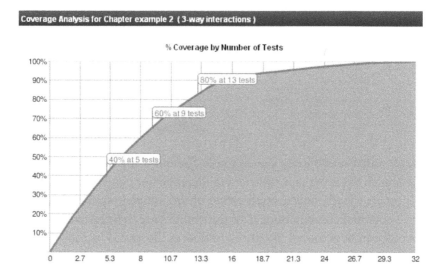

FIGURE 14.2

14.8 COMBINATORIAL COVERAGE

When two-way coverage is requested (as in Table 14.1), the test cases generated are guaranteed to provide 100 percent two-way coverage but they also provide a certain percentage of higher-order coverage. To illustrate that point, consider potential three-way interactions among hardware, find, and cart. As shown in Table 14.3, 75 percent of three-way interactions (six of eight) are covered when we request two-way coverage. Similar analysis could be done in relation to interactions among other variables.

TABLE 14.3

Potential Three-Way Interactions

Hardware	Find	Cart	Test Case Number
PC	Books	Add	1
PC	Books	Delete	5
PC	CDs	Add	3
PC	CDs	Delete	Not covered
Mac	Books	Add	Not covered
Mac	Books	Delete	4
Mac	CDs	Add	6
Mac	CDs	Delete	2

14.9 CASE STUDY: REMITTANCE PROCESSING— INDIVIDUAL RETIREMENT ACCOUNT

One hundred twenty-six test cases were identified using a business-as-usual approach. An analysis of these cases identified four missing pairs—that is, four instances of potential dual-mode defects were not tested in any of these 126 cases. The functionality being tested required six parameters, each with between two and four potential values, as illustrated in Figure 14.3. Applying the DoE-based method generated a total of thirteen test cases to achieve 100 percent two-way coverage or forty-eight tests to achieve 100 percent three-way coverage.

The manually developed plan contained a great deal of redundancy and was hence quite inefficient—lots of wasted effort. Figure 14.4 illustrates the extent of inefficiency in the manual plan. When a test plan, such as this one, has six parameters each single test case can be decomposed into fifteen potential dual-mode defects being tested for. Efficient test plans will test for as-yet-untested two-way defects with each new test case, whereas inefficient plans will test for the same potential defect again and again. DoE-based methods optimize plans generated to maximize efficiency.

14.10 SUMMARY

In our experience the DoE-based approach to software test case design has proven beneficial in every case we have encountered. It won't solve every conceivable test problem you will encounter, but it should certainly be one of the tools in every tester's bag of tricks. Give it a try—we think you'll like it!

IRA Remittance				
Plan (3)	Plan A	Plan B	Plan C	
Tax Year (2)	2009	2010		
Initial or Recurring (2)	Initial	Recurring		
Receipt Method (4)	Check	EFT	LBX	ACH-EFR
Bank (3)	"Bank A"	"Bank B"	"Bank C"	
Check Number (3)	Valid	Invalid	Blank	

FIGURE 14.3

	Original Test Plan			
Test No	Plan	Tax Year	Initial or Recurring	Receipt Method
1	Plan A	2009	Initial	CHK
2	Plan A	2010	Initial	CHK
3	Plan A	2009	Initial	CHK
4	Plan A	2010	Initial	CHK
5	Plan A	2009	Initial	CHK
6	Plan A	2010	Initial	CHK
7	Plan A	2009	Initial	CHK

	Times Tested	
	Original Plan (out of 126)	Prioritized Plan (out of 13)
Potential single-mode fault: Plan A	43 X	5 X
Potential dual-mode fault: Plan A and Initial	21 X	2 X
Potential triple-mode fault: Plan A and Initial and CHK	7 X	1 X
Potential quadruple-mode fault: Plan A and Initial and CHK and 2009	4 X	1 X

FIGURE 14.4

14.11 TO LEARN MORE

The following articles and links provide additional perspectives on DoE-based test case selection methods.

All-pairs testing: http://en.wikipedia.org/wiki/All-pairs_testing

"The Combinatorial Design Approach to Automatic Test Generation," *IEEE Software,* September 1996, pp. 83–87, http://www.argreenhouse.com/papers/gcp/AETGissre96.shtml

Elfriede Dustin, "Orthogonally Speaking," http://www.stickyminds.com/getfile.asp?ot=XML&id=5031&fn=Smzr1XDD3130filelistfilename1.pdf

Hexawise blog: http://hexawise.wordpress.com/

Madhav Phadke, "Planning Efficient Software Tests," http://www.stsc.hill.af.mil/crosstalk/1997/10/planning.asp

NOTES

1. Rick Kuhn, Raghu Kacker, Yu Lei, and Justin Hunter, "Combinatorial Software Testing," *Computer*, August 2009, http://csrc.nist.gov/groups/SNS/acts/documents/kuhn-kacker-lei-hunter09.pdf.
2. Hexawise, http://hexawise.com/examples/telecom_example.pdf.
3. James Bach and Patrick J. Schroeder, "Pairwise Testing: A Best Practice That Isn't," http://www.testingeducation.org/wtst5/PairwisePNSQC2004.pdf.
4. Michel Bolton, "Pairwise Testing," November 2007, http://www.developsense.com/pairwiseTesting.html.

15

Clean Test: Suggestions for Reducing Costs by Increasing Test Craftsmanship

Curtis Stuehrenberg

> In software, 80 percent or more of what we do is quaintly called *maintenance*: the act of repair. Rather than embracing the typical Western focus on producing good software, we should be thinking more like home repairmen in the building industry, or auto mechanics in the automotive field.
>
> **—James O. Coplien**

The opening statement is the primary thesis of Robert C. Martin's collaborative work *Clean Code: A Handbook of Agile Software Craftsmanship* [1]. The idea of software development as primarily maintenance is the impetus for all his later suggestions regarding better practices, which he groups under the term *software craftsmanship*. The software craftsman to Martin and his colleagues is an experienced coder who has spent energy and effort developing their skills and techniques over years of study and practice. It's difficult to give these distinguished authors justice when summarizing an entire work seminal to the craftsman movement, but for our purposes I believe a working summary is possible. A software craftsman is a skilled artisan apparently able to balance immediate pragmatism with a longer-term focus on reducing the amount of work they (or more likely someone else) must do tomorrow. The craftsman coder knows a small investment in time today can save days or weeks later on, but more important he or she has developed a sense of which small investments will reap the greatest rewards.

How a craftsman coder achieves this is summarized in the "Manifesto for Software Craftsmanship" authored in 2009. The craftsman manifesto elaborates the four cornerstones of the agile manifesto and is quoted here in its entirety [2].

As aspiring Software Craftsmen we are raising the bar of professional software development by practicing it and helping others learn the craft. Through this work we have come to value:

Not only working software, but also *well-crafted software*
Not only responding to change, but also *steadily adding value*
Not only individuals and interactions, but also *a community of professionals*
Not only customer collaboration, but also *productive partnerships*

That is, in pursuit of the items on the left we have found the items on the right to be indispensable.

As you can see, the "Manifesto for Software Craftsmanship" calls for a professional community to create well-crafted software that steadily adds value for sustaining partnerships. If there is a better definition for quality in software and how it's different than testing, I have yet to find it or read it. The wording is important and should be exciting to software test professionals on a second reading. Terminology and language specific to coders has been removed, to be replaced or expanded with terms implying team (or community) orientation on an ever expanding view of quality. The manifesto is a call for everyone involved in creating software to consistently develop their craft and their products, not just people who write code.

The initial genesis of the craftsmanship movement was borne out of frustration coders felt at having to "fix" someone else's code or worse, their own code. The entirety of clean code is concerned with tips and tricks for generating software that is easily maintainable and does what it's supposed to do. Or at least it does what you think it's supposed to do when you're looking at it in a debugger or another development environment. The craftsman was called on to "always leave the campground cleaner than they found it," which led to discussions on refactoring and other process improvements. Once the genie of process improvement was out of the bottle, the parties involved soon realized simply writing cleaner code would not address the issues of maintenance and tedium. So only a few years after writing a book concerned solely with coding, the members called a group together and wrote a manifesto for all software development groups.

The movement called on all people to develop their craft, to steadily add value, to develop a community of professionals, and to foster productive partnerships, but chances are also good you've never heard of them. You may have never heard of them because we as testers have not been overly concerned with the very points they bring up about community and partnerships. Thus when a group outside our discipline or industry innovates, we seldom notice. Unfortunately this focus on our individual concerns has been at a cost, and at a cost to our employers, customers, coworkers, and everyone else we should be considering as partners.

15.1 WHY CRAFTSMANSHIP MATTERS

To put it even more bluntly, the true cost of a product is the total of all costs incurred during its lifespan, not just those incurred during design and deployment in a single release. The authors of the manifesto remind us that software development is a communal activity involving more than a single person writing code. If software is 80 percent maintenance as Coplien claims, this must include testing. If 80 percent of what we do as testers is maintaining existing testing product, then does it not stand to reason the same standards and techniques for reducing the time spent maintaining code could also be applied to maintaining tests and test products?

Craftsmanship then matters to the tester for the same reason it matters to the coder. Well-crafted tests require less effort to decipher, plan, maintain, and communicate. Less effort maintaining and reusing your tests means less costs associated with them throughout the entire life cycle of the product. You can reduce your effort by adhering to the four parts of the craftsman manifesto. But how do you adhere to the manifesto as a tester? How do you help foster a community of professionals that creates well-crafted software steadily adding value for sustainable partners?

First, plan the appropriate testing for the task. Second, know your audience and keep them in mind at all times. Third, don't rely on someone else to clean up after you, even yourself. Fourth, refactoring and redesigning are not tools for excusing halfway effort. And fifth, there will be no second chances to get it right due to the escalating debt you're currently compounding. These are the five basic principles I will explain to demonstrate how a small amount of time invested early in a single project can have long-term time and cost savings against both active and passive costs across multiple projects.

15.2 SOFTWARE TESTING GENERAL PRINCIPLES

To talk about software test craftsmanship, we first must establish some general principles for software testing itself. This exercise is unfortunately necessary due to the distinct lack of any universally recognized review board or body of knowledge with regard to the software testing industry. Standards bodies such as the IEEE make the apparent mistake of defining software testing by the artifacts and tools used rather than the basic function. If we are to discuss craftsmanship, however, we need to identify the function of software testing rather than the role or product. To answer the question of what it is exactly we as software testers are expected to do, we need to ask what is our function. The two questions are inseparable.

First we should talk about what software testing is not. The function of software testing is not to run tests. The function of software testing is not to verify or validate. The function of software testing is not to uncover bugs or defects. All these activities are ancillary to the primary function of the software tester on a project. Experienced or trained software testers use all these and more as tools to help them perform their function. To confuse the function of a tester with the running of a test is to confuse the role of a carpenter with the mitering of dovetail joints.

15.3 WHAT IS THE FUNCTION OF SOFTWARE TESTING?

The function of a software tester is to communicate the experienced behavior of a software solution when compared against the expected behavior at a specific point in time. That's it. The software tester's primary project and departmental role is communicating. The primary (and in some cases only) deliverable is the information required by whoever has been burdened with project decision-making authority. The information is then used to inform their decisions up to the ultimate decision of whether to ship. How the tester arrives at that information can be an ancillary deliverable depending on the audience. However an audience inured to simply receiving raw data should not distract us from what we are truly being paid to do as testers.

Software engineers produce code that performs functions completely devoid of any communication they may or may not choose to make. You don't need the developer to tell you they designed their buttons to be black font on gray. You simply look at the product and can see it. The same is not true of testing. Communication will usually come in the form of instructions or help text, and is added as a courtesy if necessary. Software testers, on the other hand, cannot simply hand over their product for their audience to use and provide courtesy communication. In order for their work to be useful, it must be communicated rather than used. The primary product of software testing then is information.

15.4 SOFTWARE TESTING AS INFORMATION

Information provided by software testing are reports detailing the experienced behavior of a product solution in relation to its expected behavior at the point in time it was experienced. This information is then used by the recipients to inform their decisions with regard to the management and budgeting of the project as it progresses. Ultimately it is used to inform the decision-making process on whether to release the product to the customer(s).

That's a lot to process, but in essence it simply means the software tester tells the actual decision makers how a project is doing. The decision makers then have the ability to make informed decisions about scheduling, staffing, resources, feature sets, and marketing. Making these decisions is vitally important to most companies; getting them right is almost nearly as important. Test is there to make sure everyone who needs it has enough information to feel comfortable in their decisions. The various artifacts and frameworks exist as a method for guiding and framing this conversation in order to reduce the real risk of making decisions without the "right" information.

As a final note on this topic, right information is that which informs the audience to the level appropriate to their needs. It is not information that conforms to a predetermined template or format. Determining right information is simple—you ask. Then after you deliver you ask again and correct.

15.5 TESTING ARTIFACTS AS INFORMATION-
    ## GATHERING TOOLS

Test plans are a dialogue between the test team and the rest of the project. A good test plan provides information on what the team values and prioritizes as higher risks than others. The good test plan also helps provide a common language or jargon for the different groups to communicate when discussing the testing efforts themselves. A test plan is a living document changing with the group as it matures and improves its communication.

Test cases, on the other hand, are a conversation the test team has with itself. Very few managers or architects will read through individual test cases in an effort to gain information on the testing. Instead they will trust in the planning and ask for higher level status reports used for communicating trending analysis. Team communication with itself is also why most individual test cases are badly written. In the rush to churn out test cases for features, bugs, reports, or other supposed goals, the test team often finds itself developing a unique system of shorthand. The team falls back on generic and vague tools/frameworks or simply abandons the careful use of test cases (or charters) all together in favor of free form efforts, which are then used to backfill the requested reports.

Bad test cases are a primary drain on mature products for one simple reason; bad test cases do not go away after you ship the project and have your release party. Bad test cases remain in place, waiting to drive the format of all future testing, divert personnel who could be working on new feature sets, or perhaps exist only to be ignored until something called a "regression pass" is scheduled in which case all productive activity is halted in favor of a semiregular attempt to decode what was meant at the time the test cases were authored.

The problem of long-term planning for a product release is not unique to software testing. Several books and publications have been addressing this issue for software developers and project managers for quite some time now. The basic problem is defined as a lack of managing efforts for the total value of the product rather than the immediate project. The classic spiral cycle of plan, design, develop, accept, deliver, and support was an early attempt to acknowledge the cyclical nature of the total product. Unfortunately, companies practicing this method still tended to treat each release as an independent if connected activity. Design was connected to develop and planning, but not to acceptance or support.

Fortunately paradigms have emerged in recent decades outside the software industry specifically addressing the need for long-term efforts at management and analysis when valuing our current actions. These new paradigms run strictly counter to the traditional costs accounting methods somewhat appropriate to manufacturing. Peter Drucker sums up these paradigms in his book *Management Challenges for the 21st Century* as a combination of activity rather than cost-based costing and managing for the economic reality of the entire cost chain.

15.6 MANAGING THE VALUE STREAM

Activity-based costing is an accounting method uniquely appropriate to service- and knowledge-based work as it accounts for both the cost of performing an activity and the cost of not performing the activity. It does this by assuming there is only one cost, that of the entire system. Unlike traditional cost accounting, activity costing does not assume the activity being performed is either necessary or being performed in the correct location or time. In the words of Drucker, "Activity-based costing asks, 'Does it have to be done? If so, where is it best done?' Activity-based costing integrates what were once several procedures—value analysis, process analysis, quality management, and costing—into one analysis" [3].

Managing for the economic reality of the entire value chain is a bit more esoteric as a concept but still should be readily grasped by the software quality assurance professional. To truly understand this concept you must first understand there are no individual costs or cost centers for a service organization such as a software company or bank. The only cost they have is the total cost of the entire system. Or as Drucker neatly summarized, "What matters in the marketplace is the economic reality, the costs of the entire process, regardless of who owns what" [4]. Japanese companies with their networks of *kereitsu* are probably the best known examples of managing the economic realities of their products, but they were not the first. GM initially started this trend by purchasing outright part suppliers and setting up a network of licensed dealers and service mechanics. Using these techniques, GM and later Japanese companies like Toyota were able to control to greater and lesser degrees the activity costs associated with producing their product throughout its entire value stream.

To reiterate then, activity-based costing directs the inclusion of value for both activities performed (or active costs) and activities not performed (or passive costs) into costing exercises for any product. Value stream management further directs the effort to include the total costs of a product no matter whom or what currently owns it within your process or management workflow. Managing the whole value for software then concerns itself with the entire life span of a product (or company). Individual releases are not autonomous entities but are parts of a continuous whole in the minds of your customers, which is your economic reality.

15.7 SOFTWARE CRAFTSMANSHIP AND TEST CRAFTSMANSHIP

The software craftsman movement referenced at the beginning of this work restates value stream management by using the word *maintenance*. Taken in context of value stream management, maintenance of software can be seen as not just the act of supporting a prior release. Maintenance when used in this manner can also be seen as building off someone else's work to add new features or redesign existing ones to meet current needs. Software craftsmanship is the art of designing and writing features that are easy to intuit, support, adapt, and use both now and later when someone else has to do it. Test craftsmanship is the art of doing the same for test cases and other artifacts.

Lack of craftsmanship is the statement of problem I am defining within this work. To truly reduce the costs of testing the software tester needs to stop looking at each release as a single effort to be completed and archived. It's a ubiquitous issue because software testers have historically borne the brunt of schedule and resource pressure. Pressure of this nature has caused a certain self-defeating pragmatism to seep into the craft of software testing with the theorized results of shipping a single release becoming the primary goal. As testers we scramble like mad to cover as much functionality and as many combinations of interactions as possible in the time frame, negotiate what should not be released, get it out the door, and then spend a little while catching our breath before starting it all over again.

These behaviors have led to a preponderance of bad testing using bad software tests. Quality in our own product has been sacrificed on the altar of convenience, leading to untold costs later on when we've hopefully moved onto a different project. Of course we're then inheriting the bad tests left by someone else doing the same thing, which convinces us it's just the nature of testing itself.

It doesn't have to be this way. But to talk about what it should and can be, we first need to talk about what's truly awful with the way we generally test software today.

15.8 BAD SOFTWARE TESTS

Discussions of value stream management for software development are useful because if we apply these analysis principles to the artifacts produced during a particular phase, we soon arrive at a working definition for both bad and good ones. Specifically we arrive at definitions for bad and good software tests and other artifacts.

Bad software tests are ones that do not communicate the intent and frame the reports in a context easily understood by the interested audience. Bad tests are not to be confused with useless tests. Useless tests are ones that do not communicate intent even to the authors. Useless tests are usually either generated by programs, models, or other automatic methods or else are generated simply to satisfy some framework or best practice standard dictating a certain number or form of test cases should be generated.

Bad software test cases are generated by individuals for communicating with themselves at a specific point in time but hold no value beyond that moment or person. The communication is meant to be instantaneous and self-referential. In most cases even the author of the bad test case is hard pressed to interpret the intent of the bad test case once the specific moment has passed.

A bad test case, plan, charter, or other artifact is then something documented as a means to communicate only to the author or a similar small audience in a language or form only meaningful to the author or other small audience at a particular point in time. Immediate pragmatism is the general motivation for writing bad test cases, but the results are far reaching and can be quite costly.

15.9 THE TOTAL ACTIVITY COSTS OF BAD TESTS

Bad test cases cost effort, time, and resources over the entire life span of a product because all the knowledge and experience referenced, logged, and stored within them is essentially meaningless for future work. Personnel must be diverted from analyzing and creating test cases for new or updated features toward translating existing test cases or creating wholly new ones from scratch for features that have not changed. Software projects often pay this cost as a hidden tax by treating software releases as if they were independent cost centers rather than continuous work building on each other. Another way project teams pay this cost is in ramping up time whenever a new person is added to the team or switches roles however briefly. If the software tests do not communicate well, any person lacking experience in their language and patterns will need to learn them (and fast) to be of any use to the testing efforts.

Finally there is a growing popularity in a particularly favorite strategy of mine consisting of making the whole issue of the test cases someone else's problem by removing the communication out of it all together and concentrating just on the reporting. This technique is mistakenly called automating. The strategy is to gather all the bad tests together into one giant consolidated debt obligation and turn it into a report with no need for test team communication at all. The test team will simply trigger a machine to run the test cases for the team. The machine will not need a person to explain the test cases to it and a new person can start the test cases as easily as the last. It's a good strategy and it usually masks the problem of the bad tests, until they start failing. At that moment the problem will be brought out of the closet and paraded in front of management and the rest of the teams for all to see. Failing automated tests tend to bring a lot of attention down on them, which is not a good thing if the test team doesn't actually know what they're doing or why they're still being run.

15.10 GOOD SOFTWARE TESTS

If bad software tests incur unnecessary costs for a team, good software tests actually reduce activity costs associated with testing. Good software tests communicate their intent with little to no team-specific domain knowledge, reducing training costs for new team members, passive costs associated with imparting knowledge to other groups, and easily present themselves as candidates for reuse and repurposing for other projects. Good software tests are not hard to write, manual or automated. They are, however, a little more costly initially since they require a few extra analysis and review steps in order to make sure they adhere to value stream management practices.

15.11 APPROPRIATE EFFORT

Finding the appropriate level of effort and verbosity in a test case is a process of trial and error. A good test case is descriptive enough to easily communicate intent and requirements but not so descriptive as to be inflexible or actually obfuscate the intent. What is true for good test cases is also true for every other testing artifact. A test plan no one reads is a waste of effort and money. If a majority of your proposed audience simply reads the executive summary, simply produce an executive summary document and let the minority ask you for the rest and give sound reasons for requiring it. It may seem contradictory for me to now advocate less communication, but that is not actually what I am doing. Documents are not communication. They are artifacts we use when communicating. Most test cases, plans, and specifications are currently authored using stock templates manufactured for other projects, other teams, and other decision makers with very different styles of communicating. The worst of these offenders are the so-called best practice documents generated by certification boards or educators with every possible permutation of project and technology in mind. The vast majority of real estate on these documents is wasted space in that no one (including the author) ever reads again once it has been committed to paper and agreed upon.

Good software tests, plans, specifications, and charters contain only information pertinent to the intent and understanding the author wishes to communicate at the time they were written. Templates have their uses in that they often provide an excellent mnemonic device for review during the authoring. Good software tests thus do not have blank areas waiting to be filled or out-of-date information no one has bothered to update in months because it's too much work. Good software tests are read in their entirety by the executors because they contain information important to conducting the tests. Good software tests guide the testing without dictating. Good software tests are easy to update and maintain as the audience for their information changes.

15.12 KNOW YOUR AUDIENCE

There are two audiences for a test case and four roles in the communication it represents. The first role is the author who seeks to document his or her intent and expectations in the form of a test case. There is the executor who must experience the product in a manner directed by the test case and report those experiences back. There is the collator who takes the reported experiences and consolidates or collates them into a form consumable by a wider audience. And finally, there is the consumer who uses the communications to inform himself or herself of the product and project. During the best of times, the only roles directly interacting with the actual test case are the author and the executor. The two roles can usually afford to develop a shorthand language for their own use so long as they are the only ones concerned. Unfortunately if there are issues at any point, any and all roles may wish to interact directly with the communication in the specific test case. This means people who were not involved with the natural evolution of the shorthand will now be forced to take a crash course in it if they wish to understand anything about it.

The same is true of the two audiences, the current roles and the future roles. Value stream management means keeping in mind the future holders of the roles involved in your test case and not assuming either the test case will not last or the future people will have full recollection of the current communication forms. Good test cases are designed as living documents meant to grow and evolve with the product rather than exist trapped in amber as a testament to what existed at one time. Expectations of future users who may not share the knowledge and experience of the current team should always be accounted for when designing a good test case.

But as I stated earlier in the section on appropriate effort, detail is not the way to plan for future audiences. Designing test cases for reuse, maintenance, and shared effort is the proper way to craft a test case for a long-term plan; a dilemma object oriented design addressed years ago when it comes to software coding best practices. Unfortunately many testers are not familiar with the concepts of inheritance and abstraction, much less design patterns and higher level concepts. This is why a lot of testers write bad tests, claiming a more authentic vision of the user experience, all the while relying on coders working in their departments to clean them up when the tests are handed off to be "automated."

15.13 YOUR MOTHER DOESN'T WORK HERE

The assumption someone with more experience, knowledge, training, or expertise can and will follow behind the bad tests is pervasive and false.

No one can magically turn your bad test cases into good ones through the judicious application of a tool, a template, a framework, a language, or a standard. Bad test cases submitted to a tool or to a team for automation become bad automated test cases where their cost is actually worse than a bad manual test case. A bad manual test case relies on a human who can make rational judgments regarding what they think they are being told to do. Rational humans can ignore, interpret, or blunder their way through a decent test pass using bad test cases. Computers cannot. Computers only do exactly what they are told each and every time they are told to do it. A computer will never halt a test case midway through and ask what the test case is attempting to validate because it doesn't appear to make sense. Bad automated test cases represent active costs in the costs incurred transforming, authoring, maintaining, and researching when they fail. Bad automated tests also represent passive costs in lost opportunities or false assumptions based on faulty communication. Unless there is a concerted effort to completely redesign and refactor test cases during the transformation into automation, all you accomplish in automating bad test cases is the removal of the one check you have against them—the testers themselves.

15.14 REFACTORING IS NOT REDESIGNING

There is a tendency when writing bad software tests to trust in a system of refactoring or redesign to give the author or someone else a chance to fill in the blanks the current author is leaving out of a sense of urgency or convenience. This is unfortunate because it violates the definition of refactoring, is not actually redesigning, and is probably a moot problem because neither will ever likely occur.

To address the issue of it violating the principles of refactoring, I will turn to Martin Fowler. In an article for *Distributed Computing* he defined refactoring as "the controlled process of altering the existing software so its design is the way you want it now, rather than the way you wanted it then. It does this by applying a series of particular code transformations, each of which are called *refactorings*" [5]. In other words refactoring in this context is indeed the act of refining a test case, but only to refine your communication to reflect new understandings. It is not meant to fill in gaps causing confusion or misunderstanding about those understandings.

Redesigning a test case, on the other hand, is the act of altering the test case to reflect new understandings based on alterations outside the tests themselves. A hallmark of a good test case is it lends itself easily to redesign since the assumptions and intent are readily apparent. If a feature is changed or a new feature is added, good test cases allow the test team to easily focus on which tests will be affected and which can be expanded or used as templates for new tests.

Finally this whole discussion is more than likely moot for your organization. If you are currently under so much pressure to produce test cases as to justify writing bad ones, you will probably never have a few free moments to go back and complete the test cases you know are incomplete or incomprehensible to anyone else (including yourself in six months). The test cases will remain as they are and will affect the language your team and project develops when communicating. Soon the incomplete tests will seem natural and even more efficient as you find yourself producing more test cases quicker than you thought possible.

Six months later you'll be called back into a war room meeting to answer questions about a defect reported by important customers. The war team will want details about your testing, but cannot get it from your tests. So the war team spends more time and energy calling you into the meeting to interpret. If you're lucky, you'll actually know what the bad test cases imply. More likely is the scenario where you too will be baffled and so will be forced to fall back on either generalities, forced admissions of truth, or outright lies in order to buy yourself some time; none of which will answer anyone's questions, identify gaps in the process, and will actually cost the company money from lost opportunities and misallocated resources.

15.15 SKYROCKETING INTEREST RATES ON QUALITY DEBT

As was implied earlier, bad tests have a way of compounding their costs over the lifetime of a project. If test cases are an evolving pattern for communication between test and the current as well as future project members and customers, bad test cases are the foul language of that communication. As the bad test case count grows, it becomes easier on the team to simply conduct all testing along the framework of the bad ones. The apparent effort to refactor or completely rewrite the test cases into good ones will continue to grow as each new bad test case is added to the pile.

Eventually the team will be forced to abandon the test cases completely and start fresh, hire extra personnel to work outside the normal project structure to convert bad to good, or simply keep adding bodies to the teams while chalking it up to natural product growth and maturity.

15.16 CONCLUSION

As I stated earlier, it is not hard to write good software tests. All it takes is a commitment from the test team to constantly improve its craft and communication abilities outside the team. It also takes commitment from management to support these efforts even if initial budgeting or scheduling appears to be suffering. If you are working on a startup or other proto-typing project where long-term value management means thinking three months into the future, there will be pressure to abandon craftsmanship for pragmatism to deliver as fast as possible.

This is a mistake.

Today's one-off prototype design for presentation at a convention or to a customer has an annoyingly regular way of becoming tomorrow's product; the test cases associated with it following right along like baby ducks following their mother.

I have a personal anecdote I tell about this situation that never fails to amaze, but I sometimes suspect it fails to educate. A friend (and colleague) of mine was working as a developer on a "one-off project" for a client in order to demonstrate a possible application of a framework the client was developing. He had a good relationship with the tester on the project, even if it did involve a sort of friendly rivalry. The tester and he developed a lot of temporary test cases and workarounds designed just to make sure the prototype would work long enough to present. He and the tester then parted company. Fast forward four years and my friend received a phone call from a company in Florida. It seemed they'd purchased a tool from the framework company for which he'd done the prototyping work. Evidently they'd had a problem with the product and ran the internal diagnostic tools. The tool tossed back a strange error naming my friend and helpfully providing his cell phone number.

Depending on my audience, I usually am greeted with astonishment for varying reasons when I tell this story. I'm usually accused of making it up completely. Often people are astonished someone would keep the same phone number after moving up to Seattle from Florida. Very few people actually see the moral of this story. Even though my friend was working on a one-off prototype, the bad test cases cost his client and him later. It cost him usage minutes and possibly embarrassment as he explained what had actually happened. It cost his client a customer now probably thought less of them as a supplier. It cost the customer because it had an error it couldn't diagnose nor know whom to call since the test case was bad, a tad humorous, but bad.

Bad test cases cost the software industry untold amounts of money every day of every month of any year. Every time a company is forced to accept it taking three to six months for a new hire to be independently productive and not reducing the efficiency of another experienced resource, that's an unnecessary cost. Every time a company is forced to "restart" its test efforts from scratch because a change in product scope causes a cascading effect where no one is sure what's applicable anymore, that's an unnecessary cost. Every time a team has to be pulled off current work to support investigation into a customer reported defect to determine if it's something new or something old, that's an unnecessary cost. Every time... well, I think you probably get the point by now.

Bad test case craftsmanship and bad code craftsmanship are probably the two most unnecessary costs incurred as part of doing business by software companies today. Robert Martin and other writers have told the world the emperor has no clothes when it comes to coders. It's time testers were held to the same standards.

NOTES

1. The epigraph to this chapter is from the foreword to Robert C. Martin, *Clean Code: A Handbook of Agile Software Craftsmanship* (Upper Saddle River, NJ: Prentice Hall, 2009).
2. The Manifesto for Software Craftsmanship was authored in 2009 by a group of noted software development leaders in the Agile development movement. These leaders included (but were not limited to) Robert C. Martin himself as well as Corey Haines, Dave Hoover, and Paul Pagel. Since then the group has expanded to include

later signatories as equal adherents and contributors to the software craftsmanship movement. You can read the manifesto and become a signatory at the Web site http:// manifesto.softwarecraftsmanship.org.

3. Peter Drucker, *Management Challenges for the 21st Century* (New York: HarperCollins, 1999), pp. 111–112.

4. Ibid, p. 114.

5. Martin Fowler, "Refactoring: Doing Design after the Code Runs," *Distributed Computing*, September 1998.

16

Rightsizing the Cost of Testing: Tips for Executives

Scott Barber

Note to readers: This chapter has been written specifically for senior managers and executives (subsequently, executives) [1]. For the purposes of the discussions in this chapter, an executive is a person who has both the authority and responsibility to allocate the overall budget for software development activities, decide whether testing and testers are owned and managed by projects or are part of a centralized testing service, decide which software will be built or bought, establish or modify project timelines and release dates, or make equivalent decisions in other areas of the corporation such as marketing, product support, or human resources (HR). If this doesn't sound like your role and you don't at least have significant influence over decisions such as these, you are likely to find much of what is contained in this chapter to be beyond your ability to implement. If this is the case, don't feel discouraged or stop reading—the information contained in this chapter can still be immensely valuable to you as you find yourself interacting with executives. Maybe you can even convince your favorite executive to read this chapter and discuss its contents and implications with you as they relate to your corporation. And who knows; maybe one day in the future you'll find yourself in an executive role, dusting off this chapter to help you with a challenge you never imagined you'd be facing when you read it the first time.

16.1 TESTING IS JUST ANOTHER OPERATING EXPENSE—MOSTLY

As much as corporate executives may wish that it were not the case, testing will simply never be anything other than an operating expense (OPEX) unless their corporation is in the business of providing testing services as a revenue stream. No matter what fancy accounting is applied to try to make testing appear less costly or what new age calculation is used to justify the cost of testing in terms of return on investment (ROI), for most companies there is simply no direct revenue derived from this expense. For all that it can be painful to admit, testing in most cases is just as much an OPEX as facilities rental, human resources, and the "free" coffee provided to employees in the hopes that it will make them more productive.

Naturally, everyone would notice very quickly if someone were to stop paying the rent on the office, eliminate HR, or sell the coffee pots in an attempt to make a company's bottom line look better as a particularly difficult quarter is coming to a close. In fact, doing any one of those things would probably lead to a near immediate revolt, followed by virtually every employee's resume showing up on every job board in the area. Eliminating these OPEXs under the banner of saving the bottom line would be tantamount to drilling a hole in the hull of a sinking ship while proclaiming that this would help the flood waters drain.

To illustrate, let's take a look at how this worked out for Life Insurance For Testers, Inc. (LIFT). One day, after a particularly bad quarter, the entire functional testing team for LIFT's online policy application product was simply let go [2]. There were a few questions, and some other members of the software development team were nervous for the next few weeks, but there was no revolt among the remaining employees; there wasn't even any whining. Business basically went on as usual. Some of the remaining members of the team spent a little more effort checking their work, but they felt like they had more time to do so, since they weren't being bogged down in dealing with all of those bug reports, "ridiculous demands" from the testers, and incessant questions from product managers about why the testers were finding so many bugs in the first place. In fact, development seemed to be a smoother, happier, faster process—at least for a while.

But then, shortly after one of LIFT's periodic feature upgrade releases, the number of fielded support calls went up dramatically. Before the team could get a patch fix coded and released, LIFT started receiving negative reviews in consumer reports online and in print, and both the new customer policy rate and the term policy renewal rate dropped significantly [3]. There still wasn't a mass revolt, but by the close of the following quarter, LIFT's bottom line was worse than it had been before the testers were let go.

In case you may be wondering, this isn't some dark fairytale I've created to make a point. LIFT itself is a fictitious company, but the LIFT scenarios in this chapter are markedly similar to situations I have firsthand experience with, either as an employee or as a consultant called in to help plug the hole in the hull and bail out the flood waters for companies who have made decisions like these. Over the course of my career, I've witnessed and participated in both failed and successful rescue attempts related to testing cost reduction attempts gone awry. Each situation has been different in significant ways, but one thing was the same every time: when the executives were faced with the fact that their boat was taking on water faster than it was before they trimmed or cut the testing OPEX, they were always initially baffled by how that decision could have had such widespread negative consequences. After all, what executive would knowingly make a decision that's doomed to leave the corporation worse off than it was before and then stick around to watch it happen?

One of the reasons that situations like this occur, and, to varying degrees, occur frequently is that testing is different from most other OPEXs in several fundamental ways:

1. Much more so than facilities, HR, and the presence or absence of available coffee, good testing is often almost entirely transparent at the executive level. It's only when the product is of unacceptable quality that testing is likely to be brought to the attention of executives. After all, executives do tend to have offices, make use of HR services, and drink coffee. But few executives (chief technology officers who got their start as developers could be an exception) make use of a corporation's software testing services very often, at least if things are running as they should.

2. It also takes a relatively long time for too little, poor, or entirely absent testing to cause a problem that is noticeable at the executive level. Unlike when a company switches to a less expensive brand of coffee, which will be noticed within minutes of the first people arriving at work the next day, switching to a less expensive brand of testing might take several release cycles to attract executive attention.

3. From the outside, it is nearly impossible to tell if a software product is good as a result of a good testing program or if it's good because of great development (in spite of poor testing). The converse is also true; from the outside it is very difficult to tell if a product is of poor quality due to poor development, poor testing, a combination of the two, or some other problem such as the product being poorly conceived. True, it is sometimes also difficult to tell if coffee is bad because of

bad beans or bad water, but that is a problem far less complicated (and less expensive) to solve.

4. Even when companies must consider scaling back on facilities, HR programs, or coffee, the reasons these items were valued in the first place are rarely questioned. The question asked when those decisions are made is almost always a form of the following: "Is the added expense of such high quality facilities, services, etcetera, still justified for the incrementally higher value it adds, compared to less expensive options in the face of [insert current situation here]?" But when software product development expenses seem to be outweighing the perceived value obtained from those expenses, one of the questions that is frequently asked instead is "Why are we spending all that money on testing anyway?"

For an executive, all four of these items are worth noting. It's easy enough to avoid the challenges associated with the first three items if executives make some time to get to know their testing program. I'd go so far as to recommend that executives go to the test lab every now and again to lend a hand with the testing for a couple of hours—mostly because I can think of nothing that will increase familiarity with the product more than to spend some time testing it but also because this will give hands-on executives a feel for what their testers do and what challenges they face. Who knows, the visiting executive might even become aware of a challenge that is particularly debilitating to the test program but can be resolved easily through executive channels to increase cooperation and productivity all around.

But whether or not an executive has the opportunity to do some testing of his or her own before deciding whether or not testing costs need to be reduced, the decision must be based on what is being spent on testing vs. the value the company is receiving from that investment.

16.2 EXECUTIVE TIP 1: CHANGE THE QUESTION

If you are an executive who is serious about rightsizing the cost of testing within your corporation, the first thing you need to do is invert this question [4]. Rather than "What value are we currently realizing as a result of what we are spending on testing?" the more useful questions to ask are

"What value do we *want to be* realizing through our testing program, and how much are we *willing to* invest to realize that value?"

Unlike facilities, HR, and coffee, it is at best very difficult to calculate the ROI of a testing program [5]. In fact, it's much like calculating the ROI of auto insurance. The ROI of auto insurance is a big negative number if you own your car outright, live somewhere that you won't go to jail for being an uninsured driver, and never have a claim-worthy incident, but all it takes is one stray roofing nail to puncture a tire on the big rig that you happen to be ever so carefully passing and suddenly that big negative number becomes a big positive number. So which number are you going to use for your ROI calculations? I submit that, absent the development of a highly reliable testing actuarial table, that entire line of thinking will occasionally produce a number that makes sense in retrospect, typically by luck, but most of the time it will simply lead a corporation down a path of gross over- or underspending on testing programs without anyone ever correlating the degree of spending with realized value.

Instead of counting on Lady Luck to smile on you or burying your head in the sand until the testing actuarial table appears, it seems a far better choice to start the rightsizing process by identifying the desired business-level value propositions for your testing program, prioritizing them, and then assigning an acceptable cost to the highest priority value propositions [6].

16.3 EXECUTIVE TIP 2: FOCUS ON VALUE TO THE BUSINESS

Identifying the desired value proposition or outcome [7], of a testing program probably sounds like either a redundant task or a complete waste of time, but neither is likely to be the case. Very few testing programs are conceived and maintained with a focus on value to the business. Most testing programs are built on or gradually shift to a focus on project-level or tactical value. As an executive, you certainly don't want to minimize the importance of tactical value, but at the end of the quarter you still need to be able to justify the dollars spent on testing to superiors, the board of directors, investors, and shareholders. If your justification starts and ends with "Testing is just part of how we develop software products," you'll likely be told to bundle it in with the rest of the project costs and let the project managers figure out for themselves how to pay for testing without reducing the product's bottom line [8]. At least, that's what I've most frequently seen done in that situation.

But the truth is that testing does, or at least should, provide business-level value that can be monetized. Here are some examples of how:

- Testing can be the key to preparing for and passing regulatory audits, thus reducing both preparation costs and risk of having to unexpectedly invest in corrective action to pass a potentially more rigorous reaudit.
- Testing can be a very strong defense against claims of negligence, faulty advertising, and service level agreement (SLA) violations (of course, it can also be a very weak defense if the testing wasn't done with this in mind), thus reducing the likelihood of legal action being taken against the company and reducing preparation costs should a suit go to court.
- Testing can help prepare support center staff to field questions about changes and known issues in the product prior to release [9], thus reducing call duration and callbacks while increasing customer satisfaction ratings of support calls immediately following release.
- Testing can provide you with relative quality and stability comparisons from release to release, thus reducing the likelihood of product reviews calling out a downward trend.
- Testing can provide you with necessary information for assessing the relative risk of releasing on schedule versus delaying a release to improve the product, thus allowing you to make an informed decision about which course of action will be less costly overall.
- Testing can provide information about weaknesses in the product, thus enabling you to develop risk mitigation strategies or make other executive-level decisions regarding the product or project.
- Testing can provide start-point data and cross-validation for capacity planning models, thus increasing the accuracy of the models and reducing the likelihood of either overspending or running into unexpected capacity limits.
- Testing can identify candidate builds for prerelease sales demos, along with training materials for sales staff, thus preventing the sales staff from stumbling upon defects and tarnishing the product's credibility in front of potential buyers.

Note that only you and your staff can determine the strategic value of benefits such as these to the business, and that it will be up to your senior staff, generally the beneficiaries of the value, to monetize that value. Also note that these strategic value propositions are not costly add-ons, but are all things that a testing program can provide to the business while already involved in the processes of providing tactical value in such ways as:

- Finding discrepancies between requirements or specifications and what is being delivered, thus reducing the chances of delivering a product that ends up needing to be rebuilt immediately before or shortly after release due to an oversight or misinterpretation
- Detecting issues (bugs) in the product in time to resolve them prior to release when it is cheaper to fix the software or otherwise correct the issue
- Freeing up developers to spend more time focusing on new development and issue resolution and less time focusing on issue detection, thus shortening development cycles and potentially reducing staffing needs, improving the quality of the product, and improving staff contentment
- Serving as the end user's representative to ensure that usability concerns and priority user issues are discovered in time to be addressed appropriately, thus reducing the risk of widespread user complaints, bad press, reduced sales, returns, and so forth due to incorrect assumptions about what matters to the user
- Assisting in determining the scope and impact of detected issues, thus reducing the time needed to decide on a course of action, and decreasing the likelihood that such decisions will be challenged, both at the time and in subsequent scenarios when unexpected problems might crop up

Of course, these are not all or even most of the potential value propositions a testing program can provide; they are just a small sampling. In fact, many of these particulars might not even be all that interesting to your organization. The important part to recognize here is that testing provides both strategic and tactical value propositions and once identified, they can then be prioritized and given a monetized value that we'll refer to as the target cost of the value proposition [10].

Once you've identified, prioritized, and determined a target cost for the desired values, you can quickly estimate whether you have a financially balanced testing program by subtracting the current cost of your testing program from the target cost of the benefits already being realized.

Naturally, you could do this by applying a weighting scheme to the target costs to account for the degree to which their associated benefits are currently being achieved; sum the target costs of what you want, then subtract the cost of what you have to get an estimate of how much you have available to spend to add additional value propositions while remaining balanced; or applying any of a number of other kinds of analysis you favor [11]. The key is recognizing that the calculable value is there in the first place.

16.4 EXECUTIVE TIP 3: DISTRIBUTE TESTING COSTS CAREFULLY

Many organizations assign the costs associated with testing to a single ledger account, typically either the general and administrative (G&A) account or the account that includes the product group or department that "owns" software development. Either of these assignments, or an entirely different one, may be appropriate, so applying a cost allocation model will help determine what cost assignments will really work best for your organization [12].

If you are not familiar with management accounting or cost allocation, here is a quick overview to illustrate how this tip can work in action. First, an account is a subset of a corporation's financial records. Accounts generally map to functional areas or business units of the corporation for the purposes of simplifying financial tracking and accountability of these areas. For our purposes, we'll refer to those functional areas or business units as divisions. Generally speaking, assets, liabilities, equity, expenses, and revenue are tracked within each account.

To illustrate, let's return to LIFT. Needless to say, the eventual fallout from the dismissal of the online policy application's functional testing team attracted executive level attention. As a result of its executives' investigation into how this had happened and how to keep it from happening again, LIFT determined that some organizational changes were necessary to tie financial accountability to the responsibility for delivering value across its testing program.

LIFT tracks its finances across five divisions: G&A, IT, sales & support, product development, and compliance and legal defense. LIFT's desired value propositions for its testing program are the same as the ones discussed earlier. And, as it turns out, each of LIFT's divisions is the primary beneficiary of at least one of the desired value propositions, so LIFT executives have decided to assign the target cost for new propositions and the actual cost for propositions that are already in place to the division that each proposition primarily benefits. The finalized division assignments for LIFT's propositions follow:

G&A—Provide release-to-release comparisons, provide release readiness information, identify areas of weakness to feed risk-mitigation plans

IT—Provide input data and cross-validation for capacity planning

Sales and support—Identify candidate builds for prerelease sales demos and train sales staff, assist in preparing support center for pending release

Compliance and legal defense—Prepare for compliance audits, provide support for legal defense

Product development—Provide project team with information related to correctness, completeness, and overall quality of completed and in-progress development

LIFT chose to allocate costs in this manner as a way to ensure that the executives in charge of each of these divisions was clear about what portion of the testing program their divisions were responsible to fund, and these executives could be sure that their divisions were receiving the desired value as a direct result of their investment. Under this organizational model, if a division wants more value from the testing program, then that division knows that it will need to foot the bill. If the division determines that the service isn't as valuable as what it is paying, it can choose to pay for less and get less in return. This also means that since the product development division only funds a portion of the testing program, this division can only eliminate the portion of the program it is funding, thus mitigating the risk of the entire testing function for a product being eliminated without the involvement of executives from all of the affected divisions. Again, as an executive, this is a line of thinking I suspect you are familiar with [13].

16.5 EXECUTIVE TIP 4: DEMAND ACCOUNTABILITY FROM MANAGERS OF TESTING PROGRAMS

Things get a little more complicated when one or more of the divisions determine that they want more value but shouldn't have to pay for it or determine that they aren't receiving value equivalent to what they are paying for. There are three primary reasons complications arise when testing programs aren't delivering the desired strategic value:

1. Most executives have approximately zero experience testing software.
2. Most test managers have approximately zero training or experience in business management.
3. Test managers are used to being held accountable for the accuracy, not the value, of the information they provide.

It is common for test teams to have a single-minded focus on identifying defects and championing to have those defects resolved. When asked to provide executive summaries of the collective strategic business implications of those individual defects, testers widely resist [14]. This resistance is generally the result of a confluence of experiences and feelings, the most relevant and common being:

- They recognize that they don't know what risk mitigation measures or fail-safes are in place in production that they have missed in their analysis.
- Previous attempts they may have made to provide this type of information anyway have often been dismissed in an embarrassing or frustrating fashion.
- They feel these additional tasks take time away from their primary mission.
- The request simply doesn't make sense to them.

The first step in resolving this situation is two-way education. Executives need to educate testers, not only about what information they want and how they want it presented, but also about why they want the information and what decisions or actions will result from their having it. Testers need to educate executives about what information is reasonably obtainable and what that information does and does not mean. Only after this cross-education takes place can the test team work productively with executives to determine what information they can exchange to address the company's concerns.

For example, LIFT's executives liked to use statistics based on tests or test cases, and expected such measurements as the number of tests planned, the number executed, and the number of passes and fails to assess the current goodness of the product and the current degree of completeness of testing [15]. This seemed completely reasonable until LIFT recognized that neither test nor test case is a static unit of measure. *Test*, in testing terms, is a less fancy word for "experiment," and *test case* is a fancy way to say "container for one or more tests." After coming to this realization, LIFT executives quickly learned that the number of tests or test cases being planned for each release was really only directly related to the number the test team believed it could accomplish given the parameters of the project. So completing or not completing all of the planned tests was actually an indicator of the test team's estimation skill, not an indicator of whether the desired or necessary testing has been accomplished. What LIFT executives came to understand was that the only way a test group could plan to conduct exactly the right number of the right tests to expose all of the defects that matter would be if they knew what all the defects were and how to find them before they started planning.

LIFT executives came to this realization without even considering that counting tests or test cases doesn't account for the fact that many items that reduce the quality of software products do not lend themselves to binary pass–fail characterization nor the fact that the one particular failing test could be more strategically critical than the combined failure of all of the others. LIFT executives did come to realize, though, that statistical analysis of numbers of tests or test cases can reveal important trends, but goodness and completeness won't be among them. They also learned that achieving the desired value from their testing program involved collaboration in determining what value was desired, what measures or metrics were indicators for that value, and how and when to present those measures and metrics.

It is not necessary for every executive to be aware of this particular metrics disconnect, let alone to be aware of all the other measurement and metrics challenges related to software testing. However, it is critical that the executives who rely on information obtained from a testing program are aware that such challenges do exist and are common. With this awareness, instead of asking for a particular measure or metric, informed executives will be far more likely to engage in a discussion about what value they are counting on receiving from the testing program and collaborating with testers and test managers to devise a measurement or metric that provides that value.

For this to work, the most successful executives will take an approach like the following:

- Kick off discussions with requests like the following: "I need some kind of indicator of [area of interest]. What do you recommend?"
- Be open to learning and collaborating.
- Ensure that the managers of the testing program know that they will be held accountable for providing whatever measure or metric they agree to accurately and in a manner that delivers the desired value—at least if they want to continue receiving funding from the division that the participating executive represents.
- Help testers and test managers understand that they will likely need to change or enhance what they are doing to collect the data that feeds those agreed-upon measures and metrics.

In short, managers of the testing program will need to learn to be accountable to the executives in charge of the divisions that are funding the testing program to ensure that those executives are getting appropriate value for their investment, and those divisions' executives will need to learn how to work with the managers of the testing program to design the appropriate measures and metrics to be used to deliver that value.

16.6 EXECUTIVE TIP 5: KEEP TACTICS AT A TACTICAL LEVEL

To this point in this chapter, we've not considered the possibility that the testing program might turn out to be simply unable to provide the desired value with the funding available, or using its current methods, tools, or techniques. Nor have we considered what might happen when the testing program is faced with the reality that its income is being reduced while the demand for produced value is on the rise. This is where the other chapters of this book come in.

In today's climate especially, we are all certainly familiar with the desire for increased efficiency: the appeal—if not the outright necessity—of doing more with less. Every executive who has not yet, at least once, called a middle or line manager into his or her office to tell that person that he or she needs to figure out a way to cut costs in his or her department without degrading the service it provides or delaying project completion, will surely find himself or herself in exactly that position soon. In my experience, this is a fairly common occurrence, except when it comes to test programs. Every time I have encountered cost-reducing measures in a testing program, I have found that those cost-reducing measures to have been decided upon and implemented by an executive more or less independently of interaction with any members of the testing team involved. Whether this happens because of poor lines of communication between departments, a lack of understanding on the part of decision-makers of what testers' contributions to such conversations could be, or a company's sense that testing, like free coffee, is just a necessary luxury whose corners are convenient to cut, my experience strongly suggests that the approach doesn't work out very well.

Part of being accountable, across departments and administrative levels, is being able to apply cost-cutting measures when necessary. Like everyone else, the managers of your testing program need to be held accountable for their program. These managers may need some assistance and training before it's reasonable to hold them solely and independently accountable for big-picture cost-reduction measures, but they are the only ones who can determine what costs can be reduced without significantly degrading the value of their testing program. To use your testing program to its full potential as a source of actual value in your company, it will be necessary to enable the testing team to participate in making these kinds of decisions. In fact, if they aren't the people who put this book in your hands in the first place, you would probably be well served to put copies into their hands so they can consider the cost reduction and cost optimization measures presented in the other chapters as a first step in providing more comprehensive value to your company while doing the work they already do well. Ultimately, the executive who provides his or her testing team with whatever other support and resources team members need to be successful will soon be able to step back and let them prove to the whole company that they deserve the managerial position they occupy.

16.7 SUMMARY

These tips are the result of applying a systems thinking approach to some of the most serious and difficult costing, value, and accountability challenges of managing testing programs that I have encountered over the course of my career. These particular tips draw inspiration from the balanced scorecard approach to corporate performance management, total cost management (TCM), activity-based management (ABM), transfer pricing, target costing, and cost allocation, and have evolved over several years, many clients, significant trial and error, and countless hours of exacting peer review. My goal when writing this chapter was to give executives with at least some degree of responsibility for a software testing program suggestions for how to right size their programs by balancing the programs' costs with the value they provide.

I do not expect that these tips will magically solve all of your company's challenges related to testing costs versus value, but I do believe the principles on which they are based are sound and worthy of your consideration. There are as many possible solutions to an individual company's challenges as there are companies who wrestle with them, and there is not now, nor will there ever be, a one-size-fits-all model for balancing software testing costs versus value. I do believe, however, that to find the right solution for your company, a business-level, systems thinking approach (or an alternate method applied at the same level with equivalent scope) is necessary.

I have shared my thought process, problem-solving approach, and key references in this chapter as one example knowing that you will have no choice but to do your own problem solving to design a solution that is appropriate for the corporation you serve. But I hope I have been successful at inspiring you to design a successful solution of your own and to bring your executive voice into a collaborative exchange with your testers and test managers. Such an approach will be sure to lead to realistic, mutually beneficial value increases for your company as a whole.

NOTES

1. By senior managers and executives (subsequently, executives), I'm referring to people who have titles like director of X, vice president of Y, chief Z officer, managing director, and president. Some companies will have additional titles for peers to these positions on the organizational chart. For example, technology companies may have a chief X architect. For the purposes of this chapter, these actual titles are not important. What is important is to note that within this chapter, executives are considered to be individuals within a corporation who have primarily strategic roles, as opposed to line managers or team leads who have primarily tactical roles.
2. Depending on what industry you work on, this group might also be known as quality assurance (QA), system test, or even business analysts. The title isn't important to the illustration. What is important to the illustration is that I am referring to whatever group is primarily responsible for finding bugs and submitting bug reports.

3. If your company develops software that is only used internally, your users may not have the ability or influence to choose an alternate solution, but they certainly can, and will, make it clear that they wish they could. In this case, it is those internal users who will complain—and who may eventually lead an actual revolt.

4. Changing the question is my variation on the systems thinking principle known as formulating the mess. See Russell L. Ackoff, *Creating the Corporate Future* (New York: John Wiley & Sons, 1981).

5. It is less difficult but still far from mechanical to calculate the ROI of changing or upgrading a particular aspect of a testing program.

6. The idea of monetizing benefits that have no direct financial value comes from an extension of traditional benefit cost analysis known as social return on investment (SROI). See Peter Scholten, Jeremy Nicholls, Sara Olsen, and Brett Galimidi, *SROI: A Guide to Social Return on Investment* (Amsterdam: Lenthe Publishers, 2006).

7. Starting with the desired outcome and working back to where things are today, as used here, is an application of interactive planning, specifically the idealization phase, as documented most succinctly in Russell L. Ackoff, "A Brief Guide to Interactive Planning and Idealized Design" (May 31, 2001).

8. An example of throughput costing.

9. Some contributions for which testers are highly valued as part of support center preparation include writing or contributing to FAQs, sharing known workarounds, and having a tester switch places with a support representative during beta release to provide knowledge transfer, cross-training, and a voice for the support center during this last chance to raise and fix issues prior to release.

10. This is actually a hybrid of activity-based costing and target costing applied to a service model as opposed to a product model.

11. This process amounts to applying your favorite performance management method. If you aren't currently using a Performance management method or your current performance management method doesn't handle this scenario particularly well, you might consider balanced-scorecard-derived or -inspired approaches, which I've found to be particularly effective.

12. Tip 3 applies the management accounting concepts of transfer pricing and cost allocation, and presumes that the desired outcome is a purposeful, open, multiminded system with a divisional structure. See Jamshid Gharajedaghi, *Systems Thinking: Managing Chaos and Complexity; A Platform for Designing Business Architecture* (2nd ed., Burlington, MA: Butterworth-Heinemann, 2005).

13. This is a representation of interactive management within a purposeful, multiminded system, as described by Jamshid Gharajedaghi (2005).

14. Few testers will resist presenting business implications, user implications, support implications, and so forth for individual or closely related defects. Here, I am referring to collective implications of the current state of the product as a whole.

15. For more information about the challenges of test-case-based metrics, see Cem Kaner, James Bach, and Bret Pettichord, *Lessons Learned in Software Testing* (New York: Wiley, 2001). For more information on measurements and metrics, see Jonathan G. Koomey, *Turning Numbers into Knowledge,* (2nd ed., Oakland, CA: Analytics Press, 2008).

Afterword

About twenty years ago, one of our editors was reading the manual for Wizardry, a fantasy adventure game. The very back of the book contained a dictionary that defined terms. The last entry began with the letter *Y*; there was no entry for *Z*. It looked very much like this:

> **You:** Have reached the end of this manual. We've taken you as far as we can; the rest is up to you. Not get out there and play!

We don't know how you feel as readers, but as authors, we have a similar feeling. It's been a pleasure putting this book together. It's been an honor knowing that our words may affect the way other people develop software—an honor we take seriously.

But you have reached the end of the manual. From here, you'll have to take the ideas, dissect them, determine what fits for you, and give it a try.

The good news is that in the twenty-first century you don't have to be a stranger. Most of us blog, or you can join the discussion on the Software Testing (http://groups.yahoo.com/group/software-testing/) or SW-IMPROVE (http://tech.groups.yahoo.com/group/SW-Improve/) discussion lists, or on LinkedIn. We're sure that if you try the ideas in this book, the authors would appreciate hearing from you over e-mail.

But you have reached the end of this book.

So get out there and test!

Appendix A: Immediate Strategies to Reduce Test Cost

Matt Heusser

In the first chapter, I made a simple claim that reducing the cost of testing is easy: just test less. It didn't take long for us to realize things are not that simple; testing less means missing bugs. But that first chapter brought out another idea: we could save money by reducing waste in the test process. If we define waste as non-value-added activity, we should be able to reduce waste without incurring risk. Taking things just one step further, there may be some activities we do that offer a little value for much cost that you could think of as mostly waste. We might benefit from eliminating those activities as well. So without further ado, please allow me to introduce twenty-five strategies to reduce test cost, both right now and in the long term [1].

A.1 CUT YOUR DOCUMENTATION TO A MINIMUM

Documentation can be surprisingly expensive. First you have to write it; then you have to maintain it. Plus, it has value only when people read it, which—surprise—takes time.

Although you might want some documentation, a first step is to minimize it. For example, say you are testing a spreadsheet. Do you really need four pages of documentation about environment, setup, versions, preconditions, and such in order to test the bold button? Could you just have a cell in a spreadsheet that says "Test the Bold button," along with a pass–fail cell and some notes?

At the highest level, this sort of "test plan" is really just a list of the major features of the software, with perhaps a list of who is assigned to test what and the status they have. Your test planning will probably be somewhere in the middle. My advice: watch where time is actually being spent and where value is actually being added, and adjust your plan to create the most bang for the buck.

A.2 MAKE THE COST OF CHANGING THE DOCUMENTATION CHEAP

Consider the cost of e-mailing files, or keeping them on a network drive, or having only one person at a time with write permission, in the context of the earlier example where the test plan is a list of features. We could make this cheaper by putting the test plan on a wiki or, for that matter, on a whiteboard. Sometimes, the simplest solution is a whiteboard.

A.3 NEVER BE BLOCKED

Blocked is a key word. Replace it with *waste*. In other words, when you hear, "I'm blocked," think instead "I'm generating waste." If that is true, then testers should never be blocked; there is always one more thing they can do to influence the outcome. Some things testers can do while they are blocked:

- Interview customers for test ideas
- Pair with the developers to learn the system
- Work with project or product management to pair with another tester on a different piece of functionality in the same project

One more time, with feeling: "I'm blocked" is two words, ten letters. For our purposes, we're going to consider it a four-letter term—it's a swear word.

Three strikes and you are not out!

A.4 ELIMINATE MULTIPROJECTING

Testers that are blocked are likely taking on side projects. The cost of switching between projects turns out to be surprisingly high. By the time the tester has four or five different projects, each blocked, he or she is basically getting nothing done, just cycling through work. So eliminate multiproject work for testers. But, you say, the tester is blocked? See A.3.

A.5 AUTOMATE ENTIRELY REDUNDANT PROCESSES

A good, thinking tester who is exploring and learning is generally much more valuable than an automated script pushing buttons. Sometimes, however, the work of testing is entirely pushing buttons—say, for example, creating a test environment or driving the test environment to an interesting place from which to jump off into real testing. If team members can identify and automate these simple, straightforward, clearly definable business processes, they can then shift their time to work on more interesting paths in the software.

A.6 START WITH SOAP OPERA TESTS

Imagine insurance software with twenty different possible combinations, from age to sex to smoker to known medical conditions. The easy thing to do is to create a test case for each combination in isolation. That's a reasonable approach, but it would take a while to do, and bugs tend to hang out in complex interactions between inputs. So even testing all twenty might not find all the bugs.

So test all twenty at the same time. If a bug exists somewhere in the rating factors, it is likely to fall out, and if the software passes all twenty combinations at the same time, it is likely in decent shape.

Using *soap opera tests* [2] early in the process can give us a quick, cheap, and reasonably good evaluation of the status of the software under test. Hey, wait a minute—isn't that exactly what software testing is?

A.7 START WITH QUICK ATTACKS

Quick attacks are a subdiscipline of software testing that enable testing on virtually any kind of graphical-based software with very little to no understanding of the business logic [3]. Quick attacks basically overwhelm the software with invalid input, too much input, and input out of range.

Like soap opera testers, quick attacks involve a rule of thumb: if the software handles the obvious exception conditions well, it is likely in good shape. Likewise, if the developers left holes and errors in the exception conditions, it is likely they left holes and exceptions in the main business logic. Using quick attacks allows the tester to find bugs early, learn business rules, and perform a quick assessment of the software—all at the same time.

A.8 TEST EARLY

With test early, you might build and deploy incrementally; you might not. The point is to develop some features, along with the capability to drive those features, very early in the process. So although the entire software might not be delivered to test, you might be able to complete, say, the search function and deploy that. The tester might be driving the software through an application programming interface (API) or a simple stub test tool the programmers wrote.

The general idea here is to have programmers complete an entire feature, end to end, and hand it over to test as soon as possible. This way, the testers don't have to wait for a "complete" build (rule A.3), and the bugs will be found while the code is fresh in the programmers' minds. Although most modern incremental "methodologies" insist on this type of delivery, you don't have to be doing this to test early.

Even if you are doing Kanban, XP, or Scrum, and have test early, take a hard look at the time difference between developer done and actually testing. Is it measured in minutes, hours, or days? If it's anything more than an hour, it might be worth a little investment to see if you can shrink that number.

A.9 DEVELOP A REGRESSION-TEST CADENCE, AND KEEP IT LIGHT

As a general trend, we think it's safe to say that the pace of software release schedules is compressing. That means companies that used to release once a year are releasing twice a year, those that used to release every six months are releasing every three months, and those that used to release one a month are releasing every two weeks.

Notice that as we ship new versions of the same software more often, regression testing as a percentage of the test (or even project) budget continues to expand. For some teams, the entire "iteration" may become shorter than regression testing used to take. That means we need to get really good at regression testing and flipping releases around. Suggestion: Take a hard look at your regression testing. What can be cut? What can be automated? What can be done more effectively in less time with less paperwork?

Another idea: Say your software has different major components or the pieces are compartmentalized (the graphic layer vs. the back end). Instead of doing the same tests every time, the release can be focused on one component or another. In that case, you may be able to contain and cut testing costs from other components. For example, if you only work on back-end issues for a browser-based application, you may be able to severely limit your browser-compatibility test and graphical user interface (GUI) testing.

In graduate school I was taught that, conceptually, any code change could break any other piece of the application, so you need to retest everything every release. Thus, a very small checking at the end of a test cycle creates the obligation to rest the entire system anew. Practically, however, we know that is not true. A senior tester with a good nose for the code, working together with a developer, may be able to limit types of tests from a regression run with very little risk. For more about that, see the next section.

A.10 TEST THE THINGS THAT ACTUALLY YIELD BUGS

If you have regression tests you run for every release that never seem to find bugs, see if you can find a way to limit how many of those run. Perhaps you can run them every third release, or a third of them per release, or run just enough of them that they would uncover a major defect if it was introduced in that code.

A.11 ELABORATE—AND COMMUNICATE—A TEST STRATEGY OR TRIAGE STRATEGY

Doing fewer tests than we envisioned in order to hit a date is a sort of test triage. The simplest way to do it is to ship when you run out of time, but triage can be done well. One way to do it is to list features by how critical they are, and then go down the feature list in order for a first pass of, say, an hour each. If you complete that first pass, you go in more depth—say, two hours each—and so on.

A second way to do this is to create a testing contract with management: you might only promise to test the "happy path" of the software, for example, and be very specific about what the happy path is. Testing the happy path might mean that business customers should be able to do day-to-day operations, but bad input could lead to bad output.

"So what," you say. "If the customer gets a yucky error screen, press the back button, reload, and enter a correct value." For certain internal applications, that might be a reasonable level of quality. The problem will be the vice president who didn't get the memo. So if you do triage tests, make sure everyone knows how the decision was made, what the decision was—and make sure that the decision makers feel like part of it. It's amazing the difference between "Why didn't QA find that bug?" and a C-level executive saying, "Yes, I know, that was a calculated decision. It was my call to skip testing on that component."

A.12 DECREASE YOUR TIME SPENT REPRODUCING THE PROBLEM

Sometimes the reproduction strategy for a bug is obvious: a certain function fails in a certain browser, a certain button is gray when it should be enabled—something like that. Other times the tester needs to take steps to reproduce the problem. If the tester can't reproduce the problem, he or she may need to experiment, and that can mean time lost.

If your team is spending a lot of time on bug reproduction, look for ways to lower it. You might have the server store a log somewhere of every action it receives, or find a tool to record exactly what the tester is doing and make a screencast that can be played back [4].

If the defects that are hard to reproduce fall into a specific pattern, you might talk to the development team to see if those defects can be prevented.

A.13 DO A LOW-COST BETA PROGRAM OR PRERELEASE

If you have some way of segmenting your users and sending the curious ones to a sort of managed beta, you could release early and engage the users in helping to test. These kinds of efforts take management work. You'll also need some infrastructure (to figure out which users get which builds), and on Web-based projects, you'll likely need some sort of production monitoring.

Nothing is ever free, but a managed beta might be cheap. For more information, see "testing in production" in the index of *How We Test Software at Microsoft,* by Alan Page, Ken Johnston, and Bj Rollinson. Another, similar option is to engage a company like uTest to help with beta testing (more on uTest in A.24).

A.14 RECOGNIZE AND ELIMINATE PROJECT WANKERY

Getting better requirements, having more time to test, doing architecture and code reviews—these can all be good things. They can also be colossal wastes of time. Go ahead and experiment with these practices, but view them as experiments. After you've tried them once or twice (or if they are currently mandated), ask yourself: Are we going to have fewer defects down the line because of these meetings? Did we add value to the project by having the meeting? Is this going to decrease overall cost? If the answer is no, change the format. Consider doing the reviews at your desk [5]. If that doesn't work, consider dropping them.

A.15 STOP FIGHTING TO MANAGE THE PROJECT

It's easy for the test team to fall into the position of spending its time arguing about what decisions are made and how. If you find yourself in that position and testing is suddenly busy, consider limiting your role in the project. You can do this with a conversation with the development lead and the overall engineering manager.

For example, the ship–no-ship decision: instead of arguing over whether the software is ready to release, make the defects visible to everyone, and let senior management decide if it should be shipped. Imagine saying something like this: "We're going to stop fighting you over issues a, b, and c. We yield to a, b, and c. We're going to focus on testing. If a, b, or c fail, don't complain to me. The decision is yours." Consider how liberating that might be.

A.16 IF YOU'RE GOING TO FIGHT, WIN

If you do give on some issues, you may just want to pick a few battles. If you pick those battles, fight to win. Otherwise, you're just wasting time. A few times in my career, I remember saying something like "Oh, what's the use? You're going to decide to do branch-per-issue anyway. I just want to state for the record that I am against it." When I think of those times, I never do so with pride. I should have argued for my branching strategy or not at all. Anything in the middle is just a waste of time.

A.17 WALK AROUND AND LISTEN

What is the test team (and, for that matter, the greater project team) actually doing all day? Are they actually testing the software? Are they collaborating with peers, learning about the project, and reducing project risk? Or are they doing other stuff? Can the other stuff be eliminated? If I had to take a guess, on the projects I have worked on where the project manager was complaining about the impossible project with the insane deadline, there was generally at least one person standing around doing nothing all day.

Now, perhaps that person didn't have skills. Perhaps he or she was a net negative-producing programmer or tester—someone who took more time to baby-sit than deliver value. Most likely, he or she had a credible story about being "blocked" (see A.3). But just by walking around, I could tell that this guy wasn't actually doing anything.

Find that guy. Find the dozen who are in a similar boat but only part time. Find something constructive they can do, if it's only to run to a sandwich shop to buy the team lunch.

Three strikes and you are not out! There is always one more thing you can do to influence the outcome.

A.18 WRITE TEST AUTOMATION THAT ATTACKS THE BUSINESS-LOGIC LEVEL

It turns out that graphical test automation can be either surprisingly brittle (because you checked everything, and something not important moved, so you flagged an error) or miss bugs (because you didn't check everything, and something you failed to check went awry). Wouldn't it be nice if you could just look at a pure input–output "field" level? In many cases, you can. If the programmers provide setups and scaffolding, testers may be able to write tests that exercise the business-logic-level functions of the application. These tests will generally run much faster and be less brittle than GUI tests.

The GUI will still need to be tested by a human, but if the tester can gain some confidence that certain key presses go to the business-logic level, he or she can move on and let the (fast) automated tests verify those dozens (hundreds? thousands?) of possible inputs for a given function.

In most cases, test automation is an investment: in the short run, testing costs will go up. Starting at the business-logic level might make it possible to see returns in days and weeks, not months or years.

A.19 DEVELOP A TEST AUTOMATION LIBRARY

If you do want to test at the graphical level or want to have more powerful business-logic tests, you may want to develop reusable functions. For a GUI, that might be log in (taking username and password as parameters, then pushing the login button), search, tag, and so forth. At the business-logic level these will probably be object-oriented functions. For more about developing reusable test assets, see Karen Johns's chapter, "Cost Reduction through Reusable Test Assets."

A.20 DEVELOP OR HIRE EXPERTISE

Many experts suggest having a stable, predictable, repeatable test team so that if anyone leaves they can be easily replaced. That might free you from the tyranny of the prima donna employee—but it won't cut your time to market. Worse, it could likely mean defects missed and passed on to the customer.

Be it expertise in programming, domain experience on the software, quick attack skills, the ability to setup and tear down test environments quickly—whatever it is, expertise can help you decrease time to market and can be cheap to create. As a test manager, you can foster expertise with brown-bags and pairing; when you look to expand your team, look for skills that round out the team.

A.21 GET A RETURN FROM CONFERENCES, OR DON'T GO

As writers and speakers about testing, we are all for conferences. What we are saying here is to expect (no, demand) a return on investment from your conferences. A few things to get from conferences:

- Expect employees to write two single page or less, "What I learned" documents. The first will be things for us to do on Monday, the second, strategies to pursue over the next year.
- Use conferences to attract talent. Send your employees equipped with business cards and a list of open positions.
- Use conferences to retain talent. Build the conference into each employee's annual professional development goals, and he or she will be more likely to stick around to attend it.
- Use conferences to grow your network of friends with specific expertise (see next section).

Finally, if your staff comes back with ideas to implement on Monday, move heaven and earth to let them try. Otherwise, you've wasted a week of staff time and got no return. (For more on this, see A.25.)

A.22 BUILD A SOCIAL NETWORK

The value a tester can add to an organization is more than what is in his or her head—it includes any knowledge that tester can pull out of any friend, colleague, former coworker, peer, relative . . . anyone. Getting involved in local users' groups, attending conferences, collaborating over the Internet—it does more than give you a nice feeling. Done well and with integrity, it will result in an increasing list of people with skills you do not have, people willing, even eager, to share ideas if you tap them on the shoulder.

Want to talk about decreasing the cost of testing? Consider the difference between, on the one hand, being blocked by a performance testing problem for a month and then calling a consultant, and, on the other, making calls to a few friends, asking some questions, and spending a couple of days on exploration to solve the problem directly.

A.23 EXAMINE INVALID BUGS CAREFULLY

Take a look at how many bugs are being marked as invalid, or needing a reproduction strategy, or wrong for some other reason. Each of those bugs means a tester and a developer both invested time for no benefit. If enough bugs are invalid, take a look at why, and try to prevent it in the future.

Looking at the last five to ten invalid bugs, with an eye to preventing them in the future, might just be a great subject for a lunchtime brown-bag session.

A.24 BUILD A TEST MODEL THAT DEALS WITH THE NATURAL UP-AND-DOWN STAFFING NEED FOR TEST RESOURCES

The vast majority of test projects have an ebb and flow. If the testers remain constant, you'll either be stuck at times with the test team too small (and everyone else billing, and the project delayed) or too big (and extra testers costing the company money). So you'll want to build a staffing model that allows you to scale up and down quickly. You could do this by bringing in tech support to test, by having a beta program, by bringing in an out-sourcer for rapid test augmentation (hey, we've got a chapter on that), or by working with a company like uTest that delivers on-demand testers.

We find that few programmers make excellent testers, because the mental shift from creation to destruction can be hard. Also, programmers typically cost a fair amount of money, so ramping up testing by employing programmers as testers is rarely cost effective. However, in a pinch, if testing is a bottleneck, programmers can add a lot of value. It can be good to have the developers share the pain of testing, but we often find that their time can be better spent writing test tools.

A.25 ASK THE TEAM TO IDENTIFY OPPORTUNITIES TO DRIVE OUT WASTE, THEN IMPLEMENT THEM

The mind of a good tester doing testing is likely inquisitive, curious, and critical. So when it comes to defined process, the tester is likely to think, "Why do we waste so much time doing [thing]? I would think we could get by without it or get the same benefit from doing [cheaper thing]." But he or she is likely scared to say anything unless you ask. Likewise, if you ask and don't follow through, he or she will be even less likely to mention it next time. So ask your staff for ideas to eliminate waste. They'll likely come up with ideas that are hard. Those ideas may involve challenging senior management, or the programmers, or other business units. The ideas may cost you some political capital. You may not end up doing them. But you're at the end of the book. If you ask your staff for ideas to cut costs, and they give you ideas, and you don't implement them, don't blame us.

A.26 CONCLUSION

Three strikes and you are not out!
  Three strikes and you are not out!
    Three strikes . . .

NOTES

1. This list was inspired by a checklist that Dr. Cem Kaner came up with while we developed the preface. I thought you might appreciate a quick tips list, so I took the checklist idea and ran with it.
2. I believe the term *soap opera testing* was coined by Hans Buwalda, in honor of soap operas, where an incredibly unrealistic combination of events happen to people in a very short period of time. In any event, I'd recommend his article on the subject as a good introduction: http://www.logigear.com/resource-center/software-testing-articles-by-logigear-staff/246-soap-opera-testing.html.
3. For more on quick attacks, consider James Whittaker's "How to Break Software," the quick attacks session in the Black Box Software Testing online course, or my article "Ten Quick Attacks for Web Based Software," available online at http://searchsoftwarequality.techtarget.com/tip/0,289483,sid92_gci1510258_mem1,00.html.
4. As of this printing, SpectreSOFT makes an always-on screen-capture tool. If describing what the user does to create the bug is a problem, you might consider a tool like Snagit by techsmith, using it to record the problem, then attaching it to the defect "ticket."
5. Dr. Adam Porter at the University of Maryland has done some interesting research in this area. When he looked at the effectiveness of code reviews, he also looked at how long it took to find an empty conference room and hours where all the right people were available and found that it could take weeks to set up a code review. By that time, the programmer probably forgot why he or she made certain key code decisions. Porter also found that the problems found during these code reviews were more likely issues of style. Even if they found defects, his analysis was that the defects were unlikely to actually be fixed. I'll leave it to you to consider the value of such a practice.

Appendix B: 25 Tips to Reduce Testing Cost Today

Catherine Powell

You've just finished reading Appendix A and have many strategies to implement, but don't know exactly where to start. Or maybe you just finished Appendix A, and you're scared you don't have the authority to implement those strategies. Perhaps you skipped right to Appendix B because you know you don't have the authority to even get started. Good news: this chapter is all about how to get started. It's about the things the technical staff can do right now, today, to reduce the cost of testing, with or without any authority or mandate.

None of these tips takes more than half a day, and you can implement them all without permission or time or money. Pick one. Any one. And do it today. Do one more tomorrow. Take baby steps. Big changes come from starting with small things. Use this chapter in one simple way:

- Pick something.
- Do it.
- Pick something else.
- Do it.

No one change will make a huge difference. But every change will make a difference. And every change is doable. Make enough single simple changes, and you'll come a long way. It's your choice—pick a tip and repeat it in a variety of contexts, or pick a context and apply a variety of tips. Either way, I'm confident you'll look around in a while and be amazed how far you've come.

B.1 CUT YOUR DOCUMENTATION TO A MINIMUM

Just like we refactor code to make it more DRY (don't repeat yourself), we need to refactor our documentation so that we don't repeat ourselves. The magic words here are "incorporate by reference." Find something in your documentation that you've been copying and pasting, and incorporate it by reference. Replace those copies with a simple note: "See XX," and then put it—just once—at that location.

B.2 MAKE THE COST OF CHANGING THE DOCUMENTATION CHEAP

There are many tools for collaboration: source control, wikis, whiteboards. You probably already have a tool that allows concurrent updates of the same thing and that provides access to everyone on your team, so use it. Even if you have to do more formal reporting outside your group, do your internal reporting quickly and easily, and then have your quality assurance lead, quality assurance manager, or (if you share the role) quality assurance engineer responsible for reporting put it into the formal protocol. Start by collaborating on the documentation within your team; once you can show it's working it will be easier to repeat this tip with documentation that goes outside your team.

My favorite method is to get a whiteboard and write each of the major features on it, each with a column for overall test status and critical notes, such as blockers. Put four different colored markers next to the whiteboard so your teammates can update their status.

Congratulations, status updates are now a sixty-second process for most of your test team. You can easily apply this concept to other areas of documentation—moving them from shared Word documents and laborious e-mails to wikis and whiteboards.

B.3 NEVER BE BLOCKED

Most of never being blocked is making sure that you have other things to do, even when you can't proceed on your main task. This tip is about preparing to be blocked; don't wait until you're blocked to do it.

Make a wish list of the things you wish you could do but you don't have time for on your whiteboard, a sticky note, or in your PDA. For example, a list can include "configure e-mail send on successful build of release branch," and "cross-reference unit test coverage info with defects per source file." Don't spend more than ten minutes on this list; otherwise it will get too long. Then put the list aside. Next time you're blocked, pull out your list. Now's the time to do something on it!

B.4 ELIMINATE MULTIPROJECTING

Unfortunately, we don't get to pick everything we work on; at some point you may be assigned to multiple projects. This tip is about dealing with that reality. Pick a single project and create a meeting in your calendar for you and that project, and spend that block of time working on that project only. The more often you can do this, the better. The idea is to minimize task switching. Turning off your e-mail, instant messenger, phone, and putting a "do not disturb" sign on your chair while you are testing are also surprisingly effective.

B.5 AUTOMATE ENTIRELY REDUNDANT PROCESSES

Automation doesn't have to be big, or hard, or part of a framework. It can be a simple shell script or a batch file. It can be something you run manually on your own (think log parsers, for example). Find a repetitive task that you've done at least twice in the last month and automate it. Then check your automation tool into the source repository so everyone can use it. If you don't do automation, take this as a chance to try it out. After all, this is for your use; it doesn't have to be fancy. Start small by simply batching up the commands you type into a shell script.

B.6 START WITH SOAP OPERA TESTS

Soap opera tests can be some of the more fun things you'll try, especially if you do it as a team. One-upping each other to get wild and crazy soap operas is in a small way a team-bonding experience. Hold a contest with your team to come up with the craziest soap opera for your product. Then try it. Bonus points if it reveals a show-stopping bug.

B.7 START WITH QUICK ATTACKS

A quick attack is just that—quick. Even with deadlines and assigned work and no authority, it is still likely you can find time to drop some quick attacks into whatever piece of code you are currently working on. Put down the documentation and put down the test management tool, just for half an hour. We can document whatever we find and the test cases we did afterward. Pick a screen in your application and spend 30 minutes doing a quick attack on all the fields in that screen. (If you don't know how to do quick attacks, check Note 3 in Appendix A. You may have to spend twenty more minutes reading an article; it'll be worth it.)

B.8 TEST EARLY

This is a bonus: two tips in one. If you're in an Agile environment, go through your last iteration and identify how long it took you to start testing each story after it was done, then come up with one idea to start each one faster. If you're in a more traditional environment, go find your friendly local developer and offer to spend half an hour working with him to "pretest" his feature together. If the developer looks at you funny, offer to bring the doughnuts. He still might not enjoy it, but at least he'll like the doughnuts, and you'll have gotten some good testing done while showing him a few things.

B.9 DEVELOP A REGRESSION-TEST CADENCE, AND KEEP IT LIGHT

The confidence to not regression test something comes from knowing the system well and understanding how it interacts with its components. Part of that is creating a testing-oriented system diagram so you can figure out what components relate to what other components. Use it to identify what needs to be regression tested and what you can safely skip.

Get the test team together and draw the system as you see it, with its dependencies, on the whiteboard. Ask your team to expand on the drawing. Then spend an hour or so discussing what that means for different fixes or feature changes and where those are likely to break other things.

It never hurts to have an architect validate your diagram. Once again, doughnuts are great bribery material, if necessary.

B.10 TEST THE THINGS THAT ACTUALLY YIELD BUGS

Remember that testing-oriented system diagram you created in B.9? Now's the time to use it. Compare that diagram to the new features in that release, then pick one area that is on the top of your "must regression test" list and one area that is on your "we don't have to regression test" list. Then do it with just one area and with just one release. This is the tip to prove to yourself that it's OK to not regression test everything every time but to focus your testing efforts on areas that are at higher risk of having new problems.

B.11 ELABORATE—AND COMMUNICATE—A TEST STRATEGY OR TRIAGE STRATEGY

Test groups live with a test or a triage strategy day in, day out. Other groups aren't as close to it, so they need reminders of the content and norms of a test or a triage strategy. This is where status updates come in. Create a status update that you can frequently publish. Then publish it at least twice a week for the rest of the release. If your release is in under a month, publish the status update daily. Be sure to include the must-fix bugs and a summary of new bugs found.

B.12 DECREASE YOUR TIME SPENT REPRODUCING THE PROBLEM

Next time you find an unreproducible problem, set a timer for a reasonable amount of time. Depending on your culture, this might be an hour or two. Spend no more than that time box attempting to reproduce the problem and gathering information. When time is up, send the irreproducible bug over to development with two or three ideas for extra logging or information that will help track down the problem if it happens again.

B.13 DO A LOW-COST BETA PROGRAM OR PRERELEASE

This is another bonus two-tips-in-one, and this time they're reciprocal. First, do a beta test of one. To do this, get an account rep to bring a friendly customer to your offices. Let this friendly customer use the newest software for an hour or so. Sit next to the customer and watch what he does and what questions he asks. Have a frank conversation afterward about what he thinks, what he likes, and what he didn't understand or felt was missing. Getting fresh eyes—and customer eyes—on your program early will help you learn better what to look for in the product and will lend weight to your feedback going forward. After all, you've now been trained by the customer.

Second, go do a ride-along. This is a half-day or one-day task, no more, and you'll need your account rep again. Go with the account rep to a friendly customer, and just shadow the customer for half a day or a day. Don't ask too many questions, and don't show the customer how do to things or a better way to accomplish tasks. Your job is to keep quiet and take a lot of notes about how this customer actually uses the software in the field. Add half an hour to share this information with your team—it's a pretty good bet customers are using some parts of your product in ways you hadn't dreamed of. Learn from your actual end users. If the customer is open to it, record him with your phone or at least take pictures. Pictures are worth a thousand words when you're trying to remember what the customer did.

B.14 RECOGNIZE AND ELIMINATE PROJECT WANKERY

Recognizing and eliminating project wankery is a difficult strategy to accomplish quickly within a test team, but it can be done. Think of the project meeting that makes you roll your eyes; yes, that one. Then skip it. Whether it's a code review or a Gantt chart update or a status meeting, plan to skip it. To avoid making the people who are invested in the process angry, make sure you tell them you won't be able to make the meeting (no need to explain why) and send out your information—updates, notes from a private code review, and so forth—when the meeting would have started. Keep in mind that your ultimate point is to prove that the necessary work can get done and that the product won't suffer if you don't go sit in this meeting. Swapping a meeting for a brief written report is a good bargain in service to your overall goal.

B.15 STOP FIGHTING TO MANAGE THE PROJECT

This tip comes with a rule: no whining. If you want to manage a project, please go apply for project management or program management positions. If you don't want to manage a project, then you don't get to complain about how it's being managed. It's natural to want to show off what you think and to prevent other people's mistakes. If this is your job, then by all means do it, but it's probably not part of your job. A year from now, this decision probably won't matter, anyway. So don't let the things other people can do interfere with the things that only you can do.

Next time you see someone in another group (development or product management) making a decision you don't agree with, don't do anything. Don't complain about it, don't go to your boss. Just let it be.

B.16 IF YOU'RE GOING TO FIGHT, WIN

The last tip counseled you to keep your mouth shut on a decision you didn't agree with because it probably didn't matter much in the long run anyway. Now you are being told to do the opposite. Sometimes the decision really does matter in the long run. When it's truly important, you need to be able to sway the decision your way; you need to win. Winning starts well before decision time, and whether you win a decision or not will come down to your reputation, your argument, and how much support you've garnered to your side before you present your position publicly. This tip is about what to do before there's even a fight to win.

Explain yourself. The next time you are making a decision, sit down and write out why you're making that decision, including the pros and cons of the choice you are making. Then give that explanation to your boss and ask for his or her feedback (not his decision but simply his feedback). For example, if you're trying to decide how much time to allot to a certain test, write down why you decided to give two of your team members three days to do it (why not one team member for six days?). This is a decision that is entirely yours to make, and you're not asking your boss to do it. What you're doing here is honing your argument presentation and seeing how others—who will likely have to support you in future fights—react to your fighting style.

B.17 WALK AROUND AND LISTEN

If you're a test lead or a test manager, take fifteen minutes to walk around the office in the morning. Repeat your fifteen-minute walking circuit that afternoon. Don't interrupt anyone, and don't talk with them. (It's OK to say hi back if someone greets you.) Just watch and listen, and notice who doesn't seem to be doing anything either time you walk by. After your circuit, sit down for ten minutes with everyone who was not accomplishing anything and ask what you can do to unblock them or help them find a project to do.

If you're a tester, keep a "done" list for a day. Every time you finish something, put it on the list. At the end of the day, go over the list and look at how many of them were tasks (checking e-mail, updating a status report, attending a process meeting) and how many of them actually helped a larger project (a test session on a new feature, implementing a quick log parsing script). You can't eliminate tasks completely, but every day should include at least half project work.

B.18 WRITE TEST AUTOMATION THAT ATTACKS THE BUSINESS-LOGIC LEVEL

Find a non-graphical user interface (GUI) portion of your application and write one test that uses that portion of your application instead of going through the GUI to accomplish the task. For example, if you are working on a Web application, write a test that posts a form directly instead of logging in through the UI. You can later expand on this to try all sorts of usernames, passwords, users that don't exist, and so forth, and it will run much more quickly than the same tests run through a GUI (and be easier to maintain). Don't know how to automate below the GUI? Stop by the doughnut store and bribe someone to show you how.

B.19 DEVELOP A TEST AUTOMATION LIBRARY

Your tests almost certainly do some things over and over. Parsing log files or checking values in a database are good examples. If you've already got code for this, put that code into a separate function, and change everything that does it to call that separate function. You can think of this as abstraction, object orientation, or common sense, but if you don't want the same code cut and pasted all over in your product, you don't want it in your test automation either.

For this tip in particular, doing it the first time is the hardest and the most time consuming. Once you have your test code set up to use a separate library or a separate function, adding more libraries and functions is much easier.

B.20 DEVELOP OR HIRE EXPERTISE

Spend fifteen minutes and figure out the expertise of each member of your team. Then take another fifteen minutes to figure out where you need experts that you don't have. These are the areas you should be considering for training or hiring: to fill your expert gaps. For example, if you have a GUI expert and a database guru and someone who knows the most complex product module inside and out, then you don't need to spend too much time worrying about those areas. Instead, you should be looking for training in automation or load tests (where you currently lack an expert).

B.21 GET A RETURN FROM CONFERENCES, OR DON'T GO

At the next conference you or someone goes to, play find an expert. Have them bring back a business card from someone with experience in an area your team lacks. For example, if you don't have any performance testers on staff, have them seek out a performance tester at the conference. Then follow up with the expert—a quick e-mail is fine—to establish a relationship. Later, when you have a question about performance testing or need to hire someone like that, you will be able to reach out to the expert. (Oh, and a dirty little secret about all the experts? They don't have to be the famous testers, and they're probably really flattered you remembered them.)

B.22 BUILD A SOCIAL NETWORK

Pick your favorite testing site (Software Testing Club, StackExchange, etc.) and answer one question. It won't take more than an hour of your time. Next time you have a question, go to the same site and ask it. This tip is completely useless if you do it once. If you do it once a week, though, it will start to add up, and you'll build a network of testers you can rely on. Don't be surprised if this helps you get your next job, too—after all, you've now got public evidence of your competence.

B.23 EXAMINE INVALID BUGS CAREFULLY

It's time to do some data mining in your defect tracking system. Create two reports: (1) number of bugs marked invalid by reporter; and (2) number of bugs marked invalid by feature/module. Take that report and go talk to the reporter with the most invalid bugs. Pick a handful to walk through with him and spend thirty minutes brainstorming how to decrease that rate. Then take the report to the owner of the feature/module with the most invalid bugs. Pick a handful to walk through with him and spend thirty minutes brainstorming how to increase teamwide knowledge of his module/feature so the number of invalid bugs decreases.

B.24 BUILD A TEST MODEL THAT DEALS WITH THE NATURAL UP-AND-DOWN STAFFING NEED FOR TEST RESOURCES

This tip applies if you have a staff of testers already or if you're a tester on a team. Spend fifteen minutes brainstorming on the topic of what do to when you're idle. This should result in a list of things testers can do when testing on the product is relatively light. For example, it might include "create a virtual machine image with each of the last three releases for upgrade testing," or "go through the test boxes and update the wiki documenting their use and location, or create a brown-bag lunch presentation on my area of expertise for the rest of the test team" (see B.20). Next time you're idle, you'll have something to accomplish; something, that is, other than a long lunch.

B.25 ASK THE TEAM TO IDENTIFY OPPORTUNITIES TO DRIVE OUT WASTE, THEN IMPLEMENT THEM

Remember that last rant you got from one of your team members talking about how stupid it was that X, Y, Z? Pull it out. If you don't have any rants, ask your team to describe one thing that they find wasteful. Then find a way to change that one thing. You don't have to finish (for example, eliminating the test plan is probably not going to happen), but you can start. For example, instead of eliminating the test plan, you might cut one section that, frankly, no one reads anyway. This is another tip that will never end; you can repeat this forever.

Appendix C: Is It about Cost or Value?

Jon Bach

If you need a leaky pipe fixed now, you might call a plumber. If you need a meal prepared tonight, you might stop by a take-out place. This is called *outsourcing*. Some people confuse it with the word *offshoring*—the principle of using a different country's labor (usually overseas from the United States) to do work you won't or can't do without great expense. But is that really true? And if it is, how do you know? This appendix is about contexts for measuring value (benefits in return for cost), not price.

I'm a test manager for hire. I'm a vendor. I'm here to help because you asked, and chances are good you asked me at the last responsible moment, which is why I'm responding rapidly. I'm assuming you have a testing problem and need it solved fast. You might be calling me because:

- You want to know if you did the right things.
- You are worried you missed something.
- You're hoping I can find kinds of bugs your teams can't find.
- You're counting on the fact that I have some expertise that you don't.
- You need to expose some meaningful risks.
- You want me to provoke some conversations.
- You just lost members of your test team because of a layoff.

As of this writing, I work for an outsource test lab in Seattle. My title is "manager for corporate intellect"—basically, an ideas guy who can represent how we think about and execute the mission, tactics, and story of testing.

We do rapid testing. My brother James Bach invented rapid testing and cultivated it with the help of testing luminaries like Michael Bolton and Cem Kaner. Think of rapid testing like a martial art. It's the "skill of testing any software, any time, under any conditions, such that your work stands up to scrutiny" (James Bach, Satisfice, Inc.).

I mention that because, usually, a service company like ours is called in an emergency to augment an existing testing effort. The problem is if you look at our hourly rate compared to hourly offshore rates, we're not cheap. Dollar for dollar, test labs offshore are much cheaper by a factor of five, but then again, they're not often able to respond in a situation that calls for a rapid testing response. We know this, that's why our philosophy is to make the sales conversation about *value*, not price.

When I was first asked to write a chapter for this book, I had an issue with the title *Cost of Testing*. I subscribe to the context-driven school, which means I believe phrases like "best practices" and "cost of testing" depend on many different contexts—each of which can be hard to measure.

In this context (in this appendix), the cost we're measuring is labor, and I have some strong feelings about that because it seems many in our industry distill testing to a commodity. That is to say, they think testing is the same hourly activity everywhere and needs no skill, so why pay more when you can ship it overseas to where it tends to cost less per hour?

At a keynote address in 2010, Cem Kaner said, "There are green bananas, and ripe bananas, and rotten bananas, and big bananas, and little bananas. But by and large, a banana is a banana." Some people think he was trying to minimize the skill of testing, but those are people who don't know Kaner's work. Kaner help found the context-driven school, and he was talking about a certain kind of testing.

He said, "You are a commodity (banana) if your client perceives you as equivalent to the other members (bananas) of your class." Those that think one tester is as good as another will go offshore to find testers. And why not? It's cheaper per hour. They'd be silly not to.

But given that one tester is not as good as another, much in the way one car performs differently than another, what could you do to find one that was better? And if you did, under what criteria would you agree they would be worth the price over another tester?

Not long ago before the economic downturn in 2008, there was a notion in our business called "backshoring" or "reshoring"—projects that went overseas where the labor was cheap, only to have the project fail because of lack of skill, lack of infrastructure, difficulties in working across time zones, thick accents, poor communication, and lack of focus on testing as a service. Some businesses learned their lesson and started to bring projects back onshore. Quardev was on the receiving end of a backshoring product in 2008, and I was glad to see it.

But the autumn 2008 economic downturn happened and businesses either got amnesia about the lack of quality offshore or decided it was worth the risk to maintain offshoring as an option.

Now, back to the price issue.

I know several consulting jokes that are downright humorless. I got the feeling that everyone thinks the same about consultants:

1. They charge too much.
2. They don't know how to execute tasks they tell you to do.
3. They write reports that are too long.
4. They use buzzwords like "synergy" and "improvement opportunities" when more familiar words will suffice.
5. They tell you things you already know.
6. They abandon you after they get their money.
7. They're generally unethical.

I don't get it. I've had no formal training in how to be a consultant, but it seems to me that the practice of consulting comes from a desire to provide something called value, which, for me, turns out to be antithetical to the consulting jokes.

Here's my strategy:

1. Charge a fair price.
2. Have some ideas about how to execute what you recommend.
3. Write reports that tell the story you need to tell.
4. Write simply.
5. Tell them what you found out and call them "findings."
6. Talk about what you hope to do next or how you see yourself being involved.
7. Discuss your code of ethics.

I do confess to doing something consultants do in almost every joke you will read about them—I use buzzwords sometimes. Here's one to use: *value driven.* To me, it's just a way of saying "guided by the notion of what's important with respect to your values." I use this because my first order of business with a potential client is to communicate—asking questions about their values, such as:

1. What's important to you?
2. What does success look like?
3. What's the worst that could happen?
4. What would you like to do less of?

5. What would you like to do more of?
6. What do you wish were different?
7. What problems are you trying to solve?
8. What's working?
9. What would you start doing, stop doing, or keep doing?

As I get answers to these questions, I look to see if my client appreciates the thoughtfulness I'm offering. I also look for patterns in their answers that may give me a hint as to what they value. I look for patterns that suggest notions of innovation, leadership, fun, heroism, maturity, learning, reliability, and integrity.

My company has values, too. They define our corporate culture and happen to be values we want to preserve, whether we're five people or five hundred people. The magic thing about that is if we ever hire an outside consultant to come in and help us with a problem, this may be a good starting point for discussions about how we got to where we're at. But hopefully, the consultant would ask: "How did you come up with these values, and what happened along the way where you might have lost perspective?"

This is the approach I take on software projects. I like to speak to the very top tier of management, and I also like to spend time with testers side by side on the keyboard to see how testing actually gets done. Somewhere between the tester's communication of mouse clicks and keystrokes to the CPU and the CEO's communication of the company vision statement lies the problem—and it's usually one of pathology.

For example, if the company values heroism, I watch to see if it values heroism in a pathological way—if it relies on heroes to solve major problems every time, which can be just as bad as valuing maturity.

My brother once wrote an article titled "Enough about Process, We Need Heroes." When I started as a tester, this was a paper that influenced my approach to testing. I considered myself heroic, and the paper validated the value of that. I felt like a hero and it was the call to heroism that most spoke to me when becoming a tester. Years later, after trying to be heroic on many software projects—staying late, working smarter, anticipating needs, looking more deeply for problems than the established path—I began to burn out because the company I worked for took advantage of that. Out of that fatigue came a paper idea: "Enough about *Heroes*, We Need *Process*." After all, having defined process cures the need for heroes.

These days, experience has made me swing back to center—a place between heroism and process. Sometimes you want heroism, sometimes you want process. As I consultant, I'm now on the lookout for too much heroism or too much process and what an imbalance of each might mean for a company.

An important book that helped me feel prepared (and at the same time, validated me despite my inexperience at the time I read it) is Gerald Weinberg's *Secrets of Consulting*. It's refreshing, honest, and full of his style of consulting which flies in the face of convention (for example, he offers a money back guarantee for his work). What that book taught me most was that you can be of great value just by listening or getting people to talk about how they're going to solve their problem. It's important for me to find resources like these—resources in books, but also in people. Robert Sabourin is a fellow software testing consultant who believes in finding what the client values and working from the top (executive) as well as from the bottom (the entry level intern helping test for the summer).

Sabourin set the example for me a few years ago when he called the outsource company for which I work. He was looking for a test lab that could meet requirements for one of his clients. Some were technical requirements, but he also had soft requirements that he called values. For example, in our first few minutes on the phone, Sabourin's value-driven questions were his way of communicating what was important to him:

1. What was our approach to the work?
2. What kind of people did we have and how were they hired?
3. Were we the kind of lab to admit that we had limitations?
4. Could we work weekends?
5. Were we committed to helping him run meaningful exploratory tests as well as scripted tests he created?
6. What kind of reports could we give and could we be ready to adapt if needed?

All of these were value driven, but they were also value seeking—to increase the likelihood that we could work together not only on this project but perhaps follow-on projects, too.

I forget where I learned it, but an indicator of values between two companies that have never worked together can be exposed through a simple communication strategy during the pitch meeting. While other salespeople are polishing their PowerPoint presentations in the reception area, you are the one that simply takes out a sheet of paper during the pitch and ask: "Can we work right now on one of the problems you're having?"

No matter the technique, I want you to bear in mind that even if you do not know the approach or strategy or techniques or advice at the time you are asked to consult (or at the time you are interviewing consultants), it is the way you *probe* for values—thoughtfulness, enthusiasm, and an earnest interest in the work—that may lead you to find the best fit, sooner.

C.1 WHAT CLIENTS HAVE ASKED US

Your bug database or mine?
Can I get the same tester as before?
How do you train?
Can I get resumes from your staff?
To what associations do you belong?
Can I see the templates you'll use?
Can I customize the status reports you give?
If I need to postpone or cancel, what's the penalty?
Can I talk to a tester in the lab?
What are your working hours?
Will you work overtime or weekends?
What's your hiring process?
Will we be billed for the hours we don't use?
How do you measure test coverage?
Why didn't you catch that bug?

C.2 WHAT WE HAVE ASKED

Your bug database or ours?
Can I talk directly to a developer?
What are your working hours?
Do you work overtime or weekends?
What's your triage process?
When do you plan to ship?
Will we work onsite or here in our lab?
Do you use any existing tools that would be of help?
Can we see your existing bug database?
Did you want to devote time to regressions?

How often will you be giving us builds?
What are the minimum hardware requirements?
What kinds of users is this targeted for?
Has this been tested before?
Would you be a reference?

C.3 DETERMINING COST

If you're deciding whether to use a test lab based on pros and cons, you might make this list:

Pros	Cons
Price	Tricky terms and conditions
Listed in approved vendor list	Teleconferencing is a limitation
Big/scalable	Accents are difficult to understand
Discount for prepayment	Time zones mean we wake up early
Good terms and conditions	Virtual private network (VPN) access is slow and risky
Can work onsite	Potential security breaches
Lab space is available	Lawsuit jurisdictions
Time zones give more coverage	Unstable political systems

There are an equal number of pros than cons. But look closer. Are the line items really equal? Do they have the same value to you? Maybe being big is a bad thing. Maybe they came across as impersonal or have an IT bureaucracy where you would get lost in a sea of other requests more important than yours. Maybe it's really important to be in the same time zone, so that would be a deal breaker. Maybe using a VPN and opening security holes is a deal breaker.

One way to approach the value versus price question in a pro–con list is to use a spreadsheet to do some simple weighted averaging. Table C.1 shows a decision to compute a desirable Internet service provider by listing the options and criteria of the available choices and then ranking the importance of each on a scale of 1 to 10. You then rank (or give weight to) each of the three criteria, and that acts like a multiplier on the values, resulting in the lower section. In Table C.1, Company C would be the preferred provider based on the weighted values.

Likewise, the cost of something isn't just about price. It's all of the context and values and weighting and considerations that go into the

TABLE C.1

Which Test Lab to Hire?

		Criteria*			
		Price	Philosophy	Skills	
Options	Company A	3	5	7	
	Company B	4	5	4	
	Company C	5	8	10	
	Company D	7	1	2	
	Company E	8	3	1	
Weights		2	1	3	
					Ranking
Results	Company A	6	5	21	5.33
	Company B	8	5	12	4.17
	Company C	10	8	30	8.00
	Company D	14	1	6	3.50
	Company E	16	3	3	3.67

* Based on ranking of 1 to 10.

computation. For example, printers these days are really inexpensive (one hundred dollars or less), but buy one and you'll find that even though the quality is good, what you didn't account for is the high price of the ink cartridges which can cost up to half the price of the printer.

What I urge you to do is list all of the things that matter to you—all of your hopes and ideals and values. Put them into a list and give a gut-feeling ranking to each of them on a scale of 1 to 10. Share it with the people on your team who are charged with making a decision. Add, delete, modify. But also stay alert to new context that emerges once the decision is made.

Are the testers finding good bugs? No? Maybe the test design is tremendous. Maybe that's the real value. Maybe they are asking great questions and provoking good discussions about risk and product design. Table C.1 is an evaluation heuristic that may help you pick a vendor, but it may also help you decide to keep a vendor. Both are an evolutionary evaluation. Then again, you know this because it's just like software testing. To know the cost of testing, you have to know the context of testing, the value of testing, and the questions of testing. You can buy a cheap car for five hundred dollars and maybe it's just what you need. You can buy a new car for fifty thousand dollars and maybe it pays for itself in the benefits you get from it.

Also, you can reframe any problem to convey the value. One company that made rubber gloves said to its employees "We not making gloves, we're saving lives!" The same can be true for people who have five thousand friends on Facebook. Some may be baffled at what it means to have five thousand "friends" and assume the person has such low standards for friendship that they would accept anyone as a friend. But what if the person with five thousand friends was a professional recruiter? In that context, it's not about friendship; it's about the power and value of having five thousand connections to meet an urgent request.

For the question of hiring a test lab to do rapid test augmentation, you may be able to reframe the conversation to your stakeholders and decision makers—helping them realize that you're not hiring them to find bugs, you're hiring them to assist you in gaining more visibility about the value you are offering to your customers.

Appendix D: Cost of Starting Up a Test Team

Anne-Marie Charrett

D.1 TEST TEAM DESIGN

A cost-effective test team is one that meets your organizations needs. But understanding those needs and providing a viable solution is not easy. Although companies will often see the symptoms of poor quality, often they fail to understand the underlying issue. Sometimes companies will try to solve the symptoms by adding structure, often in the form of a formalized software testing process, giving the appearance of testing but often failing to improve the quality.

Without the insight of a software tester it's often left to developers to decide what is the best testing approach. Yes, occasionally there will be someone in the company who did testing once and provides a smattering of information. But there's not a lot of information available on the practicalities of starting a test team. And that's a shame, because making an ill-informed decision can be costly to a small business.

Making the right decisions up front can mean fewer mistakes resulting in greater savings. Testing is not a neatly packaged commodity, with "one size fits all" neatly written on the outside of the box. It's a complex and living entity, and its shape and structure will vary in purpose and design based on the company's ethos and belief system. A test team that has been structured and designed to work with the company will be more cost effective and in turn improve the quality of the testing performed.

One way to get a deeper understanding of the real quality issues within your company is to start asking questions of yourself and your stakeholders. The following will take a look at some of the possible questions to ask.

D.2 STAKEHOLDERS

Cem Kaner in his Black Box Software Testing foundation course describes software testing as "an empirical technical investigation conducted to provide stakeholders with information about the quality of the product or service under test." This opens the concept of stakeholder to anyone who cares about the quality of the product, and you may find stakeholders in departments that initially appear to have little direct connection with testing. For example, marketing may find the information gathered from performance testing to be beneficial when making claims about the product. Sales may take an interest in testing as an additional resource for sales demonstrations. Having an inclusive policy will help you design your test team in a way that will meet these stakeholders' needs.

Not everyone you speak with will end up being a direct stakeholder in testing. However, as you discuss testing, identify individuals who are supportive and willing to champion on behalf of testing. These people will be needed to guide the organization through change and be there for support when controversial decisions need to be made. Most important, you need the support of influential individuals in high-level management to provide credibility to any changes that result from testing. Without high-level management buy-in, adding testers may be like "inflicting help" on the company [1].

Not all stakeholders will be enthusiastic about testing. It may be that some departments will fail to understand the benefit of a tester until they see that tester perform. You may find as your testing progresses that some stakeholders will join in, others may drop out. Its good to keep the door open to all stakeholders, even those who may initially see testing in a negative light.

A company asked me to create a test process for them, something to add structure. My first request was that I speak to the key stakeholders to understand the issues they had, but also to ask them for ideas on how to approach solving the problems. What I got was an insight in to the underlying problems that existed within the communication and some excellent ideas. When I went to build the process, I made sure I incorporated sufficient ideas from people to enable them to identify with the process.

D.3 TEST TEAM BUDGET

You may feel designing a test team is a worthless exercise because your budget restricts you from many choices. For instance, you may wish in the long term to have an in-house tester but existing finances prevent you from making that choice. One option is to perform some up-front analysis to understand your goals, but then stagger the implementation. The short-term choices you make come together to achieve your final long-term goal. It also means that your implementation is more accommodating to unforeseen changes that happen to your company.

D.4 TEST TEAM PURPOSE

Why do you want a test team? A question like this gives insight into how testing is perceived in your organization. I've found that the response is often varied, based on role and personality. Sometimes the answer can be negative. Often different answers within a team conflict with one another. But all this is worth knowing. Differences in opinion can suggest that issues may arise in these areas. Confusion or ambiguity suggests potential risk [2]. Differences in opinion will influence how your team is structured.

Knowing the purpose of the team and the problem that testing is trying to solve is essential. As I mentioned earlier, it's possible that the solution is better achieved in a different way.

A common reason why companies want a test team is that they perceive that testing provides visibility and structure to the development process. They make the tester the enforcer of software quality. There is an inherent problem with this approach. Michael Bolton, in his talk "Two Futures of Software Testing," explains:

> Although testers are called the quality gatekeepers . . .
>
> - They don't have control over the schedule.
> - They don't have control over the budget.
> - They don't have control over staffing.
> - They don't have control over product scope.
> - They don't have control over market conditions or contractual obligations.

Testers do not have the authority to enforce such change and setting this expectation up front often leads to many difficulties and conflict within the project team.

Perhaps the reason for the team is to improve quality? A software tester can help do that in many ways:

- Testers can find bugs and inform developers.
- Testers can identify risks that threaten the value of the product.
- Testers can highlight visibility and structure issues within the team (they just can't fix them).
- Testers add to the overall knowledge of the system.

Many see the test team as performing multiple roles. This is very common in small businesses where testers end up being installation experts, presales demo experts, and customer support. It's good to understand that's what you're expecting right from the start. The expectations set for the team that is performing multiple roles are different to that performing solely a testing.

These factors will affect the decisions you make about your team makeup. For example, if providing demos to customers is an essential requirement from your test team, then perhaps considering outsourcing your testing is not the most appropriate decision.

It's also a good time to review your company's mission statement and understand your current company's philosophies and approach to business. If your approach to business is intimate and you believe strongly in the value of face-to-face discussion, outsourcing your testing to China is probably not going to bring you much satisfaction, regardless of the amount of money you might be saving.

D.5 TYPES OF TEST TEAMS

You've assembled your stakeholders and you have some understanding of its purpose. What is the test team going to look like? There are a number of paths you can take in creating your dream test team and I've outlined some options next.

D.5.1 In-House or External Test Team

For the purposes of this chapter, in-house testing is an independent test team that resides within the company [3]. External test teams can be an independent company. They can also be an independent test team within an external development house. Either way, from the perspective of a small business, the test lab is external. There are perceived benefits and risks to both approaches.

D.5.1.1 In-House Test Team

You can create an in-house test team by employing one tester with the tester performing independent testing alongside the developers. Having a test team that sits with your developers is a real bonus for small companies. It allows the test team to communicate with developers helping them to clarify requirements and resolve issues quickly.

The tester also benefits from being close to the many other stakeholders involved in testing such as customer support and marketing. A tester that is embroiled in company business can often pick up potential bugs and issues way before coding begins. An onsite tester speaks to company employees on a daily basis and by nature is more aware of customer-facing issues or the types of marketing information needed.

There are perceived downsides to this intimacy. Some testers feel that working closely with developers compromises their ability to detach themselves and provide an independent view. The pressure to deliver can be intense in smaller companies. A tester in this situation often needs a strong mind and good persuasion skills to ensure bugs are fixed.

Performing your testing in house requires additional hardware and software, and the overhead associated with hiring an additional staff member. The approach is also less flexible and adaptive to change, as the company is less likely to hire additional staff at peak testing times, resorting to overtime or using other team members to complete the testing. It's common in smaller companies for roles to overlap, but it may mean that other staff find their own work compromised and start resenting testing because of the additional workload it puts on their schedule. Similarly in lull times, it's not possible to lay off the tester until work starts again.

Introducing a test team has its own associated costs and risks. Developers may assume less responsibility for testing and (consciously or unconsciously) test less. Therefore it may be that introducing a tester does not necessarily mean more or better testing is being performed. In addition, for the tester to work effectively, good communication channels need to be encouraged between the testers, the developer, and other team members. This in itself requires additional time and cost to the company.

D.5.1.2 External Test Team

Testing by an external test team or test lab can be performed either near shore where the company performing the testing is based in close proximity to the company, or offshore where the testing company could be located in any country in the world.

Before using an external test lab, consider the type of testing that your company will want from the test lab. Is it to test that what's been built works correctly, or is it to test that it meets the needs of stakeholders? Understanding stakeholders requires constant communication, so you need to ask yourself, will this work well if the test team is external?

In addition, is your software complex? Does it require extensive subject matter knowledge? It may take a while for any external test lab to acquire and understand sufficient knowledge to test your product in any effective manner. Consider also that any tester that leaves the test lab takes this knowledge with him or her. This is always a risk in testing regardless of the team structure, but with a test lab you have no control over that particular tester. The risk is higher with testers in test labs that have less loyalty to your company.

The perceived benefits to outsourcing testing are mostly related to cost. Handled well, outsourcing testing can result in significant savings as all resources become the responsibility of the outsourcing partner. The company pays only for the testing effort and so it's possible to reduce the overall cost. However, as anyone who has tried this approach, outsourcing comes with many hidden costs. One common problem in outsourcing is poor communication, which can result in testing delays. It can be hard for distributed teams to resolve issues and understand bugs. This extends the testing effort and drives up the cost of testing to more than initially anticipated.

Lack of visibility to what is happening can be a real concern for you when you outsource and can eat away at trust levels. Once trust in undermined, it can be very hard to get back. Again, consistent, open communication mitigates this risk.

Sometimes it can be of benefit to outsource elements of your test team. For example, you may decide to have an internal test team but outsource any performance testing. You will still need to work out the technical details. Will the team test be using in-house applications and servers, or will the test environment be replicated elsewhere? Other systems to consider are the bug tracking system and the software configuration management. If both companies have their respective systems, how will they interact? Will you ask the test lab to adopt your tools? How will you maintain visibility over documentation and e-mails? Where will they be stored that will ensure that total team visibility is ensured? All these elements add cost to testing.

D.5.2 Offshore and Near-Shore Test Teams

It seems to be that the more distributed your teams are, the greater the need to ensure effective communication channels. It can be a real challenge to cultivate effective communication. Both teams must realize the importance of open and positive communication. This is true for both offshore and near-shore solutions. In general though, the greater the distance from your business location, the greater the communication challenges. In my experience a good deal of trust and goodwill is required for offshoring to succeed, balanced with clear expectations and deliverable outputs.

D.5.2.1 Offshore Test Team

Offshoring is a form of outsourcing where the team resides in a different country (typical countries are India and Eastern Europe) to your place of business. Done well, offshoring can be a cost effective way to get your software testing done.

To work well, you will need commitment from all parties to work as a team and communicate openly. This can be a real challenge for many people. You may find that cultural differences become more obvious when communicating at a distance. It's easy to assume that an offshore team member thinks like you and fully understands the context in which you are working. Constant communication is required on a daily basis.

More important, though, for a team to work well together you need mutual respect. Many employees view offshore and outsourced teams with suspicion, wary that their job might be the next to go. This can bias how team members work with each other. All parties must be completely committed to the offshore model and getting the testing performed well.

Offshoring that is performed in developing countries may also face more downtime than you anticipate. These problems can arise from power outages and network connectivity problems. It's a good idea to be prepared for these outages and ensure other work can be performed if such an outage occurs.

D.5.2.2 Near-Shore Test Team

A near-shore test team is an outsourced testing solution that resides close to your place of business. A near-shore test team has the advantage that it can offer your businesses with face-to-face contact. You can meet with your outsourced test team without the responsibility associated with running the team.

There are two common approaches here. One structure is that the whole test team resides in the same country as your business. An alternative and increasingly popular choice is to have a near-shore company partner with an offshore element. The near-shore partner is responsible for the testing but the customer still benefits from the reduction in costs that offshoring provides. This hybrid approach has the benefit of some face-to-face contact and still at a lower cost. The near-shore partner communicates directly with the offshore team. Make sure your near partner has worked with the outsourced element before and can vouch for their work.

D.5.3 Manual and Automation Testing

The decision on how you approach your testing can have a big impact on the type and skill set of your tester or your test lab. For example, if you have made the decision to outsource your test team and you have a long-term view of automating your testing, then you will want to ensure that the team has the necessary skills to implement automation. This is not something that you want your outsourced team to have to be trained to do adding to your cost.

D.5.3.1 Manual Testing

There are numerous benefits to manual testing but in my book it's the sheer inventiveness and creativity of a manual tester that provides the greatest benefit. A manual tester has the ability to react to the context of a project, making it flexible and responsive to change. It's this ability to quickly adapt to change that in particular suits a small business environment. In manual testing, it's possible to see the benefits of testing immediately, especially if the testing style is exploratory in nature and a tester is very quickly able to feed bugs and other information back to the rest of the team.

Manual testing sometimes has a reputation as being unskilled. This is unfortunate, as companies incorrectly assume that anyone can test well.

Good testers require excellent analytical, problem-solving and communication skills combined with a healthy dose of skepticism. There is a risk that if you only manually test without the assistance of any tools you are opening yourself to not testing in sufficient depth, often limiting the testing to graphical user interface (GUI) interactive functionality testing.

Including tools in testing can be a very powerful way of achieving added depth to your testing. A simple example would be the use of a tool to assist you in stress or load testing, something that a tester would struggle to test well manually.

D.5.3.2 Automation Testing

It is worthwhile exploring automation as a means to assist your testing. Automating the parts of testing that humans do badly is a very effective way of improving the depth and scope of your testing. Automation can be fast, very fast. What may take a manual tester days to test can often be exercised by automated scripts in minutes. It can be very advantageous to test large amounts of input data by automating the effort, and it can be particularly beneficial to automate the testing of complex calculations and algorithms.

Automated testing can also be useful in repeating the tests. A word of caution though: this type of testing is entirely confirmatory in nature and will do little to exercise the application in any new way. And in some types of testing such as performance testing, automated tools are a necessity.

Automated testing requires up-front resources before testing is due to start. A test strategy and code need to be created upfront, ready for execution at the same time testing is due to start. Also, like any code, automated scripts need to be maintained, extending the cost of the testing. This is why the promise of cheaper testing coupled with lesser resources is often a false promise.

D.6 WHEN TO BUILD A TEST TEAM

There is never a really good time to create a test team, but there is a right time to create a test team. If you are unsure if it's the right time to build a test team, why not ask yourself (and your stakeholders) this question: Is my company willing to take the risk for shipping the product as is? If a company is willing to manage the risk as it is, I recommend holding off on building a test team. A test team will identify risk but not necessarily minimize it. Managing and minimizing risk is a responsibility shared by all stakeholders. This includes developers who will need to fix code, and project managers to allocate time and resources to fix problems. If stakeholders are satisfied and can live with the level of risk at the moment, there will be little incentive to allocate time and resources for fixing newly found bugs. On the other hand, if the answer to the question is no, then yes, it may be the right time to invest in a test team.

D.7 CONCLUSION

The chances are your final approach will include perhaps a blend of more than one approach. There are no fixed rules when it comes to creating a team, just options. I've listed some ideas and approaches common to many test teams, but ultimately, the best test team is the one that works for you right now. What works for other companies, may not work for you, as you both manage different risks, have different customers, and different stakeholders.

As tides ebb and flow, so ought your approach to building a test team. What may work now will not necessarily be a suitable approach in three or five years time. By creating a short- and long-term strategy to your testing, you and your stakeholders will be open to making critical changes to your testing approach, allowing you to remain flexible, adapt, and grow as your company does.

NOTES

1. Cem Kaner, referencing Jerry Weinberg's phrase "inflicting help."
2. Confusion or ambiguity suggests potential risk. James Bach, "Heuristic Risk-Based Testing," *Software Testing and Quality Engineering Magazine*, November 1999.
3. Black Box Systems Testing course provided by the Association for Software Testing (AST) and written by Cem Kaner and James Bach.

Index

A

Acceptance-test-driven development, 204–205
Accountability, of testing programs, 253–254
Activity-based management, 258
Adzic, Gojko, 198
Agile projects, 39, 111
    acceptance-test-driven development, 204–205
    automated system tests, 205
    collaboration and, 32, 199–200
    collective test ownership, 207
    delivery, 209
    improvements based on, 30–31
    iterations, 195
    nimble planning, use in, 182, 183
    resistance to, 29, 30
    standup meetings, 200–201
    test-driven development, 206
    testing phases, 138
    transition to, 30
Amelio, Gil, 6
Apple Computer, 6
Artifacts, testing, 231–233
Automated system tests, 205
Automated unit tests, 206
Automation library, 271
Automation scripts, 174
Automation testing, 304, 305

B

Bach, James, 12, 182, 217
Backshoring, 288
Beck, Kent, 170
Beta testing, 268–269, 280
Blocking, 264, 276–277
Bolton, Michael, 182, 299
Bottlenecks, testing, 195–196
Budget, testing. See Costs, testing
Bug testing. See Defects

C

Channel stuffing, 5–6
Clean code, 228
Clean testing, 227
Code mitigation, 109
Collective test ownership, 207
Combinatorial, 216, 217
Communications regarding testing
    collaboration, relationship between, 36, 110
    configuration and change management, regarding. See under Configuration and change management
    decision makers, with, 12–13
    face-to-face, 192
    informal, 13
    real-time, 173–174
    truthfulness, 13
Compliance, costs associated with, 81
Component tasks, 4–5
Configuration and change management, 106
    communications regarding, 110–111
    migration issues, 116
    overview, 110
Constraints, theory of, 3
Continuous integration (CI), 171–173, 207–208
Coplien, James O., 227
Costs, testing
    activity-based, 233–234
    adaptation costs, 88
    advocacy costs, 85
    bench costs, 93
    budget cuts, 4
    calculating, 293–295
    cognitive costs, 96
    compliance costs, 81
    component tasks, controlling through, 4–5

current release, related to, 149–150
development-related, 80
distributing, 252–253
dithering costs, 93
documentation-related, 78, 131–132, 264, 276
domain learning, related to, 79
education costs, 91
epiphany costs, 92
experimentation costs, 91
exploratory testing costs, 81
failure costs, 24, 34
gold-plating costs, 85
internal costs, 24
interruption costs, 86
investigation costs, 91
justification costs, 91
long-term gains, 64–65
long-term savings, 64–65
maintenance-related, 80
measurement costs, 88
mitigation costs, 85
next release, related to, 150–153
open source. *See* Open source testing
operating expense, viewed as, 245–246, 247–248
operating systems, multiple, 59–60
opportunity costs. *See* Opportunity costs
optimizing, 68–69, 70
outsourcing. *See* Outsourcing
overview, 148
political costs, 96
psychological costs, 96
quality-related, 24, 36
recruitment-related, 74
reducing, 86, 169–170, 194
reporting costs, 81
resistance to, corporate, 21–23
resourcing costs, 91
right-sizing, 248–249
short-term gains, 64–65
short-term savings, 60, 64–65, 66
staff size, 3, 4
staffing-related, 74
support costs, 82
test labs, of, 293
time, relationship between, 60–62, 63–64

tooling-related, 79
traceability, related to, 80, 112, 133–134
training-related, 74
up-front costs, 98
waste elimination. *See* Waste elimination
Coverage, 120, 128
Crashes, 69, 83
Crispin, Lisa, 183
Cycles, test, 12–13, 82, 186

D

Data sheets, 162–164
Data, test, 106–107
    consolidating, 162
    database of, 164
    defining, 112–113
    reusing, 158–159, 160–162
Decisions tables, 52–54, 55
Defect management systems, 44, 173
Defects
    bug investigation, 13–14, 24
    crashes, 69, 83
    invalid bugs, 272–273, 284
    locating, 11–12
    missed by testers, 45
    net worth calculations, as part of, 41–42, 43–44
    open, 41–42, 47
    perfection, *versus,* 70
    production-based, 42–43
    risks, relationship between, 11
    showstoppers, 69, 277
    UAT, found by, 45
    user acceptance testing (UAT) defects. *See* User acceptance testing (UAT) defects
DeMarco, Tom, 6
Deming, W. Edwards, 5, 138
Design of experiments (DoE)
    abstractions, applied to, 218–219, 220–221
    benefits of, 214–215
    limitations, 217–218
    overview, 213–214
Design, test, 7
Developers. *See* Testers

Development, software
  cost management, 36, 80, 85. *See also*
      Costs, testing
  gold-plating, 85
  test-driven development (TDD). *See*
      Test-driven development (TDD)
  time resources, 59
Documentation
  clarity, importance of, 77–78
  costs associated with, 78, 131–132, 264,
      276
  customization and sizing of, 111–112
  defining, 111
  reducing, 263, 275–276
  risk associated with, 106
  traceability, 80
Dominguez, Joe, 62

E

Efficiency, 256–257
Environment, testing, 109
Experiments, design of. *See* Design of
      experiments (DoE)
Exploratory testing, 81
  characteristics of, 182
  defining, 182
  description of, 208–209
  nimble nature of, 182
  session-based test management,
      relationship between. *See under*
      Session-based test management

F

Fahrenheit/Celsius converter case, 7–8
Failure demand, 4–5
Feedback loops, 34, 132–133, 190–191
Flying Dutchman problems, 85
Fowler, Martin, 239
Full Reuse, 156
  achieving, 164–166
  benefits of, 166–167
  deliverables, 166
  overview, 159–160

G

Garmin, David A., 19, 20

Goldratt, Eli, 3
Gregory, Janet, 183

I

Implementation, 116
Infrastructure, physical, 58
Integrated development environments
      (IDEs), 58
Issue management
  migration, 116
  scheduling, 115–116
  status meetings, 115–116
  value of issues, 144–146
Iterations
  Agile, as part of, 195
  demonstrations, 203–204
  factors of, 216
  nimble test plans, as part of, 191–192,
      193
  preparing, 196–197
  releases, relationship between, 198–199
  testing, 201–203

J

Johnston, Ken, 268

K

Kanban, 266
Kaner, Cem, 12, 288, 298

L

Lean software development, 14–15, 173,
      182
  defining, 182–183
  nimble planning, use in, 183
  principles of, 183
Licensing, 59, 60
Linux, 60
Load testing, 58

M

Maintenance costs, 80
Manifesto for Software Craftsmanship,
      227, 228

Manual testing, 304–305
Martin, Robert C., 227
Metrics
    quality, 26–27, 29
    session execution, 129–130
    test completions, 130
    time-related, 131
    velocity, 126–127
Models, test, 273
MoSCoW principle, 141
Multiprojecting, 264, 277

N

National Institute of Standards and
        Technology, 182
Nelson, Lloyd, 5
Net worth
    calculating, 39–40
    defining, 39
    implementing, in testing, 41–43
    increasing, 44–45
Nimble test plans
    commitment, 186–187, 193
    communications, 192
    defining, 181
    feedback loops, as part of, 190–191, 193
    goal-oriented content, 185–186, 193
    iterations, 191–192, 193
    lightness, 184–185, 193
    multi-disciplines, 181, 182
    overview, 179–181
    practicality, 187–188
    team empowerment, 188–190, 193

O

Open source testing, 60
Operating systems, 59–60, 109
Opportunity costs
    applications, 50–51
    decision tables for, 52–54, 55
    defining, 49–50, 82
    identifying, 51–52
    limits to change, 55
    measuring, 50
    prioritizing, 54–55
    reducing, 54
    trade-offs associated with, 54, 55–56

Orthogonal, 216
Outsourcing, 66–67, 303

P

Page, Alan, 268
Pairwise, 216
Pettichord, Bret, 12
Phases, testing
    execution, 138, 140
    overview, 138
    preparation, 138
    specification, 138, 139–140
Planning and preparation, testing
    advantages of
        105–106
    cost savings associated with
        105–106
    importance of
        105–106
    nimble test plans. See Nimble test plans
Poppendieck, Mary, 14
Prioritization approach to testing
    checklist for, 108–109
    environment. See Environment, testing
    impact, 107–108
    probability, 107
Production weighting, 43

Q

Quality. See also Total quality
        management; Value
    costs associated with, 24, 36
    defining, 19, 20, 95
    manufacturing-based approaches, 20
    metrics associated with, 26–27, 29
    process controls, 29
    product-based approaches, 20
    users' expectations, 20
Quick attacks, 265, 278

R

Rapid software testing, 39
    strategy and logic of, 182
    test planning with, 183
Rational Unified Process (RUP), IBM,
        133–134

Rationality, 186–187
Recession, global, 38, 288
Recruitment, costs associated with, 74
Redesigning, 240
Redundancy, 264–265, 277
Refactoring, 239
Regression testing, 266–267, 278–279
Release cycle, 55
Requirements, 9–10
    risks, *versus,* 141–142
    technical impact *versus* business gain,
        142–143, 144
Reshoring, 288
Return on investment (ROI), 245, 249
Reusability
    data, of, 158–159, 160–162
    Full Reuse. *See* Full Reuse
    overview, 156–157
    partial, 159
    redundancy, *versus,* 157–158
RFCs, 146–148, 150, 151, 153
Risk management, 11
    areas of concern, 106–107
    coverage, relationship between, 120
    highest risk areas, determining, 68–69
    requirements *versus* risk, 141–142
Robin, Vicki, 62
Rollinson, Bj, 268
Ruskin, John, 11

S

San Francisco Depot (SFDPOT), 185–186
Scripted testing, 79, 83, 107, 277
Scrum, 266
Seddon, John, 4, 7
Senge, Peter M., 198
Session-based test management
    exploratory testing, control of, 122
    idea generation, 122, 123–124
    idea management, 124–126
    metrics, 129–130, 131
    overview, 119
    test completions, 130
    tracking session execution, 129–130
Showstoppers, 69, 277
Simple Mail Transfer Protocol, 66

Simple Network Management Protocol
        Management Information Bases,
        66
Soap opera tests, 265, 277–278
Social networking, 273, 284
Software craftsmanship, 227, 228
    importance of, 229–230
    principles of, 230
    test craftsmanship, 234
Software development kits (SDKs), 58
Stakeholders
    critical areas to, determining, 68
    influence of, 298
    testing, relationship between, 298
Status meetings, 115–116
Subject matter experts, 76
System development life cycle (SDLC), 190

T

Team, test, 297, 299, 300–301, 302–303,
        306–307. *See also* Testers
Test cases, 7, 238–239
Test craftsmanship, 234
Test design. *See* Design, test
Test execution, 7
Test management
    choices associated with, 49
    opportunity costs associated with. *See*
        Opportunity costs
    session-based. *See* Session-based test
        management
Test planning. *See* Planning and
        preparation, testing
Test-driven development (TDD)
    defect prevention via, 171
    description of, 206
    overview, 170
Testers
    collaboration between, 199–200
    conferences for, 271–272, 283
    external, 300–301, 302–303
    functions of, 230–231
    internal, 300–301
    nearshore, 303, 304
    offshore, 303
    purpose of, 299
    qualities of, 15, 107, 114
    quality gatekeepers, as, 299, 300

resistance to, corporate, 21–23
risks associated with, 114, 115
wage costs, 62–63, 288
Testing phases. *See* Phases, testing
Testing time. *See* Time, testing
Testing, prioritization of. *See*
     Prioritization approach to
     testing
Tests, nimble. *See* Nimble test plans
Throwaway tests, 174–175
Tilford, Monique, 62
Time, testing, 16–17
  accelerating, 36
  costs, relationship between, 60–62,
    63–64
  developer wages, 62–63
  optimizing, 68–69, 70
  reducing, 279
  resources related to, 59
  trade-offs associated with, 60–62
TMap Next, 138
Tools, test, 107. *See also* Scripted testing
  capacity, 114
  costs, 114
  overview, 113–114
  types, 114
Total quality management, 5. *See also*
    Quality
Total-cost management, 258
Traceability, 80, 112
  costs associated with, 133–134
Training, software
  costs association with, 74

U

User acceptance testing (UAT) defects, 41,
    43, 153
  bugs missed by testers, 45
Users, software
  identifying, 69
  quality expectations, 21
  targeting, 21
  user acceptance testing (UAT) defects.
    See User acceptance testing
    (UAT) defects

V

Value. *See also* Quality
  defining, 95
  functionality, relationship between, 29
  goals of delivery, 140–141
  issues, of, 144–146
  Manifesto for Software Craftsmanship,
    as part of, 228
  measuring, 5–6
  spectrum of, 9
  testing, of, 249–252
Value stream management, 234, 235
Velocity, 126–127

W

Waste elimination, 14–15, 174, 183, 264,
    273–274
Waterfall approach, 138
Weinberg, Gerald M., 20, 95, 291